# HURRICANES

# HURRICANES

## THEIR NATURE AND HISTORY

Particularly Those of the West Indies
and the Southern Coasts of
the United States

BY

### IVAN RAY TANNEHILL, B.S.

*Chief of the Marine Division, U.S. Weather Bureau*
*Department of Agriculture, Washington, D.C.*

GREENWOOD PRESS, PUBLISHERS
NEW YORK

# PREFACE

AN attempt has been made to set down in this book, in popular language, all the essential facts and theories regarding the tropical cyclone, and all the known history that is worth mentioning of the hurricanes of the West Indies, the United States and adjacent waters of the Atlantic Ocean, the Gulf of Mexico and the Caribbean Sea. The book has been so arranged that when the reader has found what he wishes to know about the nature of the tropical cyclone, he may obtain from the historical section an account, or at least a reference to the occurrence, of every hurricane known to have visited the locality in which he may be interested.

In preparing this book, the writer has had access to notes, manuscripts and publications of a host of students of the tropical cyclone, chiefly in the Library of the Weather Bureau which contains more than 50,000 volumes on meteorology and subjects closely related thereto. During more than twenty years of service in the Weather Bureau, all of it directly associated with the hurricane warning work, the writer has had official occasion to consult the records of a great many tropical storms. These records are found in numerous publications, some of them out of print for many years. If this book makes it unnecessary for the general reader to carry on a similar search or assists the student in finding original sources, it will justify the labor involved in its preparation.

It is hoped that, at appropriate places in the text, full credit has been given to every worker who has contributed in a substantial way to the general knowledge of the subject. The writer is indebted to many persons for aid and encouragement during the years when he was assembling the material. He wishes especially to acknowledge the advice and assistance of his associates in the Weather Bureau on examining the manuscript: Dr. W. R. Gregg, Mr. C. L. Mitchell, Dr. E. W. Woolard, Mr. E. B. Calvert and Mr. W. F. McDonald.

# CONTENTS

# CONTENTS

# INTRODUCTION

## TROPICAL CYCLONES

BECAUSE of its great size and intensity, the tropical cyclone, when fully developed, is the most destructive of all storms. Winds of the tornado blow with greater fury but they are confined to a narrow path, 1,000 feet in average width, whereas it is not unusual for the violent winds of the tropical cyclone to cover thousands of square miles. Mountainous waves accompany intense tropical storms at sea; their destructive forces are revealed in the appalling record of ships sunk or cast ashore. They cause high tides that inundate low coastal areas. Storm waves break on the shore, in some situations like a wall of water or a series of great waves. Cities and towns have been wiped out, never to be rebuilt. Though born of the tropics, some of these storms move long distances and occasionally devastate sections far remote from their place of origin. In some of the most severe tropical storms, loss of human life has been estimated at more than fifty thousand and property damage at many millions of dollars.

## ORIGIN OF THE WORD "CYCLONE"

The term "cyclone" (meaning "coil of a snake") was first suggested about the middle of the last century by Henry Piddington,[1] who was president of the Marine Courts at Calcutta. The word has come into universal use as a general term to designate all classes of storms with low atmospheric pressure at the center.

## EXTRATROPICAL CYCLONES

The earth's atmosphere is always in motion. In the general circulation there are movements of air masses on a vast scale. Lesser movements, some in the form of local disturbances, which are carried over the earth's surface in the general circulation, are always present. They are of two types. In the cyclonic type, the winds are inclined inward and more or less symmetrically around the center where pressure of the atmosphere is low. In the anticyclone, the winds are directed outward and around a center of relatively high pressure.

[1] References to the writings of meteorologists mentioned in this book will be found in the bibliography.

Cyclones are sometimes called "lows" or "depressions" and the anti-cyclones, "highs."

Of the cyclones or "lows" two classes are recognized—tropical and extratropical. Extratropical cyclones are by far the more numerous. They originate over the continents or the oceans and are of daily occurrence in middle and higher latitudes, though more frequent in winter than in summer. They are of larger diameter than tropical cyclones, as a rule, and the majority of them are rather mild in character. With anticyclones as companions, they pass across the continents and oceans in endless succession, accompanied by the ordinary changes of the weather which we experience from day to day and week to week.

Outside the tropics, the influences of lows and highs, or cyclones and anticyclones, are constantly felt. Changes of the wind, from a warm equatorial current to a cold one from higher latitudes; increasing cloudiness and rain or snow, followed by clearing weather; an occasional strong wind attending a low of unusual energy, sometimes in winter followed by the cold outflow of a great anticyclone, resulting in a cold wave or "blizzard"; all of these and many other phenomena are attendant features of the passage of disturbances in the envelope of air which surrounds the earth.

Within the tropics, weather changes are much less frequent and seldom so pronounced, as in temperate latitudes. The cyclones of the tropics are comparatively rare and have no anticyclones as companions. They are of smaller average diameter and attain much greater force.

### WORLD REGIONS OF TROPICAL CYCLONES

Tropical cyclones have their genesis near but not directly over the equator. They form over all of the tropical oceans except the South Atlantic, but not over the continents. In the western North Pacific Ocean, they are known as typhoons; in the Bay of Bengal and the northern Indian Ocean, as cyclones; in the South Pacific, eastern North Pacific, southern Indian and North Atlantic Oceans (including the Gulf of Mexico and Caribbean Sea), they are known as hurricanes. Hurricanes of Australia are sometimes called willy-willies and the typhoons of the Philippines, baguios. All are of the same general character and as a class are known as tropical cyclones.

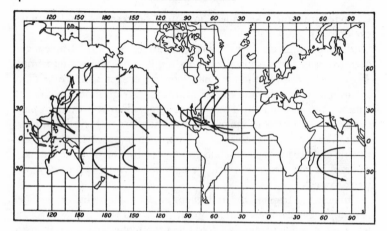

FIGURE 2. Arrows indicate principal world regions of tropical cyclones and, roughly, the direction of their movement.

### EARLY KNOWLEDGE OF TROPICAL CYCLONES

Although Piddington proposed the name "cyclone" because it expressed sufficiently what he described as the "tendency to circular motion," he was not the first to refer to tropical cyclones as whirlwinds. In his *Sailors Hornbook* he credited Captain Langford with the earliest published statement to that effect, in the *Philosophical Transactions* in 1698. Nearly fifty years before, however, a German geographer Bernhardus Varenius, treated hurricanes as whirlwinds in a book entitled *Geographia Naturalis*.

The principle of the barometer was discovered by Torricelli in 1643 and very soon thereafter it was recognized that its variations were associated with changes in the weather. A falling barometer was found to indicate the approach of bad weather; a rising barometer was found to be a sign of improving weather of a more settled type. Nevertheless, nearly two hundred years passed after the invention of the barometer without any notable contribution to the law of storms, though much was written on the subject and many references to tropical storms appeared in the narratives of the intrepid mariners of that day. One of these, William Dampier, a master seaman and world voyager, wrote an excellent description of the winds and other conditions experienced in a typhoon off the China coast in the year

1687. He came to the conclusion that there was no difference between typhoons and hurricanes except the name.

The fact that storms, both tropical and extratropical, are cyclonic wind systems which move progressively from place to place, was not definitely established until the advent of the weather map. Benjamin Franklin conceived the idea that the northeast storms of the New England and Middle Atlantic States come from the west and southwest. He cited the circumstances of an eclipse of the moon at Philadelphia which was due at about 9 o'clock in the evening but a northeast storm came up and obscured the sky at Philadelphia. Franklin was surprised to learn later, when the Boston newspapers arrived, that the eclipse was visible there and that the northeast storm arrived at Boston *later* than at Philadelphia. By correspondence he found that the storm arrived earlier in places to the southwestward of Philadelphia and later in places farther to the northeastward.

### BEGINNINGS OF THE DAILY WEATHER MAP

Invention of the synoptic weather chart, about 1819, has been credited to H. W. Brandes, a professor at the University of Breslau. There being no telegraph, weather maps at first were drawn from observations gathered by mail. Charts by Brandes were from observations taken in the year 1783. Circulation of the winds in cyclonic storms was depicted on these first weather maps which threw a flood of light on the problems that had disturbed earlier investigators.

In 1828, Heinrich Wilhelm Dove, physicist and meteorologist, showed that cyclones in the southern

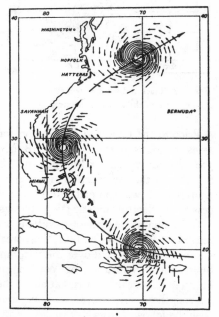

FIGURE 3. Track and wind system of a tropical cyclone in the northern hemisphere.

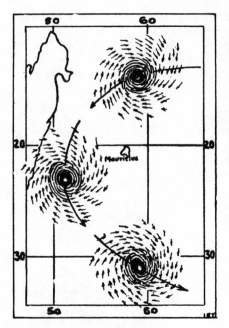

FIGURE 4. Track and wind system of a tropical cyclone in the southern hemisphere.

hemisphere rotate clockwise, that is, the winds move in the direction of the hands of a clock, while in the northern hemisphere the movement is counterclockwise. (Figs. 3 and 4.) Shortly thereafter, Wm. C. Redfield in America and Colonel W. Reid in England, described more fully the phenomena of translation and rotation in hurricanes. In 1853 Reid handed the investigation over to Captain Piddington who, in the next fifteen years, collected ships' weather observations and wrote voluminously on the law of storms. Contemporary students who contributed to the knowledge of tropical storms were James Espy and Elias Loomis.

Prior to the time that Piddington was carrying on his investigations of storms at sea, Samuel F. B. Morse was experimenting with the electromagnetic telegraph. In 1843 Congress appropriated $30,000 for the construction of a telegraph line from Washington to Baltimore. It was completed in 1844 and from that time on, the success of the electromagnetic telegraph was assured.

Collection of weather observations was greatly facilitated by the telegraph. From 1854 to 1861, daily weather observations from land stations were collected over the telegraph lines and displayed in the Smithsonian Institution at Washington. Similar collections were begun in European countries at about the same time.

From these early efforts it was apparent that movements of storms could be followed from day to day on the weather map (Fig. 5) and, shortly after the invention of the telegraph, storm warning services

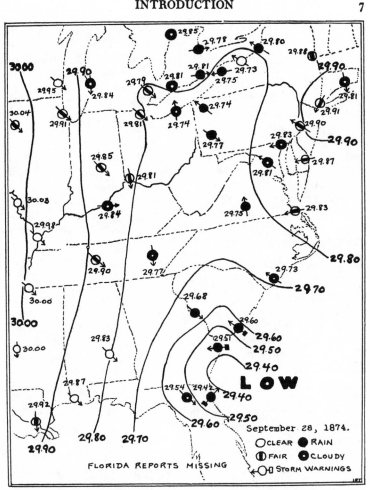

FIGURE 5. Wind direction, weather and barometric pressure from the daily weather map of the Signal Service, U.S. Army, September 28, 1874, 7:35 a.m. Hurricane moving northeastward with center off Atlantic coast between Savannah and Jacksonville.

were organized in the United States, England and France. In 1870 a Federal weather service was established in the United States, under the direction of the Chief Signal Officer of the Army. Increase A. Lapham, a civilian assistant, issued the first storm warning for the

Great Lakes in November 1870. Although Lapham was responsible for the first Government weather forecasts for the United States, in November and December, 1870, "weather probabilities" had been prepared and issued under the auspices of the Cincinnati Chamber of Commerce by Cleveland Abbe as early as 1869.

At that time the very practical and important work of issuing advices and warnings of storms was greatly handicapped by lack of prompt and effective communication with ships at sea. Weather reports from the ocean were received by mail, after arrival of ships in port, and were thus too belated to be useful in the issue of storm warnings. Dependence was placed upon continental and island reports by telegraph. A system of signals, by flags and lights, was developed to give warning to ships in port or passing in view of the display stations. When the navigator passed beyond sight of land he had no further communication with the weather station to enable him to receive warnings and advices of storms.

### WEATHER REPORTS FROM SHIPS AT SEA

This situation continued until the beginning of the present century when the invention of wireless telegraphy by Marconi opened a new field of weather service. By that time the art of forecasting the weather had made considerable progress. For information concerning tropical storms, the forecasters depended upon coastal and island station observations, gathered by land telegraph lines and cables. These supplied meagre information when the storm was located in the Atlantic Ocean, Gulf of Mexico or Caribbean Sea at a distance from fixed observation points.

Having already the facilities for collecting and charting observations and issuing forecasts and warnings, the United States Weather Bureau and other national meteorological services were enabled to take advantage of direct communication with ships at sea as rapidly as installation of wireless apparatus on shipboard progressed. The first radio weather observation received by the Weather Bureau from a ship at sea was on December 3, 1905. The message was sent from the S.S. *New York* in latitude 40°N. and longitude 60°W. The first report of a hurricane received by wireless from a ship at sea was on August 26, 1909, from the S.S. *Cartago* near the coast of Yucatan.

A system of twice-daily observations from ships, with provision for special observations at intervening hours, was soon developed and proved of great assistance in charting storms at sea. Thus, wireless did for ocean weather reporting what the telegraph had already done for the continental weather service.

## BALLOON SOUNDINGS

In the last five years the attention of meteorologists has been directed toward a solution of the problem of securing observations in the upper levels of the hurricane. The ordinary pilot balloon which drifts freely as it rises, gives an indication of the movement of the air above the earth's surface. On account of the low clouds in the hurricane area, the balloons are lost from sight before revealing any information of value. In one method of securing the observations, use is made of a small meteorograph carried up by a sounding balloon. Observers at strategic points in the South Atlantic and Gulf States are notified to release balloons when a hurricane approaches. The meteorograph makes an automatic record of atmospheric conditions as the balloon rises. The balloon constantly expands as it reaches higher levels until it bursts, dropping the meteorograph which is equipped with a small parachute. A reward is offered the finder for returning it for a study of the record.

While this method may yield important information as to the structure of the hurricane, the record is not available in time to be used for forecasting. Efforts are now being concentrated on the development of a radiometeorograph which will send signals as the balloon rises. The signals are emitted on high frequency to indicate the pressure, temperature and humidity at various levels. Use of direction-finding apparatus may also enable the receiving station to plot the course of the balloon and thus ascertain the movement of the air at various altitudes. The radio transmitter and meteorograph are combined in one unit and must be compact and light in weight.

These developments promise a much needed extension of our knowledge of the hurricane to the upper levels—an advancement which will be similar to that made possible by radio in the earlier part of the century when the reporting system was extended to ships at sea.

## RECORDS OF HURRICANES

Though the history of tropical storms in the Atlantic, Gulf and Caribbean extends back more than four hundred years, much of it is incomplete. In that period there were, however, many tropical storms of great intensity, some of them commanding an important place in any chronicle of the times because of a frightful loss of human life, widespread devastation in cities, towns and agricultural regions, and the sinking or wrecking of fishing boats, merchant ships and men-of-war.

Tropical cyclones of the southern North Atlantic Ocean, Caribbean Sea and Gulf of Mexico are known as West Indian hurricanes. The approach of one of these great storms, when fully developed, is terrifying to the inhabitants of island and coastal sections in its path and the lives of many depend upon the warnings of the forecaster who traces its progress across his weather chart.

# CHAPTER I

# WINDS OF THE HURRICANE

AT the outer limits of the hurricane, the winds are light to moderate, and gusty. As the center approaches, they increase gradually, growing to squalls, then furious gales, and finally, in the fully developed hurricane, the winds immediately surrounding the center blow with indescribable fury. On the ocean the winds of the hurricane create tremendous seas and blow the tops of them away in sheets and spray, so that the mariner can scarcely tell where the ocean ends and the atmosphere begins. On land, the crops in the field are laid waste, buildings are destroyed and trees uprooted and the débris is carried along with the winds. In ships that go down at sea and in buildings that collapse ashore, many human lives are lost. Unsanitary conditions and disease follow often in the wake of the storm, adding to the death toll.

Words fail to present an adequate description of the fury of a great hurricane. A shipmaster who passed through the center of the hurricane which destroyed Santa Cruz del Sur in November 1932, wrote in his log a description of the winds he experienced. His notations followed the Beaufort scale.[1] Hour by hour the winds increased in violence as the center of the storm approached. He recorded the winds in higher numbers of the Beaufort scale, until he wrote that it was a full hurricane, force 12, the highest number of the scale. Then, finding no adjectives to describe the violence of the winds which continued to increase, he wrote in his log, "winds infinite."

Winds at the surface of the earth are retarded somewhat by friction, even over the ocean, so that we must conclude that the strongest winds of the hurricane are at some distance above the surface.

## MEASUREMENT OF HURRICANE WINDS

It is very difficult to determine, even approximately, the velocity of hurricane winds.

On board ships at sea, wind velocities are estimated by the effects of the wind upon smoke, flags and sails, but on steamships dependence

[1] The Beaufort scale is given in Chapter III.

is placed chiefly on observations of the action of the winds upon the water. At many land stations measurements are made by instruments. Pressure-tube anemometers exposed in the air stream indicate the pressures experienced, which are directly related to the wind speed. For many years the Weather Bureau has used anemometers of the Robinson type, so called because the instrument was invented in 1846 by J. T. R. Robinson, an Irish astronomer and physicist at Dublin. It has four hemispherical cups, mounted on arms, the whole attached to a vertical shaft and geared to a dial. The relation between the rotation of the cups and the movement of the wind is determined by tests and the instrument is designed to indicate the number of miles of wind movement in a given length of time.

### DESIGN OF WIND-MEASURING APPARATUS

Many perplexing problems are involved in designing instruments to measure accurately the speed of moving air. The standard Weather Bureau anemometer, of the Robinson type, has four hemispherical cups 4 inches in diameter on arms 6.72 inches long and was originally assumed to make 500 turns per mile of wind travel, regardless of the wind velocity. (Fig. 6.)

On January 1, 1932, the Weather Bureau adopted a policy of correcting all wind velocities indicated by anemometers so that the true winds would be used in publications, telegraphic reports, and records of all kinds. For that reason, when instrumental wind records are given in this chapter, true velocities, in important instances, are added in parentheses.

One very serious problem in designing wind-measuring devices arises from the requirement that the instrument be sufficiently sensitive to respond to variations at moderate velocities and yet be sturdy enough to withstand the winds of the hurricane. In many violent hurricanes the wind instruments have been damaged or blown away before the highest storm winds were experienced. In some instances the steel towers which supported the anemometers have been wrecked. In other cases the buildings on which the instruments were exposed have been destroyed or unroofed.

High velocities, when taken from a self-recording instrument, are usually given for a period of five consecutive minutes. Extreme velocities are sometimes determined for intervals of one or two minutes. Neither of these methods gives a measure of wind in gusts of very short duration which are characteristic of the hurricane.

FIGURE 6. Four-cup anemometer of the Robinson type used by the U.S. Weather Bureau.

Instrumental records indicate that the winds of the hurricane are sometimes sustained for intervals of five minutes at an average rate of more than 150 miles an hour. There is good reason to believe that the gusts of the hurricane represent air movements for brief intervals that may reach as high as 250 miles an hour in the most violent storms.

It is evident that our information concerning wind velocities in hurricanes is fragmentary.

The highest wind velocities of record in continental United States, and probably in the entire world, have been measured in New

Hampshire at Mt. Washington. The first of these extraordinary velocities occurred at Mt. Washington at 4 a.m. on January 11, 1878. A storm of great severity (not a hurricane) moved up the Atlantic coast from Cape Hatteras. The observer at Mt. Washington wrote into the records that at 11:22 p.m. of January 10, 1878, the wind was blowing from the east, 112 miles an hour, with heavy sleet. (A note said: "Window stove in and storm shutters put up.") At 11:40 p.m., wind east 144 miles an hour, heavy snow ("the roar of the wind is deafening and the building rocks and trembles"); 2 a.m., east 159 miles, heavy snow ("another window stove in"); 3 a.m., east 168 miles, heavy snow; 4 a.m., wind northeast, 186 miles, heavy snow.

These high velocities were attributed to the severity of the storm and to the altitude of the station.[2] The highest wind, 186 miles an hour as indicated by the Robinson anemometer, represented a true wind of approximately 140 miles an hour.

The U.S. Signal Service maintained a station on Mt. Washington for seventeen years. In October 1932, a meteorological station was again opened on the summit of the mountain under the auspices of Blue Hill Observatory. Wind records obtained there are of interest as illustrating the extreme velocities recorded in very short intervals.

Records of the Signal Service in the early period of occupancy were incomplete. Ordinary cup anemometers could not withstand the terrific winds. A special anemometer of rugged construction was used. During nine months of the year, ice formed on the instrument rendering it inoperative much of the time. Following reoccupancy of the station in 1932, a special anemometer with a heating element was installed, thus preventing the formation of ice. This anemometer, which had been calibrated at the U.S. Bureau of Standards, indicated a wind of 188 miles an hour which was sustained for a period of five minutes beginning at 12:25 p.m. on April 12, 1934. The instrument was designed to indicate each 1/30 mile of wind travel, thus giving a fairly good measurement of the speed of the gusts for very short intervals.

Several gusts were timed between 12:25 and 12:35 p.m. at 229 miles an hour and at 1:21 p.m., the extreme velocity of 231 miles an hour

[2] At Lansing, Mich., December 17, 1919, a wind velocity of 186 miles an hour was measured by drift of a pilot balloon at a height of 7,000 meters above the earth's surface.

was indicated twice.[3] The observatory building shook considerably under the impact of these terrific winds. Salvatore Pagliuca, the chief observer, was of the opinion that the heavy deposit of rough frost on the observatory building so increased the rigidity of the structure that it was able to withstand the winds.

### WINDS RECORDED IN SEVERE HURRICANES

At Miami Beach, Fla., during the hurricane of September 18, 1926, a wind velocity of 128 miles an hour (true wind 123) was sustained for five consecutive minutes beginning at 7:30 a.m. The record was obtained from a three-cup anemometer. Beginning at 7:40 a.m., the wind velocity for two consecutive minutes was 138 (132 true). The rate continued above 120 miles an hour until 8:12 a.m., when the anemometer blew away. These records were obtained from an instrument at Allison Hospital about four miles east of the city of Miami. The Weather Bureau office was in a three-story Federal building and the anemometer was exposed on top of the building. The exposure at the time of the hurricane was a very poor one, there being a number of higher buildings surrounding it, varying in height from eight to eighteen stories.

A violent hurricane which passed up the Atlantic coast in August 1879 was attended by extremely high winds. At Cape Lookout, N.C., on August 18, a velocity of 138 miles an hour (105 true) was recorded when the anemometer collapsed. The wind continued to rise to an estimated velocity of 165 miles an hour. If this estimate was correctly based upon the indications of the Robinson four-cup anemometer then in use, it represented a true wind velocity of 125 miles an hour.

All of the records of winds in hurricanes were exceeded at San Juan, Puerto Rico, in September 1928. At 11:44 a.m. of September 13 the three-cup anemometer at the office of the United States Weather Bureau at San Juan recorded a velocity of 150 miles an hour for five consecutive minutes (135 true) and an extreme velocity for one minute of 160 (144 true). (Fig. 7.)

[3] In July 1934, Marvin published an analysis of the high wind record of April 1934 at Mt. Washington. The analysis was based partly on new calibration tests at the Bureau of Standards in June 1934. The higher gusts were found to be 225 miles an hour (true) and the 5-minute maximum velocities 187 to 204 miles an hour. The gusts were timed and hence were exactly determined, whereas the 5-minute winds were measured from a record sheet with consequent uncertainty as to the precise measurement, hence the range of 187 to 204 in miles per hour.

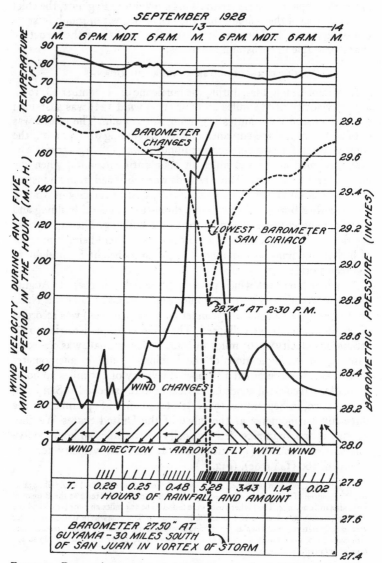

FIGURE 7. Barometric pressure, wind, temperature and rainfall in the hurricane of September 13, 1928, at San Juan, P.R. (From U.S. Weather Bureau records. After Fassig.)

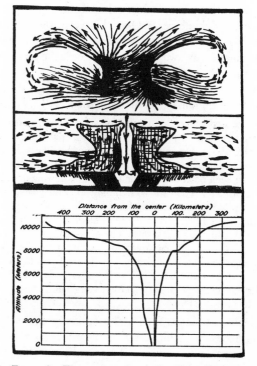

FIGURE 8. Three conceptions of cyclone structure. Upper, hurricane circulation after Hayden. Middle, vertical cross section of hurricane after Schubart. Lower, shape of the funnel of the Manila typhoon of 1882, from calculations by Haurwitz.

## THE "EYE OF THE STORM"

In nearly all tropical cyclones the highest winds are those which immediately encompass the calm center or "eye of the storm." As the calm center passes, the winds begin again, suddenly and with great violence, blowing from about the opposite quarter. The average diameter of the calm center is approximately 14 miles, though there are wide variations in individual cases. The time required for the central calm area to pass over a place depends upon (1) the diameter of the calm area and (2) the rate of progress of the hurricane.

There is sometimes a complete calm, though in many instances there are light variable breezes. Over the ocean, the seas are usually pyramidal, mountainous and confused, in the calm center. The clouds sometimes break away; sunlight succeeds the torrential rain by day and at night the stars appear.

Following is an excerpt from the account of the great hurricane of 1912 at Black River, Jamaica, written by the Rev. J. J. Williams, S.J.

Then succeeded a breathless calm for a few hours, that seemed to indicate that the very vortex of the storm was passing over us. This lull lasted for about three hours. The unnatural stillness, marred only by an occasional drizzle, was itself portentous of approaching trouble. As there had been no change of the wind, the knowing ones prepared for the worst. . . . The rain was coming in fitful gusts, when suddenly we seemed to be standing in the midst of a blazing furnace. Around the entire horizon was a ring of blood-red fire, shading away to a brilliant amber at the zenith. The sky, in fact (it was near the hour of sunset), formed one great fiery dome of reddish light that shone through the descending rain. . . . Then burst forth the hurricane afresh, and for two hours or more (I have lost track of the hours that night) it raged and tore asunder what little had passed unscathed through the previous blow.

The following extract is from a description of the passage of the ship *Idaho* through the calm center of a tropical cyclone in the China Sea, September 21, 1869, as given by John Eliot in his *Handbook of Cyclonic Storms of the Bay of Bengal*.

Till then the sea had been beaten down by the wind, and only boarded the vessel when she became completely unmanageable; but now the waters, relieved from all restraint (in the calm center), rose in their own might. Ghastly gleams of lightning revealed them piled up on every side in rough, pyramidal masses, mountain high,—the revolving circle of the wind, which everywhere enclosed them, causing them to boil and tumble as though they were being stirred in some mighty cauldron. The ship, no longer blown over on her side, rolled and pitched, and was tossed about like a cork. The sea rose, toppled over, and fell with crushing force upon her decks. Once she shipped immense bodies of water over both her bows, both quarters, and the starboard gangway at the same moment. Her seams opened fore and aft. Both above and below the men were pitched about the decks and many of them injured.

FIGURE 9. Birds on the S.S. *West Quechee* in calm center of a hurricane in August 1926.

At twenty minutes before eight o'clock the vessel entered the vortex; at twenty minutes past nine o'clock it had passed and the hurricane returned blowing with renewed violence from the north, veering to the east. The ship was now only an unmanageable wreck.

During the passage of the calm center, the roar of the hurricane winds on all sides may sometimes be heard distinctly. It has been described as a "moaning of the winds," a "roar in the air," and "a hollow and distant rumbling noise." By day the banks of hurricane clouds may be seen at the horizon. At sea, birds, exhausted, alight or fall upon the decks of the ship. (Fig. 9.)

There are few instances of a calm center passing directly over a fully equipped meteorological observatory. One such instance occurred at Manila, October 20, 1882. (Fig. 10.) The following is quoted from John Eliot's work:

At 11:46 a.m. (20th), after a violent rush from the west-northwest, Manila was in the vortex. The calm was not absolute, but with alternate gusts and lulls for about eight minutes. At 11:52 a.m. the calm was absolute for two minutes; then alternate calm and gusts from the southwest. Blue sky was not seen, but it cleared to a dense, watery vapor; the dark belt of the storm could be traced on the horizon. The diameter of the vortex was probably not more than fourteen or sixteen miles.

The most striking phenomenon of the calm center was the sudden change of temperature and hygrometric condition of the air, as revealed by the curves traced; the former from seventy-five degrees to eighty-eight degrees Fahrenheit (i.e. seventy-five degrees before passage of the center, eighty-eight degrees during passage, and seventy-five after), and the latter from fifty-three (rarely observed here and only in April and May), up to saturation (i.e. saturation before and after passage, fifty-three during passage). Persons who opened their windows during the calm were instantly compelled to close them, for the air "burned" as in the Italian sirocco.

The hurricane of September 1926 passed directly over Miami, Fla., and the relatively calm center was felt in the central and southern parts of the city, while over the extreme northern parts of the city there was no pronounced lull. At the Weather Bureau office, the wind fell to 10 miles an hour at 6:30 a.m., while at the Allison Hospital, 6¼ miles northeast of the Weather Bureau office, the wind was at that moment 80 miles an hour, having been 108 miles ten minutes before. For about 35 minutes, at the Weather Bureau office, the wind blew

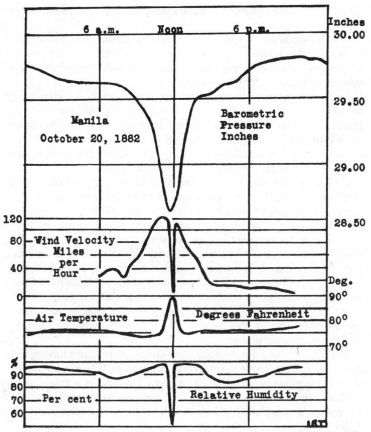

FIGURE 10.  Barometric pressure, wind velocity, temperature and relative humidity during passage of typhoon over Manila on October 20, 1882.

from all points of the compass, with velocities ranging from about 8 to 14 miles an hour.

### DESCENDING CURRENTS IN THE CYCLONE CENTER

The existence of descending currents in the central area of absolute or relative calm of the tropical cyclone has been asserted by a number of meteorologists. Phenomena which support this view are (1) the light winds, or absence of wind movement; (2) the rise in temperature noted at the center of some tropical cyclones; and (3) the low relative humidity (dry air).

Gentle winds and clear skies or broken clouds, without rain or snow, are characteristic of the center of anticyclonic systems with descending and outflowing winds, clockwise in the northern hemisphere. Descending air grows warmer and drier.

As to the cause of the temperature rise, there is a difference of opinion. Father Algué, discussing the Manila typhoon of 1882, expressed the opinion that the increase in temperature was due to the sun's heat in the clear, central region, so that the low temperatures attending cloudiness and rainfall were succeeded naturally by normal temperatures under the influence of solar radiation.

Co-Ching Chu found during the years 1904-1915 four cases of an increase of temperature during the passage of the central relative calm of typhoons. In one case the temperature rise was more remarkable than during the Manila storm of 1882. It occurred at Taito, Formosa, on September 16, 1912. Between 9 and 10 p.m. of the 16th, the barometer was 28.05 inches and, with this minimum, there was a rise of 19°F. from 75.4°F. to 94.1°F., in temperature as shown by the thermograph during a period of one hour. (Fig. 11.) This rise of temperature, taking place at about 9 p.m. and not at midday, as in the Manila typhoon, cannot be explained by the sun's radiation. Indeed, as Chu points out, a cooling would be expected, owing to nocturnal radiation into a clear sky.

The typhoon at Taito was a mature storm, its presence having been noted for six days prior to its arrival at Formosa. The wind velocities were the highest of record at Taito and Tainan. As a result of the typhoon there were 107 deaths, 293 persons were injured, 91,400 houses were completely demolished and 115,700 houses were partially wrecked.

Chu mentioned other cases, not so pronounced. In some of them the temperature rise occurred during hours of darkness. He was of the opinion that the rises in temperature were the result of a gently descending current in the "eye of the storm."

T. Okada was of the opinion that high temperature and dryness are only occasional phenomena but are not essential characteristics of the central calm or "eye of the storm." He cites the case of the Hamamatu typhoon of September 24, 1918. At 12:10 p.m., the city was within the central calm of the typhoon. The sky was covered by a thin sheet of clouds but the sun shone through for a time. At the

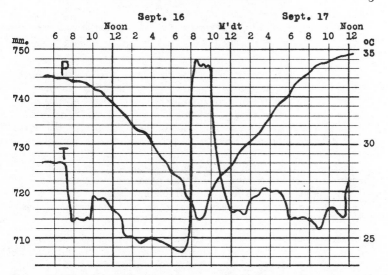

FIGURE 11. Barograph and thermograph curves at Taito, Formosa, September 16-17, 1912. *T*—temperature, Centigrade. *P*—pressure, in millimeters.

Hamamatu Meteorological Station, the temperature rose from 22°C. to 23.5°C. The relative humidity fell from 98% at noon to 94% at 12:30 p.m. Humidity observations were taken every five minutes and the lowest recorded during the passage of the calm was 92%. It is evident that the central region of this typhoon was filled with moist air.

Okada also cites the very unusual case of the Gifu typhoon, July 9, 1903. At the Gifu Meteorological Observatory, the central calm was felt from 9:50 to 10:00 a.m. The dense clouds partly disappeared so that the blue sky was visible through openings and there was sunlight. The temperature was rising as the center approached but immediately on passage into the relative calm, the temperature fell abruptly, the total fall amounting to about 2.5°C. After the calm the temperature rose again by about 5°C. in little more than an hour. Though it was relatively cool in the calm center, the humidity, which was 95% before the calm, fell abruptly to about 60%, then rose to 98% after the calm.

Bernhard Haurwitz, who studied records of the Manila typhoon and of some hurricanes of southern United States, published a paper in 1935 in which he expressed the opinion that descent of air is at least partially responsible for the warm and dry air at the center of the tropical cyclone. Referring particularly to the Manila typhoon of 1882, he says:

> The relative humidity, which was about 100 percent immediately before and after the calm, dropped to 49.7 percent. The rise in temperature may be due to insolation, according to Algué, in spite of a continuous "veil of condensed vapor." If the change in relative humidity had been caused by insolation of the same air mass that was present before the calm, we should expect to observe a drop in relative humidity to about 61 percent; but the air in the center is very much drier, indicating that in the eye of the storm we have a downward current which brings warm and dry air to the ground. This air in the center probably comes from the surrounding regions of the cyclone, and has lost part of its moisture content by precipitation during previous ascent.

There seems to be no other satisfactory solution than that of a descending air current at the center, yet, if true, it is a paradox for we must assume that the tropical cyclone as a whole involves ascending currents on a grand scale to account for the torrential rainfall and to provide an outlet for the vast quantity of air that is carried inward at the surface.

### TORNADOES WITHIN THE HURRICANE

There are few authentic records of tornadoes or violent local storms of tornadic nature occurring within a hurricane. Tornadoes are of relatively small diameter but of terrific violence. Winds of the tornado possibly attain velocities as high as 500 miles an hour. A characteristic feature is the pendant, funnel-shaped cloud which reaches down to earth, sometimes writhing about. Where this cloud reaches down to earth there is terrible destruction. The tornado can be seen; the hurricane is so vast that the observer can see only an extremely small part of the whole. (Fig. 12.)

In extratropical cyclones of middle latitudes, the tornado occurs as a rule in the southeast quadrant. Occurrences of tornadoes in hurricanes in the United States in recent years have been confined to the State of Florida; they have been observed only in the northern semicircle of a hurricane passing through the Florida Straits or over extreme southern Florida. Tornadoes were reported as occurring at Charleston, S.C., in 1811 and 1814, during the passage of hurricanes.

FIGURE 12.  A tornado. (Elmwood, Neb., April 6, 1919. Photo by W. A. Wood.)

On September 10, 1919, a tornado occurred at Goulds, Fla., a small town about twenty miles southwest of Miami. It passed Goulds at about 1:00 to 1:15 p.m., eastern summer time. A tropical storm of great energy was then central over the extreme southeastern Gulf of Mexico, having passed through the Florida Straits. Goulds was well within the hurricane area.

There were many evidences of a whirling motion of the air. Many trees were found with large pieces of tin and sheet-metal roofing wrapped around them. The roofing had been torn from buildings one mile to the east. The tornado moved from east to west in the same direction as the hurricane in which it formed.

In September 1929 a hurricane passed westward through the Florida Straits and on the 28th there were tornadoes at Fort Lauderdale, Miami, Stuart and Boca Ratone.

On the night of October 4 to 5, 1933, when a tropical storm was near southern Florida, east of Key West and south of Miami, having moved to that position from the vicinity of Havana, tornadoes occurred at Miami, Hollywood and Fort Lauderdale. At least one of these moved from east to west, whereas in this case the hurricane itself was moving toward the northeast.

### STORMS OF LARGE AND SMALL DIAMETER

Wind velocity in tropical storms of small diameter is probably as high or higher than in the great storms of large diameter. Destruction is confined to a much smaller path, however, and frequently storms of small diameter cross our coasts in sections that are sparsely inhabited so that no records are obtained from the storm center and destruction of a few scattered buildings attracts little attention. In extreme cases the winds of the small diameter storm are probably of greater velocity. In some of them the barometer at the center is in the neighborhood of 27.50 inches and in rare instances much lower, which compares favorably in that respect with the greatest of hurricanes. Since the diameter of the small storm is much less, the barometric gradient is much steeper and hence the wind velocities must be higher.

### THE LAW OF STORMS

On ships at sea passing through tropical cyclones, changes in direction and force of the wind are fully understood. A knowledge of the law of storms is an essential part of the education of ships' officers. To the landsman who experiences a tropical storm, the direction from which the wind blows, in relation to the position of the storm center, is sometimes puzzling. After the wind blows from one general direction for a considerable time, increasing in force, a calm succeeds, followed by a violent wind from nearly the opposite quarter. It simply means that the storm center has passed over the place. Nevertheless, it is frequently said that the "storm came back." When the wind blows from northeast toward the southwest, the conclusion is that the storm is coming from the northeast and moving toward the southwest. Then when the southwest wind succeeds the calm, the conclusion is that the storm has come back and is now moving from southwest to northeast. Such conclusions are altogether erroneous.

In order that seamen might easily understand and anticipate the changes in wind during the rather complex combined movements of ship and storm, Piddington used the "horn card." Such a diagram for a tropical storm in the northern hemisphere is shown in the accompanying figure. (Fig. 13.) In the southern hemisphere, of course, the winds turn in the opposite direction.

To apply the principle of the "horn card" to the landsman's purposes is very simple. A sheet of transparent paper is placed over the

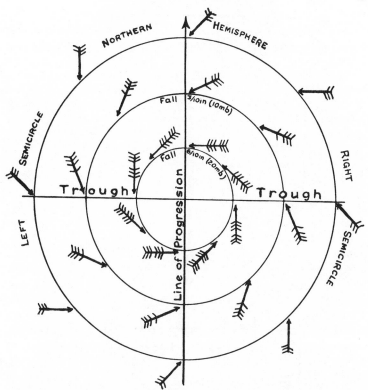

FIGURE 13. Diagram illustrating the principle of the "Horn Card."

diagram and the circular lines, wind arrows, and line of progression are traced on the paper. If desired, a diagram may be drawn to a smaller scale. It is then placed over a map, with its center at the reported position of the storm center. If the transparent diagram is moved over the map until it passes over the observer's locality, he will see the changes in the force and direction of the wind that will take place (1) if the center moves directly over him, (2) if it moves to the right of him and (3) if it moves to his left. The direction of the arrow nearest to him at any time will give the direction of the wind he would experience and the number of barbs on the arrow will indicate the wind's force.

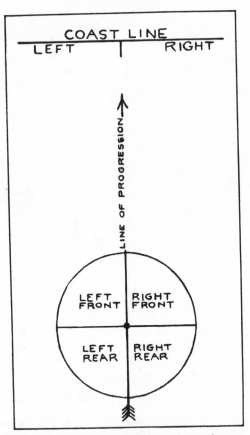

FIGURE 14. Diagram showing the quadrants of a tropical storm and the "right" and "left" sides of the path
with respect to the direction of progression.

By experimenting with such a diagram it becomes easy for anyone
to visualize the successive changes of wind direction and force in the
event that a tropical storm approaches from any direction and passes
over or to either side of the observer, and when the storm's progressive motion is in a straight line or along a curved path.

It must be kept in mind, however, that the diagram represents ideal
conditions, that the storm may not be quite circular or symmetrical,

and that the progressive movement of the storm will affect the force and to some extent the direction of the winds as they will actually be experienced.

If a tropical storm be divided into four quadrants, they are called the right front, left front, right rear and left rear, as they would be to an observer looking forward along the line of progress from the storm center. The storm is said to cross the coast line to the right or left of a place, as viewed by the observer who is supposed to be located at the storm center and looking forward along the line of progress. This is illustrated in the accompanying diagram. (Fig. 14.)

When a tropical storm in the northern hemisphere passes to the left of a place, at some distance, or directly over the place on the coast, the winds are more severe because the progressive movement of the storm augments the force of the wind. The tide is high because the winds are stronger and blow more or less directly toward the shore.

When a tropical storm in the northern hemisphere passes to the right of a place on the coast, the winds are less severe and the tide is not so high and tends to go below the normal as the storm center passes the coast line, because the winds blow more or less directly off shore. When a storm of great force passes across a coast line, there is usually very little destruction to the left of the center. On the right, serious property damage may extend to considerable distances.

These conditions are of course reversed in the southern hemisphere.

# CHAPTER II

# THE STORM WAVE

FLYING débris and wrecked buildings in hurricane winds have caused the death of thousands of people. Thousands more have lost their lives in ships gone down at sea. Yet more than three-fourths of all the loss of human lives in tropical cyclones has been due to inundations. The rise of the sea over low coastal areas not subject to overflow by the ordinary tides is sometimes sudden and overwhelming and in some situations there is no escape.

Usually the rise of the sea is gradual as the center of the storm approaches but sometimes it comes swiftly. Rising waters attending tropical cyclones have been called "tidal waves." They are not tides like the daily ebb and flow brought about by gravitational forces. The French use the expression, *raz de marée*. In connection with cyclones of the Bay of Bengal, Piddington and Eliot have called them "storm waves." These terrible phenomena are not completely understood. Some meteorologists have expressed doubts that a sudden inundation of the character of the so-called "tidal wave" can be produced by a tropical cyclone. Certainly it is a gradual process in most cases.

### INUNDATIONS CAUSED BY TROPICAL STORMS

Yet the history of these terrible storms reveals many instances of cities and towns overwhelmed and thousands of lives lost in inundations, which is evidence that such rises are not always gradual. One of the latest to be added to the long list of calamities of this nature occurred at Santa Cruz del Sur, Cuba, in November 1932. (Fig. 15.)

### DISASTER AT SANTA CRUZ DEL SUR

We have no meteorological record of this storm at Santa Cruz del Sur, because the rise of the sea carried everything before it; the observer was drowned and the instruments and records were lost. The secretary of the Municipal Administration at Santa Cruz del Sur, Senor Clemente Arias, reported that there was a rise of the sea, which means that there was a storm wave. Out of a population of about four thousand, approximately twenty-five hundred lives were lost.

FIGURE 15. Santa Cruz del Sur, Cuba, after devastation by the storm wave attending the hurricane of November 9, 1932. Photograph by the Rev. M. Gutierrez Lanza, S.J.

Although the winds of this hurricane reached tremendous velocities, estimated at 210 miles an hour in Nuevitas, the destruction at Santa Cruz del Sur was caused principally by the sea and not directly by the force of the winds.

### THE STORM WAVE AT CORINGA

Piddington quoted from an account of a storm wave at Coringa on the Bay of Bengal:

Coringa was destroyed in a single day. A frightful phenomenon reduced it to its present state. In the month of December 1789, at the moment when a high tide was at its highest point, and that the northwest wind blowing with fury, accumulated the waters at the head of the bay, the unfortunate inhabitants of Coringa saw with terror three monstrous waves coming in from the sea, and following each other at short distances. The first, sweeping everything in its passage, brought several feet of water into the town. The second augmented these ravages by inundating all the low country, and the third overwhelmed everything.

According to Piddington, the town and twenty thousand inhabitants disappeared; vessels at anchor in the mouth of the river were carried into the plains surrounding Yanaon, which suffered considerably also. "The sea in retiring left heaps of sand and mud, which rendered all search for the property or bodies impossible, and shut up the mouth of the river for large ships. The only trace of the ancient town which now remains [1860], is the house of the master attendant and the dockyards surrounding it." However, this final result was in part accomplished by a repetition of the disaster in 1839. Another cyclone and storm wave in that year equalled the inundation of 1789.

### THE HOOGHLY DISASTER OF 1737

Perhaps the greatest catastrophe of this nature was that which occurred on October 7, 1737, at the mouth of the Hooghly River, on the Bay of Bengal. A furious cyclone destroyed twenty thousand craft of all descriptions and the storm wave rose forty feet. It is recorded that three hundred thousand people perished in Lower Bengal or in the Bay. Apparently this is a favorable spot for the development of a storm wave. Another similar catastrophe took place in 1864 and approximately fifty thousand human lives were lost and one hundred thousand head of cattle drowned.

### STORM TIDES AND GRAVITATIONAL TIDES

Evidently the storm wave is facilitated by a rising ocean bed and favorable shore contours, as is the astronomical tide in like situations. The ordinary rise of the tide, from gravitational causes, amounts to only two or three feet in the open oceans. There it is of little significance; its rise and fall are gradual. When it reaches the coast, its range is often ten to twelve feet. In certain bays and channels, where the wave encounters the shores and a rising ocean bed, the rise may be twenty-five to fifty feet above low water. The times of ebb and flow of such a tide are well known; otherwise many people would be caught unawares and drowned. On the other hand, the storm wave comes so rarely to any one community that it is seldom anticipated in its fully developed form.

In some places the storm tide is never in any form except a fairly gradual rise of water; in other localities destructive storm waves are developed whenever a tropical cyclone of great intensity follows a particular course across the coast line.

### STORM CURRENTS

As a vast whirlwind of great power, the cyclone communicates its whirling movement to the waters. If it moves slowly the winds act for a longer time upon the same water area and more vigorous cur-

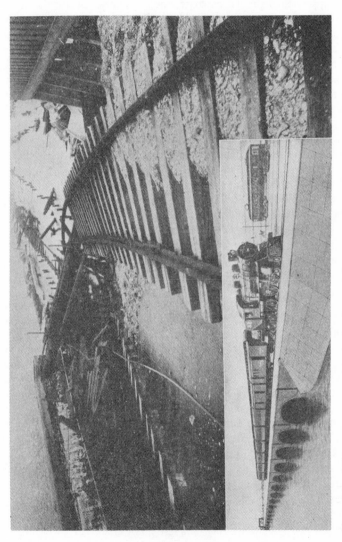

FIGURE 16. Galveston causeway after the hurricane of August 1915. Insert shows causeway before the hurricane. Destruction caused principally by wave action.

rents are set up around the storm center. This movement of the water reaches to considerable depths. When the great hurricane of August 1915 approached the Texas coast, the current set up by the storm carried Trinity Shoals gas and whistling buoy nearly ten miles to the westward. This buoy weighed 21,000 pounds, and was anchored in 42 feet of water with a 6,500-pound sinker and 252 feet of anchor chain weighing 3,250 pounds. Another evidence of strong currents is the excessive drift of vessels in tropical cyclones. Eliot says that the currents over the whole storm area of fierce, hurricane winds, agree approximately in direction with the winds and are probably stronger than is commonly imagined. He remarks that an increasing set of water to the westward at the head of the Bay of Bengal is a marked and characteristic feature of cyclone formation in the center or north of the Bay.

When the cyclone is at some distance from the coast, the first tidal effect is a slow rise in the section toward which the storm is moving. Eliot states that there is an accumulation of water at the north end of the Bay of Bengal as a cyclone approaches from the south. A similar rise occurs on the Gulf and South Atlantic coasts of the United States when a hurricane approaches.

### DEVELOPMENT OF THE STORM WAVE

The true storm wave is not developed unless the slope of the ocean bed and the contour of the coast line are favorable. Like the gravitational tide, it reaches its greatest height in certain situations. If there is a bay to the right of the point where the cyclone center moves inland, the waters are driven into the bay. With a gently sloping bed, the water is piled up by resistance and becomes a great wave or series of waves which moves forward and to the left, the principal inundation usually taking place on the left bay shore. Great storm waves which have taken an enormous toll of human lives have, so far as records are available, occurred in nearly every case in a situation of this kind.

A notable instance occurred at Indianola, Tex. The town was located about midway of the southwest shore of Matagorda and Lavaca Bays. A hurricane approached from the southeast, on August 19, 1886. The center of the storm passed inland to the southwest of Matagorda Bay (the left side), in the early morning of

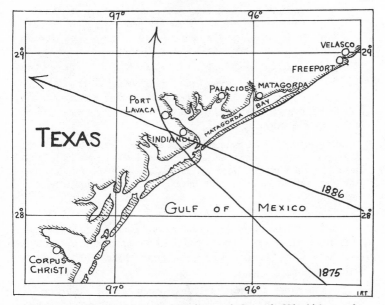

FIGURE 17. Tracks of centers of hurricanes of 1875 and 1886 which caused inundations at Indianola, Tex.

August 20. (Fig. 17.) The following is taken from an account in the *Monthly Weather Review* of August 1886:

From that time [9 p.m. of August 19], the force of the wind gradually increased, veering slightly, and about daylight the water in the bay commenced to rise rapidly. At this hour the wind was blowing at the rate of seventy-two miles an hour and the Signal Office building [the weather station] gave way; in attempting to escape, the observer, I. A. Reed, was killed by falling timber. A lamp in the office set fire to the building and, although rain was falling heavily, it was burned, and also more than a block of buildings on both sides of the street. Shortly after daylight the wind grew stronger, blowing from the east; about 5 a.m. of the 20th most of the damage to property was done.

The appearance of the town after the storm was one of universal wreck. Not a house remained uninjured, and most of those that were left standing were in an unsafe condition. Many were washed away completely and scattered over the plains back of the town; others were lifted from their foundations and moved bodily over considerable distances. Over all this strip of low ground, as far as could be seen, were the wrecks of houses, carriages, personal property of all kinds, and a great many dead animals. Very few people were able to save anything whatever, and as the houses which were left were scarcely habitable the town was deserted as fast as possible.

Indianola was never rebuilt. The town had suffered a similar calamity in a hurricane in 1875, the center of which, like that of 1886, moved across the coast line to the southwest of Matagorda Bay. (Fig. 17.) The account in the *Monthly Weather Review* for September 1875, gives the following facts:

> September 16, 1875. Rain continued and the storm increased to a hurricane from the northeast, accompanied by a disastrous inundation from the bay. One hundred and seventy-six lives were lost and three-fourths of the town swept away. The highest wind registered was 88 miles an hour when the anemometer blew away; highest wind estimated at 100 miles an hour.

A similar disaster occurred at Galveston, Tex., in 1900. The center of the hurricane crossed the coast line to the southwest of Galveston Bay. The following is quoted from the report of the weather observer, Dr. I. M. Cline:

> The water rose at a steady rate from 3 p.m. until about 7.30 p.m., when there was a sudden rise of about 4 feet in as many seconds. I was standing at my front door, which was partly open, watching the water which was flowing with *great rapidity from east to west*. The water at this time was about 8 inches deep in my residence and the sudden rise of 4 feet brought it above my waist before I could change my position.

The rise of water occurred about 7:30 p.m., September 8, 1900. The center of the hurricane was approaching the shore line to the southwestward and the east to west current (right to left) was being impeded by the shore. Approximately six thousand persons lost their lives in this inundation.

To produce a storm wave, the cyclone must move in a direction nearly normal to the coast line. Its currents are then developed to maximum strength when the storm reaches the shallows near the coast. If the storm moves slowly, the winds have more time in which to develop a storm wave.

#### HIGHEST TIDES OF RECORD ON THE GULF COAST

The highest tides of record on the coast of the Gulf of Mexico have been developed under such circumstances. (Fig. 18.)

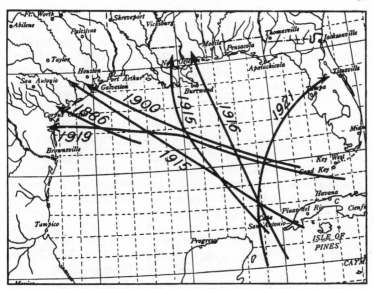

FIGURE 18. Tracks of centers of hurricanes which caused highest tides of record
on Gulf Coast.

At Corpus Christi, in 1919, the storm center passed to the left of
the bay and the waters reached a height of 16 feet on the bay shore.
The storm moved slowly and in a direction nearly at right angles to
the coast line. A rapidly moving storm in August 1916, which passed
over the same section of coast, created considerably less tide than the
slow moving storm of 1919.

The Indianola storms of 1875 and 1886, and the Galveston storms
of 1900 and 1915, created very high tides; all of them moved to the
left of Matagorda and Galveston Bays, respectively.

In 1915, a severe storm moved inland over southern Louisiana, in a
direction nearly normal to the coast line, and the highest tides of
record occurred to the right of the Mississippi Delta.

In July 1916, a hurricane moved inland to the left of Mobile Bay,
in a direction nearly normal to the coast line, and Mobile, at the upper
end of the bay and to the left, experienced the highest tide of record,
11.6 feet.

The situation of Tampa, on the western coast of Florida, is not favorable for storm tides, because the majority of severe hurricanes approach the city from the southeast or south. In October 1921 a severe hurricane recurved in the eastern Gulf and crossed the coast line to the left of Tampa, moving in a direction nearly normal to the coast line on passing inland. The waters in Tampa Bay rose to 10.5 feet, by far the highest of record.

### STORM WAVES ON SHORES OF THE BAY OF BENGAL

In the Bay of Bengal the conditions along shore are more favorable for tidal waves, especially at the head of the bay. The daily tide, due to gravitational forces, is developed to a much greater extent than the tides of the Gulf of Mexico. These conditions combine to produce much more severe storm waves on the coast of India, especially when the time of high water approximately coincides with the arrival of the storm wave. There the storm wave arrives as a sudden rise of water, sometimes as an advancing wall of water and at other times in the form of a bore. The only record of a bore produced by a West Indian hurricane was in September 1926, at Miami. There, the highest water occurred with the shift of wind at the center of the storm, and in the Miami River the tide came in the form of a bore that left a mass of wreckage from boats that had sought safe anchorage in the river.

Eliot describes several great cyclones in the Bay of Bengal, some of which were attended by pronounced storm waves. (Fig. 19.)

*The Calcutta cyclone of 1864.*—It crossed the coast line near Contai, moving in a direction nearly at right angles to the coast, at the left of the mouth of the Hooghly. The barometer fell to 28.025 inches and the calm lasted at Contai from 9:45 to 11:00 a.m. The storm wave arrived at the mouth of the Hooghly a little after 10:00 a.m., high water being due at about noon as the moon was nearly full. There was an enormous accumulation of water at the northwest angle of the bay (the left side). The storm wave was estimated to have risen 40 feet. Loss of life from drowning was estimated at 50,000 and from disease as a result of the inundation, 30,000.

*The Backergunge cyclone of 1876.*—The center moved across the bay toward the northeast, passing to the left of Chittagong, and near Backergunge on the left shore. An enormous storm wave was driven over the islands and lowlands near the mouth of the Megna. There was an unusually high tide, followed very shortly by the storm wave. The pressure of the advancing wave prevented the tidal and river

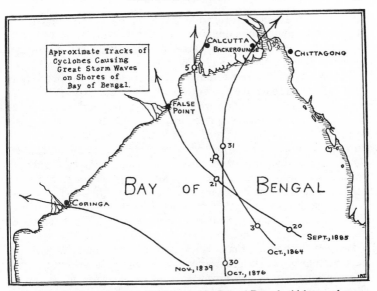

FIGURE 19. Tracks of centers of cyclones in the Bay of Bengal which caused storm waves and great loss of life; Backergunge, October 1876; Calcutta, October 1864; False Point, September 1885; and Coringa, November 1839. (From data collected by J. Eliot and H. Piddington.)

water from flowing off. The storm wave was retarded and finally overpowered the downflowing waters and rushed with irresistible force over the islands and low-lying coastal areas, covering them to a depth of 10 to 30 or 40 feet. It was estimated that 100,000 lives were lost from drowning and subsequently 100,000 more died of disease as a result of the inundation.

It has been said by several writers that this was the most extensive and the fiercest cyclone of that century.

*The False Point cyclone of 1885.*—In this cyclone an extremely low barometer reading, 27.135 inches, was recorded. The cyclone center passed over False Point Lighthouse. At the lighthouse, at 6:30 a.m., the wind hauled from northeast to northwest, continued to blow a hurricane for a few minutes, then suddenly lulled. The calm lasted until 6:50 a.m., when the wind came with redoubled fury from the south-southwest. The storm wave came up at 6:20 a.m. (before the arrival of the calm center), and swept over False Point Harbor, destroying all the houses. It rolled in a wide unbroken wave in a north-easterly direction, submerging villages and carrying away before it, with irresistible force, houses, cattle, human beings, etc. The measured height of the wave at False Point was 22 feet.

Typhoons have caused a number of storm waves. One in 1881, at Haifong, is said to have caused the death of 300,000 persons.

On January 13, 1903, the Society Islands, in the South Pacific, were devastated by enormous waves breaking over them, causing the death of 1,000 persons and the loss of great quantities of property. A hurricane had been raging and when the center of the storm reached shore, several abnormal waves broke on it, each being higher than its predecessor, until, according to accounts, a wall of water, 40 feet in height, rushed across the islands, covering them with water for miles.

A hurricane which did great damage in the southern Marshall Islands on June 30, 1905, caused a storm wave at Mille that was reported to be 46 feet in height.

However, it appears that when the storm wave coincides with the maximum height of the gravitational tide, in regions where the latter is exceptionally well developed, there is little reason for doubting that the combined effect produces a wave which may reach a height of at least 40 feet, because the gravitational tide alone, in some localities, exceeds that height.

#### THEORIES OF PIDDINGTON AND BLANFORD

Piddington, Blanford, and others attempted to explain the storm wave. It was Piddington's belief that a mass of water was raised above the level of the ocean by the diminution of atmospheric pressure and carried bodily along with the storm. He noted the fact that the true storm wave occurred only in certain situations when this mass of water reached bays or river mouths, or other confined situations.

Blanford evidently adopted Piddington's explanation. He assumed a "head of water in the central part of the vortex" and stated that "it is only when the wave thus formed reaches a low coast, with a shallow, shelving foreshore, such as are the coasts of Bengal and Orissa, that, like the tidal wave, it is retarded and piled up to a height which enables it to inundate the flats of the maritime belt, over which it sweeps with irresistible onset."

Such an explanation requires as its basis the assumption that the central mass of water is driven forward by the winds at the rear of the cyclone. It is common observation that the tide rises along the coast in advance of a cyclone when the winds are offshore, opposing the water's rise. In the cases cited by Blanford, the storm wave was not driven in by the winds at the rear of the cyclone; the wave preceded the winds. At False Point in 1885 (September 23) the storm wave came up at False Point Harbor at 6:20 a.m. while the wind was still blowing with hurricane force from the northeast; thus the wave progressed toward the northeastward *against* the wind. At 6:30 a.m. the wind shifted to northwest, followed by a calm until 6:50 a.m., when the wind came with redoubled fury from the west-southwest.

### ARRIVAL OF STORM WAVES DURING THE CALM

In the Calcutta cyclone of October 5, 1864, the storm wave arrived at the mouth of the Hooghly a little after 10 a.m. On the coast at Contai where the center passed, there was a calm from 9:45 a.m. until 11:00 a.m. so the storm wave came in during the calm. The center of this storm also passed over Tamluck where the storm wave came in between 11:30 a.m. and noon. The center then arrived with a calm lasting more than half an hour, at the end of which the rear winds of the cyclone arrived.

In the "Labor Day Storm" of September 2, 1935, on the Florida Keys (Fig. 20), a rise of water came from the southern side of the Keys; reports agreed in describing the great rapidity with which the rise came as a "wall of water" or a "high wave." The track and cross ties of the railroad were in one stretch washed off a concrete viaduct 30 feet above ordinary water level, but wave action probably contributed to this result. A cooperative observer of the Weather Bureau at Long Key, J. E. Duane, wrote an account of his experiences in the storm center, from which the following is quoted:

> During this lull the sky is clear to northward, stars shining brightly and a very light breeze continued; no flat calm. About the middle of the lull, which lasted a timed 55 minutes, the sea began to lift up, it seemed, and rise very fast; this from the ocean side of camp. I put my flashlight out on sea and could see walls of water which seemed many feet high. I had to race fast to regain entrance of cottage, but water caught me waist deep, although writer was only about 60 feet from doorway of cottage. Water lifted cottage from its foundations and it floated.
>
> 10:10 p.m.—Barometer now 27.02 inches; wind beginning to blow from SSW.

FIGURE 20. Airplane view of the rescue train that was sent to remove World War veterans and residents from the Florida Keys, September 2, 1935, and was swept from the tracks by the hurricane and storm wave.—*Courtesy Miami Daily News*

10:15 p.m.—The first blast from SSW, full force. House now breaking up—wind seemed stronger than any time during storm. I glanced at barometer which read 26.98 inches, dropped it in water and was blown outside into sea; got hung up in broken fronds of cocoanut tree and hung on for dear life. I was then struck by some object and knocked unconscious.

September 3: 2:25 a.m.—I became conscious in tree and found I was lodged about 20 feet above ground.

It will be noted that this storm wave came in during the calm.

Fortunately, along the Gulf and South Atlantic coasts of the United States, storm waves are not so readily developed as on the coasts of India, probably due to less favorable contours of shore and ocean bed and because the tide from gravitational forces is of a smaller range so that its coincidence with the hurricane tide does not result in such a great rise of the sea.

# CHAPTER III

# ORIGIN OF WEST INDIAN HURRICANES

THE word "hurricane" originally came from the natives of the West Indies or Central America. It is an Indian word. By early navigators at and following the time of Columbus, the word was variously given as "aracan," "huiranvucan," "urican," "huracan," etc. It is claimed by some to be a Carib Indian word signifying "big wind." According to Professor Lehmann-Nitsche, the god of stormy weather was "Hunrakan" to the Indians of Guatemala, from whom the word hurricane came. As a name for tropical cyclones of the West Indies, it has come into general use. Tropical storms of other parts of the world are now called hurricanes.

In 1806, Sir Francis Beaufort, a British admiral and the hydrographer of the Navy, introduced a numerical scale from 0 to 12, for estimating the force of the wind. He marked a calm as 0, light air as 1, a slight breeze as 2, etc., up to a force of 12, the highest of the scale, which he called a "hurricane." The Beaufort scale of wind force is now universally used and any wind, whether accompanying a tropical cyclone or not, if it reaches a force of 12, is called a hurricane.

Thus the word hurricane has come to have two distinct meanings with resulting confusion. It is (1) a cyclonic wind system of the tropics, which may or may not be attended by winds as high as force 12 on the Beaufort scale, and (2) a wind of force 12 from any cause whatever.

West Indian hurricanes apparently originate chiefly within certain restricted areas; one is the southeastern portion of the North Atlantic Ocean near and south of the Cape Verde Islands; another is the western Caribbean Sea. C. L. Mitchell, who traced many of these storms to a place of origin, published an account of them in 1924, in which he stated that hurricanes rarely originate over the Atlantic Ocean west of longitude 30°W. and that they never have their genesis over the Caribbean Sea east of longitude 78°W.

They seldom if ever originate over the land. On running ashore they usually weaken and disappear entirely or are transformed into extratropical cyclones, increasing in diameter and losing much of their destructive force.

## TABLE I

### BEAUFORT SCALE OF WIND FORCE

| Beaufort number | Name of wind | Specifications for use on land | Miles per hour |
|---|---|---|---|
| | | | Less than |
| o | Calm | Calm; smoke rises vertically.............. | 1 |
| 1 | Light airs | Direction of wind shown by smoke drift, but not by wind vanes.................... | 1–3 |
| 2 | Light breeze | Wind felt on face; leaves rustle; ordinary vane moved by wind.................. | 4–7 |
| 3 | Gentle breeze | Leaves and small twigs in constant motion; wind extends light flag................ | 8–12 |
| 4 | Moderate breeze | Raises dust and loose paper; small branches are moved.......................... | 13–18 |
| 5 | Fresh breeze | Small trees in leaf begin to sway; crested wavelets form on inland waters......... | 19–24 |
| 6 | Strong breeze | Large branches in motion; whistling heard in telegraph wires; umbrellas used with difficulty............................ | 25–31 |
| 7 | High wind | Whole trees in motion; inconvenience felt in walking against wind.................. | 32–38 |
| 8 | Gale | Breaks twigs off trees; generally impedes progress............................ | 39–46 |
| 9 | Strong gale | Slight structural damage occurs (chimney pots and slate removed).............. | 47–54 |
| 10 | Whole gale | Seldom experienced inland; trees uprooted; considerable structural damage occurs.... | 55–63 |
| 11 | Storm | Very rarely experienced; accompanied by widespread damage.................... | 64–75 |
| 12 | Hurricane | More or less complete destruction........ | Above 75 |

### PLACE OF ORIGIN—THE DOLDRUMS

In the tropics north of the equator the prevailing winds blow from the northeast; south of the equator they blow from the southeast. Between these two trade wind systems there is a belt of equatorial calms called the "doldrums." It appears that this is where hurricanes usually develop. The two trade wind systems are not precisely balanced at the equator, however, and in the Atlantic the southeast trades extend north of the equator, reaching farther north at some seasons than others. The belt of calm swings northward and southward with the advance and retreat of the trade winds. When the doldrums are within 6° of the equator, cyclones seldom form there, evidently because the deflective effect of the earth's rotation is slight so near the equator.

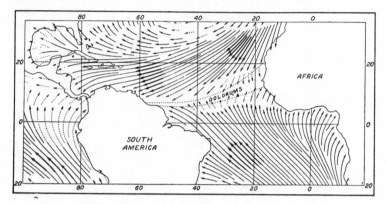

FIGURE 21.   Prevailing winds over Atlantic Ocean, July and August.
(After Bartholomew.)

The deflective effect of the earth's rotation was first demonstrated by William Ferrel, an assistant in the office of the *American Ephemeris and Nautical Almanac*, in the year 1859. If a body moves in any direction upon the earth's surface, there is a deflecting effect arising from the earth's rotation, which deflects it to the right in the northern hemisphere, but to the left in the southern hemisphere. Thus, the cyclones which originate north of the equator rotate in a counterclockwise direction while cyclones of the southern hemisphere rotate clockwise. Near the equator the deflective effect is small, becoming zero at the equator, and there is no evidence of any West Indian hurricanes originating in the North Atlantic Ocean or Caribbean Sea south of about 6° north latitude. There being no belt of doldrums in the Atlantic south of the equator, tropical cyclones are unknown there.

In the eastern North Atlantic the belt of doldrums is farthest north in August and September—about 12 to 13 degrees north of the equator. Practically all of the hurricanes of the Cape Verde region occur during those two months. The doldrum belt extends westward and slightly southward from the Cape Verde region to the northern coast of South America. Between 40° and 55°W. and just south of 10°N., in the western end of this belt, calms are found with great frequency and there is good evidence that hurricanes occasionally originate in that area. (Fig. 21.)

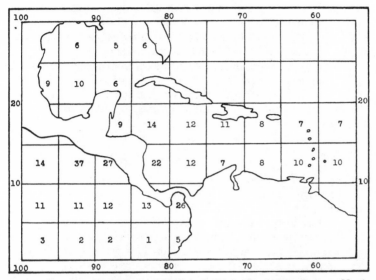

FIGURE 22. Calms in the Gulf of Mexico, Caribbean Sea and southeastern North Pacific Ocean, in October. Figures in 5°-squares show percentages of calms.

There is no belt of doldrums in the eastern two-thirds of the Caribbean Sea and no hurricanes are definitely known to have originated in that region. It is of course difficult to ascertain the point of genesis of many tropical cyclones of the Gulf of Mexico, Caribbean Sea and southern North Atlantic Ocean and it cannot be said positively that their genesis is restricted to certain localities.

Another belt of equatorial calms or doldrums is found in the Pacific Ocean. (Fig. 22.) Its eastern extremity usually lies just south of the Isthmus of Panama. Hurricanes develop there and move northwestward and northward along the western coast of Mexico. The eastern end of this belt at times extends eastward and shifts northward, according to Mitchell, so that it reaches into the western Caribbean Sea, off the Central American coast. This happens near the beginning or end of the hurricane season, which extends from June to November, roughly. The western Caribbean Sea then becomes as favorable a breeding ground for hurricanes as is the region in the Atlantic near the Cape Verde Islands. In November, hurricanes which originate in the western Caribbean Sea usually move northeastward into the Atlantic, but in other months they generally pass into the Gulf of Mexico or northward over western Cuba and the majority of them reach the coasts of the United States. Some of these storms of the western Caribbean Sea attain great violence.

The vapor-laden and heated air of the doldrums, where calms and light, baffling breezes prevail, with frequent rains and thunderstorms, is a favorable place for the birth of tropical storms. While these are the prevailing conditions in the doldrums, tropical cyclones form there only occasionally. Just what other condition or combination of conditions gives rise to the cyclone is not definitely known.

### THEORIES AS TO CAUSE AND MAINTENANCE

For many years there have been two leading hypotheses to account for the origin of the tropical cyclone—convectional and counter-current, or frontal.

According to the convectional hypothesis, a large mass of air becomes relatively warm or moist compared with its surroundings and upward motion on a large scale results. This air is replaced by air flowing in from all sides. Atmospheric pressure is relatively low over the region of active convection. Rotation of the earth causes a deflection of the inflowing air streams and a cyclone is formed. Both earth rotation and the centrifugal force developed by the whirl retard the movement of air toward the center and there is a further fall in pressure. This process continues until a vigorous wind system is developed. According to this theory there is needed but a combination of favorable conditions for convection to grow into the furious cyclonic storm. However, there must be an equally effective removal of the air carried aloft, otherwise it would tend to accumulate and the circulation would be arrested. The facts are not known, owing to lack of observations in the upper levels.

Humphreys offers a satisfactory explanation of the fact that tropical cyclones form only occasionally whereas conditions in the tropics are much more frequently favorable for vertical convection. He says that convection is nearly always limited to very restricted areas, resulting in local thunderstorms; it is only occasionally that an expansion of air takes place over a relatively large area, as a result of increase of temperature or vapor density, or both; in this latter case a cyclone forms if the requisite conditions occur at sufficient distance from the equator for the deflective effect of the earth's rotation to be operative.

The countercurrent hypothesis was first suggested by Heinrich Wilhelm Dove. He said, "it surely cannot be denied that violent storms may be produced by the sudden irruption of cold air of the polar current into warm and rarefied air of the equatorial current." All regions of frequent genesis of tropical storms are bounded by oppositely directed trade wind systems and it is reasonable to suppose that they are instrumental in the development of the cyclone. The South Atlantic is the only ocean which has no tropical region of calms bounded by oppositely directed winds and it is the only ocean without tropical cyclones.[1]

The countercurrent hypothesis with various modifications has been supported by Thom, Meldrum, Abbe, Bigelow and others. More recently the frontal concepts of cyclones in higher latitudes have been applied to the tropical cyclone by Deppermann, Rodewald, True and others. The surface of separation between two air masses with different temperatures and different movements is called a "front." The extratropical cyclone develops as a wave along the surface of separation or front. As cyclones grow the fronts tend to disappear at the surface but continue at some upper level; the surface winds then become more symmetrical, approaching the condition of a simple whirl in the lowest levels of the atmosphere.

Owing to the slight horizontal variations of temperature generally observed in tropical air masses during the birth or growth of cyclones, the fronts in relation to cyclone genesis are not convincingly shown by surface observations. The tropical cyclone, if it is developed on a front, appears quickly to grow into a more or less symmetrical wind system. However, the trade winds, the doldrums, and occasional air masses from the continents in higher latitudes provide some definite though relatively small, differences in temperature and moisture along surfaces which may properly be called fronts.

Regarding the origin of typhoons, Deppermann makes the following comment:

> For a typhoon there seems to be required a *concerted* uplifting over a considerable area, together with an air stream moving in such a direction as to bring the center of upheaval into a latitude where the Coriolis force of the earth's rotation is enough to start the spiraling of the air around the center. All these conditions are admirably fulfilled on the equatorial front, situated as it is in low latitudes and bounded by air streams which frequently meet each other at a con-

[1] Excepting, of course, the Arctic and Antarctic oceans.

siderable angle, and one of which at least, the southwest monsoon, is very moist even up to considerable altitudes. Coming now to actual facts of experience, the writer knows of no case coming under his observation in the Philippine region, in which he could observe events from the beginning, where a typhoon did not originate upon a front. In no case did a typhoon clearly originate *within* a homogeneous air mass, even the moist southwest monsoon.

### CONDITIONS OBSERVED DURING INITIAL STAGES

While the causes of storm genesis in the tropics are imperfectly understood, the conditions surrounding some of them in incipient stages are fairly well known. Contrary to the belief of many persons in regions frequented by tropical storms, they do not so far as is known grow from small whirls in the atmosphere such as the whirlwinds and dust storms commonly observed.

Observations indicate that when a hurricane is born, unsettled and squally weather sets in over a considerable area, generally involving thousands of square miles of ocean surface. At first there is no definite center; the barometer falls gradually over the whole region; the winds freshen and eventually take on a cyclonic circulation. Progressive movement of the disturbance begins; a definite center forms; and then it sometimes grows rapidly in intensity, becoming a dangerous storm.

On the weather map it is first seen as a change of the wind from its prevailing direction or as a slight fall in the barometer which causes irregularities in the lines of equal pressure drawn on the map. From that time on it is closely watched for a lowering of the pressure and a definite wind circulation about a center. Many of these slight disturbances fail to develop further; others eventually become fully fledged hurricanes.

### FORMATION OF THE HURRICANE OF OCTOBER 1926

In October 1926 a tropical disturbance developed over the western Caribbean Sea under conditions particularly favorable for observation.

The extreme southwestern Caribbean Sea is a favorable region for securing observations because of the regular reporting stations along the coast and the frequency of ships in that area, either en route to the Panama Canal or to Central American ports in the banana trade. On the accompanying chart (Fig. 23), land and ship station observations are shown for October 14, 1926, at 7 a.m. Lines, more or less circular, are drawn through points having equal barometer readings. Within the circle the barometer is presumably lower than on the out-

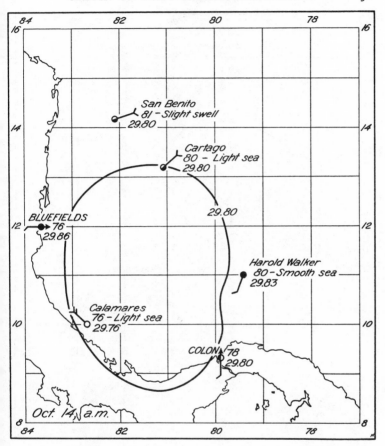

FIGURE 23.  Ship reports during formation of a hurricane in the western Caribbean Sea, October 14, 1926, approximately 7 a.m., E.S.T. (As plotted by F. G. Tingley.)

side. Within the small circle the weather at time of observation is shown; open circle is clear sky; a circle half black and half white is partly cloudy sky; and an entirely black circle is overcast or cloudy weather. Two dots alongside the circle mean rain.

Direction of the wind is shown by a line drawn from the circle to represent an arrow. The number of barbs indicates the wind force on the Beaufort scale. The arrow flies with the wind, so that the line with

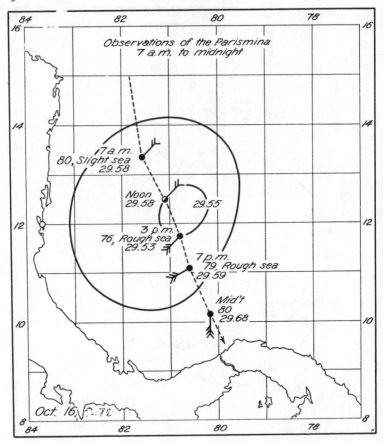

FIGURE 24. Observations taken on the S.S. *Parismina* during passage through center of tropical storm in process of formation on October 16, 1926.

its barbs extends toward the direction from which the wind is blowing. For example, the steamship *Cartago* on October 14 (a.m.) had a wind from the northeast, force 2, there being two barbs on the shaft of the "arrow."

While the barometric pressure on October 14 in the region under observation was only slightly lower than usual, there was already a fairly well established counter-clockwise movement of the winds. On

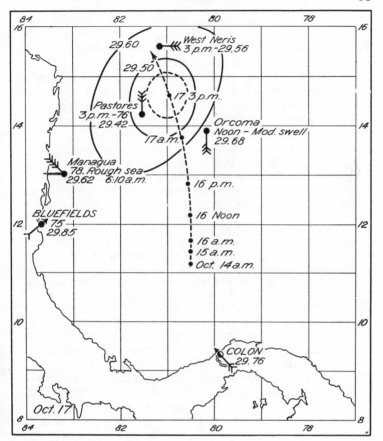

FIGURE 25. Track of center of hurricane in formation, October 14 to 17, 1926, and observations on October 17, 1926.

October 16, the steamship *Parismina* passed directly through the disturbed area, with lowest barometer 29.53 inches and wind force 5. (Fig. 24.) By that time the disturbance had begun to move toward the north and a little west. Its movement increased on the 17th; there was a further fall in pressure and winds of force 6 were experienced. At 3 p.m. of the 17th the steamship *Pastores* reported a barometer reading of 29.42 inches. (Fig. 25.) From that time on the disturbance gained force with great rapidity. On the 18th and 19th, it crossed Cuba, a destructive storm. At Havana the barometer fell to 28.07 inches and the wind reached 99 miles an hour, when the tower supporting the anemometers at the National Observatory was blown down. At Belen College, in Havana, the anemometer recorded 110 miles an hour before it was carried away by the wind. There was great damage at Havana, in surrounding areas, and on the Isle of Pines.

The observed facts regarding the genesis of the hurricane of October 1926 were summed up by Tingley as follows:

> First, slightly reduced pressure and gentle cyclonic circulation over a region some 300 miles in diameter; second, a slow transition from this state to one of storm intensity, requiring at least three days to develop winds of gale force near the immediate center, although squalls formed locally within the affected area; third, a strengthening of the southerly winds at Balboa Heights, near the Pacific entrance to the Panama Canal, and distant nearly 250 miles from the point where the center was first definitely observed to be located, 24 hours before the center was observed; fourth, a slight increase in wind velocity above the 612-meter level, also before the observance of a center, at the naval air station at Coco Solo, near the Atlantic entrance to the Canal.

STORM TRACK INTERSECTIONS AS AN INDICATION OF PLACE OF ORIGIN

From any region in which tropical cyclones originate, they move outward in more or less divergent paths which intersect the paths of those which come from another area. Cyclones which are formed in the Cape Verde region and move westward so as to approach the Gulf of Mexico or South Atlantic coast of the United States do so, no doubt, because the general movement of the atmosphere at critical levels is favorable for such a course and there is consequently a strong tendency to continue on a westerly course. When we chart these tracks we find that they intersect sharply with the paths of storms which have come from the western Caribbean Sea at various times, moving outward in more or less divergent courses. In the western Caribbean Sea there is a pronounced field of such intersections on the track charts, whereas in the eastern Caribbean Sea there are very few except in the vicinity of the Windward Islands and Puerto Rico. In the latter region, and to the eastward of the Windward Islands, there is another pronounced field of such intersections, which suggests that there is another area of tropical storm genesis in the western end of the Atlantic doldrums, just east of the South American coast, south of 10°N. and between 40° and 55° W.

# CHAPTER IV

# HURRICANE TRACKS

M UCH has been written about average storm tracks but they are of little value. If all the known tracks of West Indian hurricanes were assembled on a single chart, it would exhibit an intricate and dense pattern, covering practically every part of the Gulf of Mexico and Caribbean Sea and much of the North Atlantic Ocean. The one outstanding feature of any chart of hurricane tracks for a considerable period of years is the presence of many broad sweeping curves which extend westward or northwestward, then turning to northward or northeastward. While a large percentage of these tracks are described as "parabolic," there are many exceptions.

## SEASONAL VARIATIONS IN PATHS

There is, however, a decided variation in the movements of hurricanes from one month to another. This variation is revealed in an examination of tracks by months.

During the early part of the hurricane season, in June and sometimes July, hurricanes originate in the western Caribbean Sea. From that region nearly all of them move in a northwesterly direction into the Gulf of Mexico, crossing the coast line into Mexico or the Gulf States. During August and September, and less frequently in July and October, hurricanes develop over the eastern North Atlantic Ocean south of the Cape Verde Islands. The majority of these move in a westerly direction across the Atlantic, some of them reaching the coasts of the United States before they recurve to the northward and northeastward.

In the latter part of September, and in October and November, hurricanes are again found originating in the western Caribbean Sea. Those of the latter part of September follow much the same paths as storms from that region in June, but in October and November they are more likely to turn northward and northeastward in lower latitudes, sweeping out over Florida or the Greater Antilles.

The two types of tropical storms are illustrated separately on the accompanying charts. The first (Fig. 26) shows the tracks of tropical cyclones of full hurricane intensity which are known to have originated in the Cape Verde region during forty-six years, 1887 to 1932, inclusive, and the second (Fig. 27) shows analogous tracks of western Caribbean origin. Tracks for the first thirty-seven years of this period are as given by Mitchell in Supplement No. 24 of the *Monthly Weather Review.*

Only eight, or about one-third of those definitely known to have originated in the Cape Verde region, reached the South Atlantic or Gulf coast during that period. Six of them were hurricanes of tremendous force, some of the most intense of record, as follows:

August 1893 at Charleston.
September 1900, at Galveston.
September 1906, at Mobile.
August 1915, at Galveston.
September 1926, at Miami.
September 1928, at West Palm Beach.

Tracks of tropical cyclones of hurricane intensity which apparently originated south of latitude 10°N. and between 40° and 55°W. are also shown with the western Caribbean storms.

The track of a tropical storm is shown by a line, straight, curved, or irregular, which represents the successive positions of the exact center of the storm as accurately as can be ascertained by charting all available reports from the region. Efforts to show the width of the storm area in various stages lead to confusion; furthermore, it is not possible to assign any definite value to the width of the storm area; the winds diminish in force with distance from the center, gradually becoming merged with the general wind system of the region in which the storm is located. The wind system at any position on the track should be considered as more or less circular in form (Fig. 3) extending 25 to 250 miles, or more, in all directions from the center, depending upon the diameter of the particular storm represented on the track chart.

### AVERAGE PATH AS RELATED TO NORMAL PRESSURE

Of the hurricanes which have passed from the Atlantic into the eastern Caribbean Sea, a large number have moved in a path described as "parabolic," crossing the Caribbean, the Bahamas or the

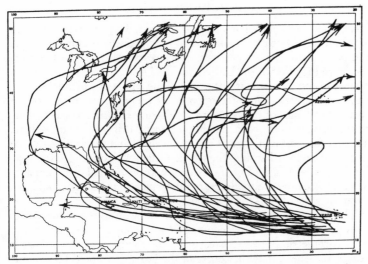

FIGURE 26. Tracks of tropical cyclones of hurricane intensity known to have originated in the Cape Verde region, 1887-1932, inclusive.

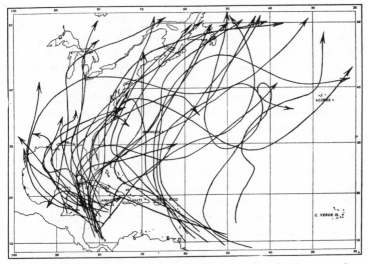

FIGURE 27. Tracks of tropical cyclones of hurricane intensity known to have originated in the western Caribbean Sea, 1887-1932, inclusive; also tropical cyclones of hurricane intensity which probably formed between 40° and 55°W. and south of 10°N.

waters between the Bahamas and Bermuda. The generally accepted explanation of this movement is that high pressure normally overlies the ocean from the Azores west-southwestward over the Bermuda region to the coast of the United States. This high pressure is part of a more or less permanent anticyclone, the winds of which move in a clockwise direction, just the opposite of the wind circulation of the tropical cyclones of the northern hemisphere. Hurricanes, according to this explanation, are carried in the general drift of the atmosphere, skirting the southern edge of the anticyclone and turning northward and northeastward around the western edge. A chart (Fig. 28), showing the average path of 130 hurricanes and the normal distribution of atmospheric pressure to illustrate this explanation, has been adapted from the work of Dr. Oliver L. Fassig.

This view was supported by E. H. Bowie, who stated in 1922, after a study of hurricane movements, that in the case of a single area of high barometric pressure, fixed in position and magnitude, there is reason to believe that the course of the hurricane would be a simple one—viz., its center would follow the outer isobar with the speed of the wind system then prevalent.

### ROTARY AND PROGRESSIVE MOVEMENTS

The progressive movement is comparatively slow. Although the winds of the hurricane blow around and incline inwards toward the center at high velocities, sometimes 100 to 150 miles an hour, this movement must not be confused with the progressive change of position of the storm itself, which averages only about 12 miles an hour. The hurricane may be likened to a top which spins rapidly but changes its position slowly.

These two distinct movements, one rotary and the other progressive, create confusion in the minds of many persons in regions subject to hurricane visitation. They conclude that the storm is moving forward at a rate of 50 to 100 miles an hour or even more and, when 1000 miles away, will arrive in 10 to 20 hours. In reality, the storm may be moving forward at a rate of only 12 miles an hour, and thus be distant more than 80 hours in time.

### HEIGHT OF THE TROPICAL CYCLONE

Hurricanes do not readily cross mountainous regions, and on reaching continental areas frequently dissipate. The reason for this is

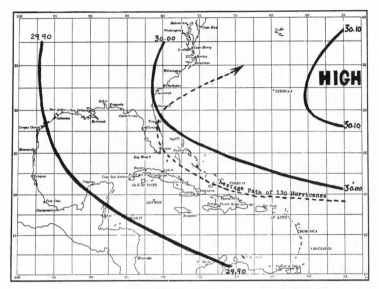

FIGURE 28. Normal pressure distribution and average path of 130 hurricanes.
(After Fassig.)

obvious when it is known that the height of a tropical storm is small. The diameter of a hurricane in some cases is not more than 50 to 75 miles, but in the majority the diameter is greater and in many instances has exceeded 500 miles. The height of the tropical storm is not so well known. Eliot estimated the height of cyclones of the Bay of Bengal at about one mile. In the Arabian Sea, cyclones are unable to cross the Western Ghats, which average about 3,000 feet in elevation with peaks reaching to a height of 5,000 to 7,000 feet. Cyclones appear to be temporarily destroyed on reaching these mountains, but in some instances redevelop on the other side. This phenomenon has been explained by supposing that the cyclone is forced into the higher atmosphere until the mountains are crossed when it again returns to the surface. Redfield estimated the height of the hurricane at one mile. Viñes, who made observations in many hurricanes, and Algué, who studied cyclones of the Far East, were both of the opinion that the height is considerably more than a mile. From a consideration of temperature change with altitude, Köppen and Haurwitz think that the pressure difference between center and periphery of

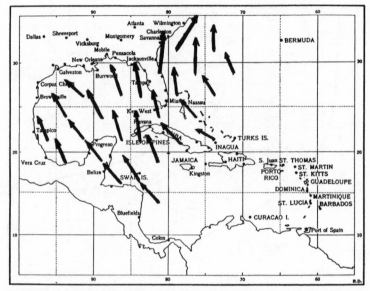

FIGURE 29. Arrows show average direction of movement of tropical cyclones in June (1887-1923). Length of arrow shows average distance travelled by cyclone centers in 24 hours. (Smoothed values after Mitchell.)

the hurricane does not disappear until considerably higher altitudes are reached, probably six miles or more.

### TROPICAL CYCLONES IN MOUNTAINS

Concerning typhoons and mountains, S. S. Visher wrote as follows, in the *Monthly Weather Review*, November 1922:

It is stated in some standard meteorologies that tropical cyclones can not cross a mountain range 3,000 feet high. This is often disproven in the Far East, for typhoons sometimes cross mountains of greater height than this in Taiwan (Formosa), in the Philippines, in Japan, and elsewhere. Mountainous Formosa often appears to deflect typhoons which approach it at a small angle, and sometimes cuts the typhoon in two, according to Froc, but, on the other hand, other storms clearly cross it with no apparent regard for its mountains, the highest of which reach over 13,000 feet. Doctor Okada reports that studies made on lofty Fuji, near Yokohama, and on the highest mountains of Formosa indicate the depth of most typhoons to be approximately 5 or 6 kilometers (16,000 to 20,000 feet).

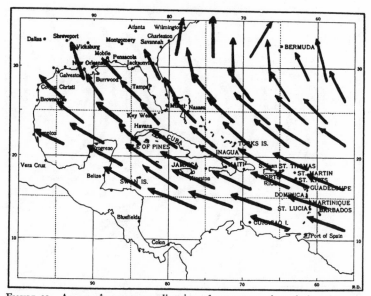

FIGURE 30. Arrows show average direction of movement of tropical cyclones in August (1887-1923). Length of arrow shows average distance travelled by cyclone centers in 24 hours. (Smoothed values after Mitchell.)

Although it is commonly stated that typhoons weaken decidedly as soon as they come upon the land, both Froc and Okada have observed many cases where this was not true in southeast China, the typhoons maintaining most of their force until encountering lofty mountains.

In any case, the height of three or four miles, possibly more, is so small in comparison with the diameter that a large tropical cyclone is actually shaped like a phonograph record disk, though convex owing to the curvature of the earth. Any interference to the flow of winds in hilly or mountainous country is likely to be fatal to such a widespread and relatively shallow circulation. The hurricane attains its greatest force over the ocean where the winds experience a minimum of surface friction.

Thus it appears that the movements of hurricanes are influenced by islands and continental areas in their paths and by anticyclones and extratropical cyclones over adjacent oceanic and continental areas. In some instances their movements have been quite erratic.

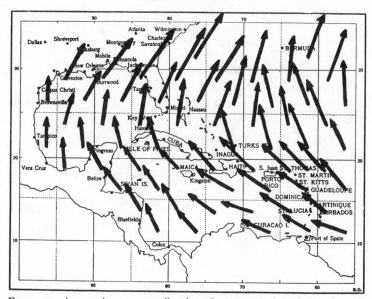

FIGURE 31. Arrows show average direction of movement of tropical cyclones in October (1887-1923). Length of arrow shows average distance travelled by cyclone centers in 24 hours. (Smoothed values after Mitchell.)

Some of these unusual movements and the explanations offered for them, will be discussed in Chapter VIII.

### AVERAGE MOVEMENT BY MONTHS

Average movements of West Indian hurricanes were determined by Bowie and Weightman (1914) and by Mitchell (1924). The accompanying charts showing average 24-hour movements have been adapted from those published by Mitchell. (Figs. 29, 30, and 31.)

Hurricanes sometimes move very slowly at the point of recurve, especially if the change of direction is abrupt. It does not appear to be definitely established that any tropical cyclone has actually been stationary at any point in its path; it is generally believed that there is practically always a progressive motion though in many cases it has been less than five miles an hour.

Fassig, who studied the movements of hurricanes with respect to the recurve, found that the average daily movement is 260 miles before the recurve and 392 miles after the recurve. He found that the average latitude of recurve advances northward, from 28°N. in June and July to 30°N. in August, then retreats to 28°N. in September and to 25°N. in October.

Speaking of the rule that hurricane tracks are found farther and farther to the westward as the season advances, Father Viñes said:

> So ancient is the belief in this rule that the ecclesiastic authority, from time immemorial, wisely ordained that priests in Porto Rico should recite in the mass the prayer, "Ad repellendat tempestates," during the months of August and September, but not in October, and in Cuba it should be recited in September and October, but not in August. All of which proves that the ecclesiastical authority knew by experience that the cyclones of October were very much to be feared in Cuba but not those of August, and that in Porto Rico, on the contrary, the hurricanes of August are disastrous, while those of October are rare.

An examination of August storm tracks immediately demonstrates the truth of this rule as regards August hurricanes in Cuba. Their course is westward or west-northwestward in most cases; those which reach Cuba have, as a rule, passed over Haiti, resulting in a considerable diminution of intensity.

Late in the season storms form over the western Caribbean Sea with a strong tendency to move northward or northeastward.

Occasionally a storm late in the season attains terrific violence and the island of Cuba lies lengthwise across its most probable path. The extreme western end of Cuba is occasionally devastated by hurricanes in August which move westward through the Yucatan Channel or that immediate vicinity. Storms which originate in the western Caribbean Sea in June and July do not frequently attain great force and their usual path is to the westward of Cuba.

Of the July storms which enter the Caribbean Sea from the east, those which pass south of Haiti eventually reach the Mexican Gulf coast west of Florida. Those which go north of Haiti reach the Atlantic coast of the United States or recurve to the northeastward before reaching the coast. In August those which pass south of Haiti move on through the Gulf or into Yucatan and few cross the Gulf coast east of the mouth of the Mississippi River. In August some of the storms which go north of Haiti finally cross southern Florida and enter the United States as far west as Alabama and Mississippi; the remainder go farther to the east and north and do not reach the Gulf of Mexico.

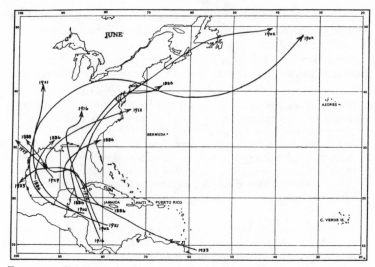

FIGURE 32. Tracks of tropical cyclones of hurricane intensity in the month of June, 1874 to 1933, inclusive. In this and the following track charts, the classification follows that of C. L. Mitchell, i.e. a tropical cyclone of hurricane intensity is one with central pressure 29.00 inches or lower and winds near center more than 60 miles an hour, at some point in the path of the storm.

As September advances, storms from the Atlantic which pass westward through the Caribbean Sea begin to recurve more sharply in the Gulf and cross the coast farther to the east. Those which pass north of Haiti also recurve farther to the east and a small percent of them go as far west as Florida.

October hurricanes which come from the east and pass north or northeast of Haiti rarely reach the coast of the United States. Those which travel westward to the south of Haiti rarely continue to the Gulf coast of the United States west of the mouth of the Mississippi. In October and occasionally in November the western Caribbean storms cross Jamaica, Cuba and Florida.

### TRACKS OF HURRICANES, 1874 TO 1933

The tracks of all tropical cyclones of hurricane intensity which are of record for the sixty years, 1874 to 1933, will be found in Figures 32 to 39. Tracks of those which were of minor force or doubtful as to hurricane intensity for the years 1901 to 1937, and for those of full

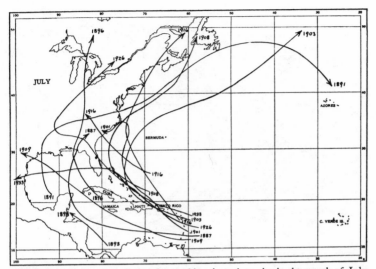

FIGURE 33. Tracks of tropical cyclones of hurricane intensity in the month of July, 1874 to 1933, inclusive.

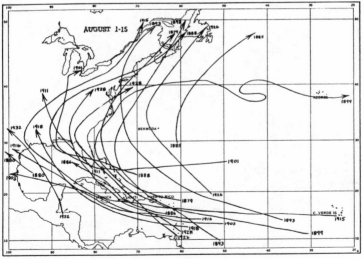

FIGURE 34. Tracks of tropical cyclones of hurricane intensity, August 1 to 15, 1874 to 1933, inclusive.

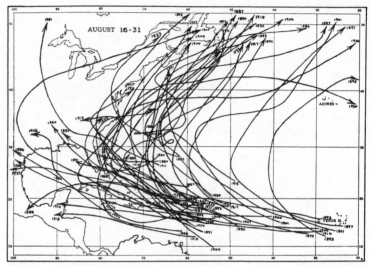

FIGURE 35. Tracks of tropical cyclones of hurricane intensity, August 16 to 31, 1874 to 1933, inclusive.

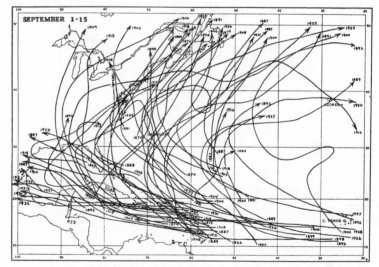

FIGURE 36. Tracks of tropical cyclones of hurricane intensity, September 1 to 15, 1874 to 1933, inclusive.

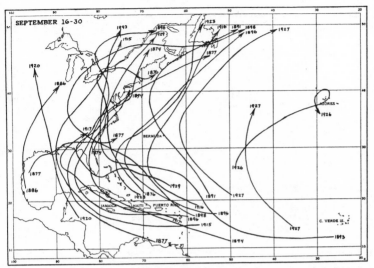

FIGURE 37. Tracks of tropical cyclones of hurricane intensity, September 16 to 30, 1874 to 1933, inclusive.

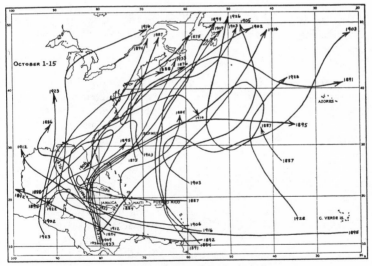

FIGURE 38. Tracks of tropical cyclones of hurricane intensity, October 1 to 15, 1874 to 1933, inclusive.

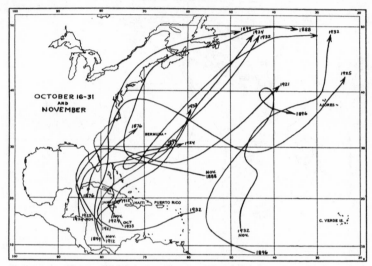

FIGURE 39.  Tracks of tropical cyclones of hurricane intensity, October 16 to
November 30, 1874 to 1933, inclusive.

hurricane intensity after 1933, will be found in Chapter XIV. Those
of minor intensity or doubtful as to hurricane force prior to 1901 are
not shown.

### LIFE OF TROPICAL CYCLONES

So far as available observations show, the average life of tropical
storms of the Atlantic, Gulf and Caribbean, is about 9.5 days. The
average life is actually somewhat longer as some are lost in mid-
ocean before they actually dissipate and others are certainly not
observed until they have been in existence for a day or more. August
storms are longer lived than those originating in any other month,
averaging about 12 days. July and November storms have had the
shortest life, about 8 days.

Some tropical storms of the North Atlantic have been tracked for
three to four weeks. Many of those originating south of the Cape
Verde Islands have been traced westward across the Atlantic and,
after the recurve, northeastward and eastward to Europe. The hurricane of August and September 1900 was followed from the mid-
Atlantic west-northwestward to the Texas coast, thence northeastward and eastward into Siberia.

Many typhoons have been traced from the Philippines to the North American coast—some of them across North America and the North Atlantic. Others have moved from the vicinity of the Philippines across the Malay Peninsula to the Bay of Bengal. One tropical cyclone first observed off the western coast of Mexico, moved across the United States and nearly across the Atlantic. Some tropical cyclones, according to Visher, have been tracked from the east of Queensland around northern and western Australia and on as far as New Zealand, a total distance of about 9,000 miles.

Of course the tropical cyclone, after it leaves the tropics, soon becomes identical in nature with the extratropical cyclone.

Extratropical cyclones, however, have been followed to greater distances. One, which appeared near Havre, Mont., on February 23, 1925, was traced by Mitchell around the globe past its starting point. It was well along on another encircling trip when it was blocked and surrounded by high pressure on March 23, 1925, in the Gulf of St. Lawrence, where it died. The distance travelled by the center of this extratropical cyclone was computed to be 21,379 statute miles.

# CHAPTER V

# RAINFALL IN TROPICAL CYCLONES

IN tropical cyclones, rainfall is nearly always heavy and frequently it is torrential, reaching on some occasions to the proportions of what is commonly termed a "cloudburst." High winds which accompany the cyclone prevent an accurate catch of the rain which falls; in some instances it is probable that not more than 50 to 75 per cent of the rain is caught by the gage.

## DEPTH AND WEIGHT OF HURRICANE RAINFALL

A fall of one inch of rain in a period of twenty-four consecutive hours is considered heavy in temperate latitudes. On a perfectly level surface, the water after an inch of rain would be exactly one inch deep. On an acre of ground a fall of one inch would amount to 113 tons of water. During the life history of a tropical cyclone, the quantity of rain which falls is almost unbelievable. Newnham estimated that in the Puerto Rico hurricane of 1899, the total weight of rainfall on that island alone was approximately 2,600,000,000 tons. On some occasions the rainfall in tropical cyclones has been so heavy that on a level surface, without any run-off, evaporation or seepage into the soil, the water after passage of the storm would have been waist deep or higher.

Rainfall on September 13 to 14, 1928, during the passage of a hurricane over Puerto Rico was the heaviest recorded there in thirty years. In the regions of greatest normal rainfall—in the vicinity of Adjuntas in the Central Cordillera and in the Luquillo Mountains— the amounts exceeded 25 inches. At Adjuntas the fall was 29.60 inches. (Fig. 40.)

## WORLD'S RECORDS OF RAINFALL IN TROPICAL CYCLONES

Tropical cyclones of the South Indian Ocean, which approach the island of Mauritius from the north, produce some very heavy rains at places on the island. One of the most remarkable falls accompanied a cyclone of February 15-21, 1896, which passed directly over the island from north to south. The greatest 24-hour fall was over 20 inches and the following totals were measured for the four days dur-

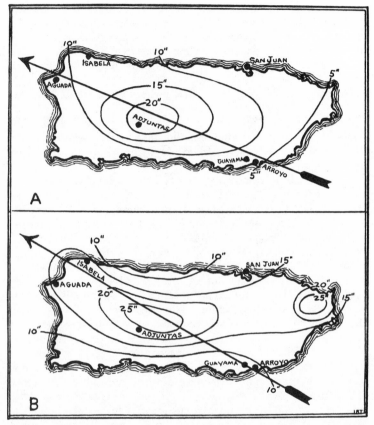

FIGURE 40. Rainfall in Puerto Rico during passage of (A) the hurricane of August 1899, and (B) the hurricane of September 1928. The large arrow shows the path of the hurricane center. Lines pass through places having equal depths of rainfall.

ing which the storm influenced the weather conditions at Mauritius: Pamplemousses, 26 inches; Reunion, 47 inches; la Marie, Tamarind Falls, and l'Etoile, 41 inches. Falls exceeding 30 inches were reported from other parts of the island.

Rainfalls exceeding 30 inches have been recorded in West Australian and Queensland hurricanes. The heaviest three-day rain in Queensland was 63 inches at Mount Molloy.

Probably the world's heaviest rainfall in twenty-four consecutive hours, was that measured at Baguio in the Philippines in July 1911. The amount was 46 inches. During the same storm an additional 42 inches of rain fell at Baguio, totalling 88 inches in four days.

At Silver Hill, Jamaica, 96.5 inches of rain was recorded in four days.

In 1913, from July 18 to 20, 81.5 inches of rain fell at Funkiko, Formosa.

At Cherrapunji, India, where the southwest monsoon strikes the Khasi Hills, the annual rainfall is thought to be the heaviest in the world, averaging 426 inches. In one day, June 14, 1876, 40.8 inches of rain fell at Cherrapunji.

Falls exceeding 20 inches in twenty-four consecutive hours have been recorded in hurricanes in the United States. In 1916, a hurricane caused the greatest floods known in the southern Appalachians. At Altapass, N.C., the rainfall accompanying the hurricane amounted to 22.22 inches in twenty-four hours.

The greatest 24-hour rainfall of record in the United States resulted from a tropical storm in September 1921. It moved westward across the southwestern Gulf of Mexico and passed inland over Mexico, after which it turned northward and crossed the Rio Grande valley into Texas. After passing inland the storm rapidly dissipated and by the time it reached Texas could scarcely be identified as a cyclone except by the torrential rains which continued northward into Texas. Within twenty-four consecutive hours, 23.11 inches of rain fell at Taylor, Tex. Torrential rains accompanying this disturbance (Fig. 41), caused the most destructive flood in the history of San Antonio. Water rose so rapidly in the streets that automobiles were deserted and the occupants sought safety in the high buildings. Five to nine feet of water stood in the large hotels, theaters and stores. Fifty-one lives were lost in San Antonio and property damage amounted to $5,000,000.

Rainfall in a single day in tropical cyclones in the instances cited equals or exceeds the average *annual* rainfall at Paris, 21 inches; London, 25 inches; Chicago, 33 inches; and San Francisco, 22 inches. These amounts include also melted snow measurements.

### DISASTROUS EFFECTS OF TORRENTIAL RAINS

In level country, such excessively heavy rains as those which accompany tropical storms are not particularly dangerous. In hilly

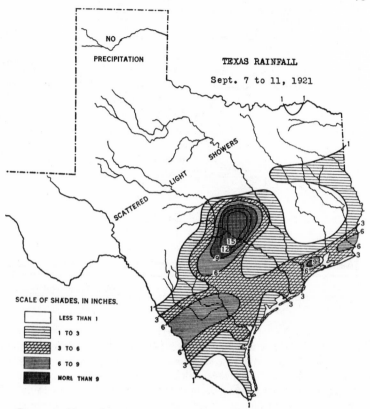

FIGURE 41. Torrential rains in Texas during passage of the remnants of a tropical storm.

or mountainous country where there is drainage down steep slopes, the results are sometimes disastrous. One of the early cases was at Dominica in 1806 (Chapter XIII). Recent examples are the San Antonio flood of 1921, the El Salvador landslides of 1934, the hurricane in Haiti in October 1935, and the typhoon rains in the valleys north of Manila in Luzon[1] in 1936.

[1] A typhoon moving on a west-southwest course across Luzon, October 9, 1936 caused heavy rains that resulted in extensive floods and great damage to property; loss of life estimated at 517 in newspapers of October 16.

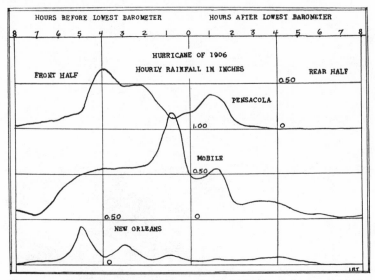

FIGURE 42. Rainfall by hours before and after passage of the center of the hurricane of September 1906, at Pensacola, Mobile and New Orleans. (From data compiled by I. M. Cline.)

The El Salvador hurricane of early June 1934[2] was attended by torrential rains; whole towns were destroyed by landslides; Lakes Guija and Coatepeque rose far above their banks; after the floods the funnel of a steamboat was seen sticking out of the water in the Lempa River, with bodies floating around it; there were also heavy rains and floods in western Honduras; a death toll in excess of two thousand was reported by relief workers from the area of hurricane rains. It was reported that the Ulua River rose more than 45 feet above its normal stage and that inhabitants at Pimienta, who fled before rising flood waters, reached a small hill, only to be drowned there as the water rose over the summit. These statements were taken from press reports following the disaster.

### DISTRIBUTION OF RAIN INTENSITY IN THE HURRICANE

Cline published in 1926 results of an investigation into the distribution of rainfall and other phenomena of the tropical cyclone. He

[2] The hurricane probably came from the Pacific side.

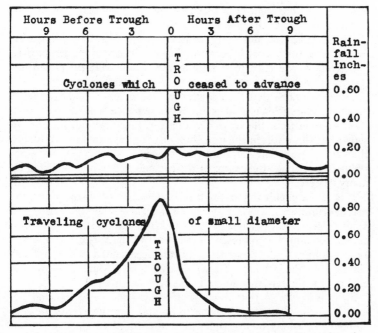

FIGURE 43.   Hourly rainfall in tropical cyclones before and after "trough" or time of lowest barometric pressure, showing difference between rainfall distribution in cyclones which ceased to advance and travelling cyclones of small diameter. (From data compiled by I. M. Cline.)

found a decided contrast in the distribution of rainfall between travelling cyclones and those which ceased to advance. According to Cline, rainfall at any given moment in the travelling cyclone is not distributed uniformly about the center, as would be indicated by a study of total falls in the path of the cyclone, during the entire period of its passage. Very little rainfall, he finds, occurs in the rear half. (Fig. 42.) Rain falls at the most rapid rate in front and to the right of the line of advance. In three cyclones which ceased to advance, he found that the area of greatest rainfall shifted to the rear of the cyclone, and that the systematic rainfall distribution of the travelling cyclone was absent. (Fig. 43.)

Cline's conclusion is that energy released by condensation of moisture in the right front quarter of the cyclone is sufficient to account for the continuous redevelopment, or maintenance, of tropical cyclones of the greatest intensity.

Father Viñes did not agree with this view. His observations indicated that the rainfall extends farther in advance of the center than it extends to the rear, in most hurricanes, but that there were instances in which the rain area extended itself farther backward.

Cline maintains that the heaviest rainfall occurs in the right front quarter of the cyclone as the result of convergence of winds there with those coming from the right rear quarter. His observations tend to show that the winds in the right half of the storm are much stronger than those in the left half, and that the circulation in general is not symmetrical about the center of the cyclone as has been asserted by many writers.

It is very difficult to portray from a collection of observations, the real distribution of winds in the tropical cyclone. The winds observed at any place, as the cyclone passes over, are a resultant of rotary wind circulation and the progressive movement of the cyclone, combined. In the right half, the progressive movement is added to the wind circulation; in the left half, the wind circulation is diminished by the effect of the forward movement of the cyclone.

So it is probable that much of the disparity between wind velocities in the right and left semicircles and to some extent the convergence of winds in the right front quadrant are only apparent, owing to the effect of the translatory movement of the entire wind system. As the storm moves inland, its wind circulation is modified by friction of land surfaces; the advancing semicircle is affected first, while the winds of the right rear quadrant continue over water surfaces. Doubtless the distribution of rainfall is affected by these conditions as the storm moves inland. Over the ocean there is very little information as to the amount and intensity of rainfall except by inference from observations at island and peninsular stations. Amounts of rainfall are not recorded on shipboard; indeed, the driving of spray by hurricane winds renders accurate measurement impossible.

Cline's investigation leaves little doubt, however, that the travelling cyclone, when crossing the Gulf and South Atlantic coasts of the United States, is characterized by more intense rainfall in the right front quadrant than in other parts of the cyclone and that so far as observations are available, little rainfall occurs, as a rule, in the rear half of the storm area.

## THUNDER AND LIGHTNING IN TROPICAL CYCLONES

Though there have been many references to lightning and thunder in tropical cyclones, information on the subject is inexact. Frequent and almost continuous lightning has been observed within the destructive wind circle of many tropical storms. Thunder is often indistinguishable in the deafening roar of the winds, falling of rain, and the noises attending the destruction of buildings; on the seacoast the sea adds to the confusion of noises. Thunderstorms are most frequently noted after the center of the cyclone has passed. For that reason, the occurrence of a thunderstorm is considered a sign that the storm will soon break away.

Father Viñes was of this opinion:

> The absence of electrical discharges within the cyclone is a phenomenon so constantly observed that whenever during a tempest the rolling of thunder is heard or flashes of lightning are perceived this is considered as a favorable sign indicating the speedy disappearance of the storm. Especially among the country folks this opinion is general and deeply rooted. The crashing of thunder and the crowing of the cock are here the barometer of the farmer during cyclones, a barometer which, as he affirms, never deceives him. As long as the rooster does not crow, nor is there heard any peal of thunder, the storm will continue to rage in full force. But as soon as the lively crowing of the cock or the pealing of thunder reaches his ear, the tempest to his conviction, is about to pass away.

As applied to thunder and the crowing of the cock, but not to lightning, there is no doubt much truth in the statement, although it seems more reasonable to assume that when these sounds reach the ear it is evidence that the storm *has already abated* sufficiently that such sounds can be heard.

# CHAPTER VI

# BAROMETRIC PRESSURES

### INVENTION AND DEVELOPMENT OF THE BAROMETER

THE barometer was invented in 1643 by Evangelista Torricelli, a professor of mathematics in the Florentine Academy. In 1670, Robert Hooke designed the wheel barometer. The aneroid barometer was invented by Lucien Vidie in 1843.[1] It is the type principally employed on board ships at sea and the majority of recording barometers, or barographs, are of this type.

The relation between the rise and fall of the barometer and changes in the weather had been recognized practically from the beginning, and even in the early days there appeared the inscriptions which are, with some modifications, still found on many aneroid barometers today: "Stormy, Rain, Change, Fair, and Very Dry." No one seems to know who originated this scheme for indicating the relation between barometer readings and weather. Even where most appropriate, at sea-level in the vicinity of London, this relation is of questionable value.

The barometer indicates the pressure of the atmosphere indirectly as the height in inches of a column of mercury that is supported *in vacuo* by the weight of the atmosphere. (Fig. 44.) As the pressure of the atmosphere varies, the mercurial column rises and falls. The aneroid barometer likewise is graduated to indicate in terms of the height of a mercurial column. (Fig. 45.)

Pressure of the atmosphere decreases with height above the earth's surface, so that it is necessary when comparing barometric pressures at different places to reduce them to a common level by the application of corrections. It is general practice to give the reading as reduced to sea-level. Other corrections are necessary for temperature, standard gravity, capillarity, scale errors and degree of vacuum, if a mercurial barometer is used. The aneroid barometer is not so reliable but is portable and easily read.

---

[1] Although the invention of the aneroid barometer has been generally credited to Vidie, instruments operating on the same principle are known to have been in use prior to that time.

### USE OF BAROMETRIC DATA IN WEATHER FORECASTING

Readings of the barometer are the most important data in weather forecasting. Barometric pressures are reported, along with other data, by telegraph and radio from land stations and ships at sea, and entered on the weather map. (Fig. 46.) Lines are then drawn through places having the same sea-level pressure, at intervals of one-tenth of an inch of the mercurial column, i.e. through all places having a pressure of 30.00, 29.90, 29.80 inches, etc.[2] The word "LOW" is entered at the center of regions where low atmospheric pressure prevails and the word "HIGH" at high-pressure centers. The former are cyclones, the latter, anticyclones.

Lines of equal pressure, or "isobars," in the hurricane are symmetrical and nearly circular in form. At the center of

[2] Some barometers, however, are designed to give readings in millibars, others in millimeters.

FIGURE 44. A pair of mercurial barometers of the type used at field stations of the U.S. Weather Bureau.

FIGURE 45. An aneroid barometer.

the hurricane, the pressure of the atmosphere is sometimes two inches or more below the normal, which is approximately 30.00 inches at sea-level.

The rate of decrease in pressure between two places is known as the "gradient."[3] The wind velocity increases with the steepness of the

[3] Pressure gradient is defined as the change of pressure per unit distance measured perpendicular to the isobars, and in the direction in which pressure decreases.

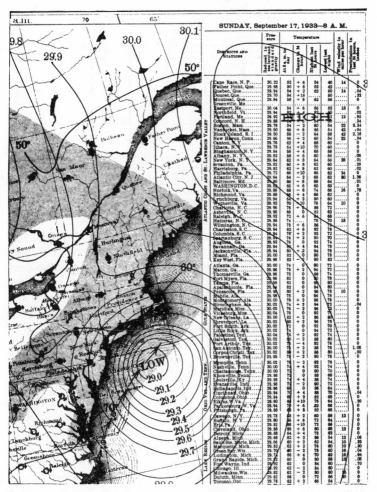

FIGURE 46. Section of the daily weather map, 8 a.m., September 17, 1933, showing isobars of the hurricane.

gradient, other things being equal, or as the difference in pressure between the two places increases. Pressure gradients in hurricanes are very steep—the barometer falls rapidly as the center of the hurricane approaches, and as the velocity of the wind increases.

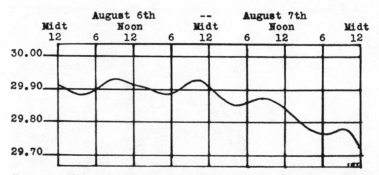

FIGURE 47. Variation in barometric pressure at San Juan, P.R., August 6 and 7, 1899, during approach of the great hurricane of August 8. The semi-diurnal swing of the barometric pressure curve is plainly in evidence even during the 7th of August when the barometer was falling steadily.

Buys Ballot, a Dutch physicist, formulated a law about the year 1857, by which the direction of the center of low pressure may be ascertained from the movement of the wind. As applied to hurricanes, the observer, in the northern hemisphere, standing with his back directly to the wind, will have the center of the hurricane to his left. Since the hurricane winds are inclined inwards, the center will be to his left and slightly to the front.

In the tropics there is, as a rule, little variation in pressure—the barometer reads about the same from day to day unless a tropical storm develops or approaches. There is, however, a slight but well marked daily swing, known as the diurnal change. (Fig. 47.)

When the hurricane is still at a distance, the barometer sometimes rises above its usual height. This, according to Father Viñes, is one of the first indications of the approach of the hurricane. Soon thereafter the barometer begins to fall. The amount of fall at any given place depends upon the intensity of the hurricane and the direction of its approach—whether the center moves directly over the place or passes to one side.

### WORLD'S RECORDS OF LOW PRESSURE

Until 1935, the barometer reading recorded at False Point, India (on the coast southeast from Cuttack), on September 22, 1885, was generally accepted as the lowest which had ever occurred in a tropical cyclone at a land meteorological station with a reliable barometer.

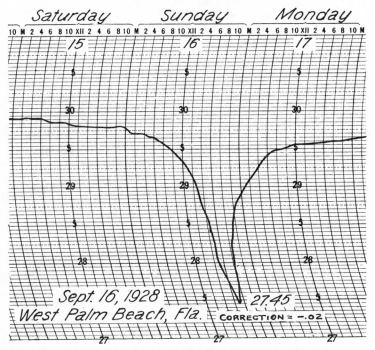

FIGURE 48. Barograph trace at West Palm Beach, Fla., September 15, 16 and 17, 1928.

The center of the cyclone passed over False Point Lighthouse and a calm prevailed from 6:30 a.m. to 6:50 a.m., the "eye of the storm." Pressure in the center of the storm reached the low point of 27.135 inches. This reading, according to John Eliot, was taken by a trained observer with a properly verified barometer.

Sea-level readings below 28.00 inches are not commonly observed in hurricanes, but there are a number of such records. In the Miami hurricane in 1926, the barometer in the Weather Bureau office fell to 27.61 inches, the lowest reading ever recorded (sea-level) in a hurricane at a regular station of the United States Weather Bureau. A lower reading, apparently trustworthy, was taken at West Palm Beach, Florida, in September 1928. The center of the hurricane passed over West Palm Beach about 7:00 p.m., of September 16. The record sheet from a recording barometer in the American Telegraph and Telephone Company office showed a minimum reading when corrected of 27.43 inches. (Fig. 48.) The West Palm Beach storm had previously devastated Puerto Rico, where extremely high wind velocities were felt at San Juan and a low reading of the barometer, 27.50 inches, was reported from Guayama.

On September 2, 1935, a hurricane of very small diameter but one of the most intense of record anywhere in the world, crossed the Florida Keys with its center on Lower Matecumbe Key from about 9:30 to 10:00 p.m. Records of the lowest pressure were secured from three aneroid barometers, the values ranging from 26.75 to 26.98 inches. However, none of these barometers had previously been compared with standard. One of the barometers, owned by Iver Olson, was shipped to the Weather Bureau in Washington where it was tested in the Instrument Division. Careful laboratory tests showed it to be an exceptionally responsive and reliable instrument and that the correct reading at the position of the needle indicated by Mr. Olson at the center of the storm was 26.35 inches. This is the world's lowest record of pressure at a land station.[4]

It is reasonable to expect lower readings from ships than from land stations, because tropical cyclones are usually more intense over the water than over land. Furthermore, nearly all ships are equipped with barometers, while they are not frequently available in the sparsely settled coastal regions where many tropical storms have moved inland.

The *Meteorological Magazine*, of February 1933, gives a number of very low sea-level barometer readings. By far the lowest is a reading of 26.185 inches on August 18, 1927, on the Dutch steamship *Sapoeroea*, in the Pacific 460 miles east of Luzon (Philippines). A barograph was on board but the pen passed off the chart and readings were made from a mercurial barometer. The lowest reading was checked by several persons.

[4] At sea-level. For comparative purposes, barometric pressures are reduced to sea-level. Pressure decreases with altitude, hence the pressures actually indicated by barometers are ordinarily lowest at the station with the highest elevation. For example, a reading of 26.35 inches is common at a height of 3500 feet above sea-level, but on reduction to sea-level a correction of approximately one inch of pressure for each one thousand feet is added, the exact amount depending upon temperature and other conditions.

Wilhelm Krebs collected reports of low barometric pressures and in 1911 published the following:

| Number | Place | Location | Date | Pressure |
|---|---|---|---|---|
| 1. | Vohemare | Madagascar | Feb. 3, 1899 | 24.76 inches |
| 2. | S.S. *Arethusa* | 13° 55′ N.—134° 30′ E. | Dec. 16, 1900 | 26.16 |
| 3. | Morne Rouge | Martinique | Aug. 18 to 19, 1891 | 26.85 |
| 4. | Basilan | Frank Helm Bay | Sept. 25, 1905 | 26.85 |
| 5. | S.S. *Laisang* | 26° 44′ N.—123° 02′ E. | Aug. 2, 1901 | 27.03 |
| 6. | Ship *Favorita* | In harbor, Apia, Samoa | Apr. 6, 1850 | 27.05 |
| 7. | Havana | Cuba | Oct. 10 to 11, 1846 | 27.06 |
| 8. | False Point | India | Sept. 22, 1885 | 27.08 |

Krebs states that Nos. 1, 3, and 8, are the only ones not completely reduced to sea-level and standard gravity. This probably explains the difference between his No. 8 and that quoted from Eliot (27.135 inches).

At St. Pierre, Martinique, a self-registering barometer, in the hurricane of August 18 to 19, 1891, gave a minimum of about 28.70 inches. The record showed excessive vibration but a good aneroid, at passage of the center of the hurricane, read 28.98 inches. Thus it appears that the reading given by Krebs was probably in error as lack of proper sea-level reduction could scarcely account for the difference.

The director of the meteorological service in Madagascar, in 1933, in reply to a query from C. F. Talman, reported that the reading at Vohemare, in 1899, No. 1 in Krebs' list, was 728.9 millimeters and that through a printer's error it was published as 628.9 (24.76 inches).

In the vicinity of Australia, tropical cyclones are sometimes called "willy-willies." Griffith Taylor, in *Australian Meteorology*, lists a number of willy-willies with barometric pressures observed in each instance. The following are worthy of note because of the low barometer readings:

| Date | Locality | Barometer Reading |
|---|---|---|
| January 7, 1881 | Cossack | 27.00 inches |
| April 2, 1898 | Cossack | 27.80 |
| January 20, 1918 | Mackay | 27.50 |
| March 9, 1918 | Innisfal | 27.80 |

Piddington published a number of instances of excessive falls of the barometer in cyclones, among which appear the following:

| Storm and Locality | Barometer Fell To |
|---|---|
| H. C. Ship *Duke of York*, Kedgeree, 1833 | 26.30 inches |
| Brig *Gazelle*, China Sea, 1849 | 27.00 |
| H.M.S. *Pluto*, China Sea (no date) | 27.55 |
| Ship *Howqua*, Timor Sea, 1848 | 27.60 |
| Ship *John O'Gaunt*, China Sea, 1846 | 27.50 |
| Brig *Freak*, Bay of Bengal, 1840 | 27.25 |
| Ship *Exmouth*, South Indian Ocean, 1846 | 27.00 |

There seems to be credible evidence that barometric minima below 27.00 inches have occurred in tropical cyclones at land stations equipped with reliable barometers. The reading on board the Dutch S.S. *Sapoeroea*, on August 18, 1927, taken from a mercurial barometer (26.185 inches), is phenomenally low, but appears to have been carefully observed and checked.

A reading, almost identical (26.16 inches), is cited by Krebs as taken aboard the S.S. *Arethusa* in the same locality but twenty-seven years earlier. There is some reason to doubt the accuracy of the barometer on board the *Duke of York*, when the reading of 26.30 inches was recorded in the Bay of Bengal in 1833. An examination of the trace given by Piddington, showing the rise and fall of the barometer on the *Duke of York* in this storm, would indicate that the storm moved very slowly or that the barometer was reading a half inch or more too low, because it rose very slowly in the three hours after the ship passed through the storm. At the end of that period the barometer had risen to 28.00 inches, approximately, and it should have risen more rapidly from such a low point. Furthermore, Piddington says the barometer on the *Duke of York* fell from 29.00 inches to 26.30 inches. The initial reading seems entirely too low.

On the other hand, Reid quotes from the *Journal of the Bengal Asiatic Society* a report of this same storm, at Saugor, stating that the barometer there fell below 26.50 inches. The mercury did not rise in the tube after the storm, as the observer expected, and he attributed it to some salt water having reached the leather bag and loosened it from the wood, which permitted an escape of mercury. However, twenty-four and one-half hours were required at Saugor for the barometer to rise from 26.50 to 28.60 inches, which lends some support to the record on the *Duke of York*.

### PRESSURES IN AREA OF RELATIVE CALM

Readings in the calm centers of tropical cyclones are secured only occasionally and we have by no means a complete check on the central pressure of any tropical cyclone during its entire life history.

Minimum readings do not always occur at the central point of the calm area. In some cases the barometer remains steady throughout the calm; in others it oscillates. In some cases the minimum is reached at the beginning of the calm, the barometer rising steadily during the calm; in other cases the barometer does not reach the lowest point till the end of the calm period. Variation in intensity of the storm itself, during passage of the calm, may be the cause of these eccentricities.

The isobars, or lines of equal barometric pressure, about the tropical cyclone are circular or nearly so within the region of abnormally low pressure. The outer isobars are not so regular in shape. Visher states that most tropical cyclones are elliptical, the ratio between the longest and shortest diameter being about three to two, though many of them are nearly circular. The elongation, according to Visher, is in the direction of travel normally, though it may be at any angle.

"Pumping" of the barometer during the passage of a hurricane is frequently observed. The barometer alternately rises and falls during comparatively short periods, sometimes with an amplitude of as much as .10 to .20 inch. Pumping is usually associated with great gustiness and is probably due principally to the effects of the wind upon the structure in which the barometer is kept, though it may be due in some instances to secondary whirls, such as the tornadoes of southern Florida and the secondary centers observed in connection with some tropical cyclones of the Pacific. There are no records of secondary centers in West Indian hurricanes, although some remarkable oscillations of the barometer were recorded on the S.S. *Phemius* in November 1932. (See Chapter XIV.)

# CHAPTER VII

## SIGNS OF THE APPROACHING HURRICANE

TO the natives of tropical and subtropical regions subject to hurricanes, typhoons, and other tropical revolving storms, the precursory signs are well known. In coastal regions, one of the first is the storm swell. The winds in the distant storm create waves on the sea. Moving outward from the storm area, they traverse great distances and break upon the shore 400 to 500 miles or more from the storm. When the wind is light, the booming sound of the surf at fairly regular intervals, is ominous. Clouds, changes of the wind, barometric pressure, rise of tide, and other phenomena, in relation to the distant cyclone, have been studied by many meteorologists.

Preeminent among pioneer observers of West Indian hurricanes was the Rev. Benito Viñes, S.J., who was director of the Magnetic and Meteorological Observatory of the Colegio de Belen, Havana. The Rev. Jose Algué, S.J., in connection with typhoons, and John Eliot, cyclones of the Bay of Bengal, were thorough students of the precursory signs of the tropical storm.

### WIND WAVES AND STORM SWELLS

Winds create waves upon the sea which move with a speed that is only a little less than the speed of the wind which produced them. Waves quickly outrun the tropical storm in which they are formed. The West Indian hurricane moves at an average rate of only about 12 miles an hour, while the waves move at rates sometimes exceeding 30 miles an hour. In the open ocean, in deep water, the height, speed and length of the waves are closely related to the velocity of the wind which produced them.

When wind begins blowing over a water surface it produces at first a series of ripples moving with the wind. As the ripples move forward with the wind, they steadily increase in size so long as the wind continues. The ultimate size of the waves depends upon the force of the wind and the "fetch" or length of water surface to windward.

After the wave moves beyond the influence of the winds which caused it, there is a change in its form. The most rapid change at first is a decrease in height. The wave becomes a relatively low, undulating movement of the sea surface known as a swell. To the mariner a swell is distinguished by two features: first, its relatively smooth, undulating form without the steep and ragged crests characteristic of waves actively driven by the wind and, second, the movement of winds and waves in different directions indicating that the waves have been formed elsewhere by winds from another quarter. There is no satisfactory definition of swells as distinguished from waves actively driven by the wind because there is an endless variety of conditions of wind and swell, sometimes with newly developed waves moving across the swells. The typical case is the sea swell moving far in advance of the storm into regions where winds are of insufficient force to produce any local confusion of the sea surface.

Waves of the open sea do not involve a bodily transfer of water and are not subject to the deflective effect of the earth's rotation; the winds, however, *are* deflected and in the northern hemisphere are directed counter-clockwise around the cyclone center. After waves are formed by winds in any part of the storm area, they move straight forward while the winds are deflected to the left in the northern hemisphere and to the right in the southern hemisphere. This is illustrated in the upper part of Figure 49. If the winds represented by the dotted areas at *A* produce waves moving in the direction of the solid arrow at *A*, the waves move straight onward as shown by the solid arrow at *B*. If the winds are part of a tropical cyclone in the northern hemisphere, they turn to the left as shown by the dotted arrows at *C*; if they are part of a tropical cyclone in the southern hemisphere, they turn to the right as shown by the dotted arrows at *D*. This deviation of wind from swell is found in all quadrants of the tropical cyclone. However, observations show that the amount of deviation in any quadrant depends upon the direction and rate of travel of the cyclone.

After the winds have turned to the left (in the northern hemisphere) new waves are developed moving in another direction. This is shown in the lower part of Figure 49, where the winds at *A* are producing the waves shown there by dotted lines; those waves grow and become the dominant waves (solid lines) moving into the wind field at *B* where new waves (dotted lines) are being developed, later to become in turn the dominant waves at *C*. Thus the dominant waves are those developed to windward.

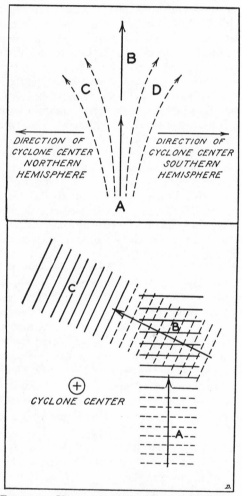

FIGURE 49. Upper section: Deviation of wind from swell in tropical cyclones in northern and southern hemispheres. Lower section: Development of dominant swells in cyclonic wind field.

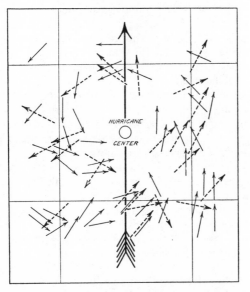

FIGURE 50. Composite chart showing wind direction
(solid arrows) and direction of movement of swells
(dashed arrows) in hurricane in North Atlantic,
August 1935.

From ship reports gathered during the progress of a hurricane in
August 1935, twelve synoptic charts were prepared showing direction
of wind and swell. The hurricane was in the Atlantic east of the
Bahamas from the 20th to 22nd, as shown by the track in Figure 112.
Each of the twelve individual maps was oriented so that the line of
progression of the storm center lay on the central meridian of the
composite chart before transferring the observations. The twelve
maps combined in this manner gave the composite shown in Figure
50. These observations show clearly the deviation of wind to the left
of the swells; that is, the observer standing with his back to the wind
would find the swells moving off to his right. The deviation of wind
from swell averaged 61° in the two front quadrants, 104° in the left
rear quadrant and only 20° in the right rear quadrant. This difference in the amount of deviation is caused by the progressive movement of the hurricane. The forward movement of the wind field in the
right rear quadrant results in a prolonged action of wind in the direc-

tion in which the swells are running; conditions are reversed in the left rear quadrant.

In front and to the right of the storm center the swells in general move forward roughly in the direction of travel of the storm. If the storm continues to move in the same direction these swells become larger and reach far in advance.

To the mariner the direction of movement of the storm swell in the open sea is significant. To the observer on shore the direction of movement of storm swells is not a dependable indication of the direction in which the storm center lies, unless he understands the effect of shallow water on the direction of wave movement. The period of waves created by a storm at sea does not change materially as the waves move out of the storm field; even when the swells reach shore, where they move more slowly, they become shorter so that the time interval is not affected. As shown in Figure 51, the wave, on reaching shallow water, is retarded and finally spills over. As each wave is retarded, the next following wave gains upon it, so the distance between successive waves is diminished. The time interval between waves remains the same.

If the shore line does not lie at right angles to the direction from which the wave comes, then one end of the wave reaches shallow water and is retarded first so that the remainder of the wave gains upon it. This results in a turning movement that tends to bring the wave front parallel to the shore line. However, this is seldom fully accomplished so that the direction of swells is usually at some deviation from normal to the shore line, though the deviation may be slight. The effect is different in various situations and can be learned only by experience.

The observer on shore should give particular attention to the period of the wave. The number of swells per minute should be ascertained by counting for three minutes. It is a valuable index to the intensity of the storm. In ordinary weather the waves on the Gulf of Mexico have a period of 4 or 5 seconds—12 to 15 waves to the minute. A fully developed hurricane causes swells on shore at some distance from the storm center with a period of 12 to 15 seconds—4 or 5 waves to the minute. In ordinary weather the waves observed on the Atlantic coast have longer periods than in the Gulf of Mexico. During the period from September 1 to 28, 1935, observations daily at five stations on the South Atlantic coast and two on the Texas coast gave an average of 7.7 waves to the minute at the former stations and 11.2

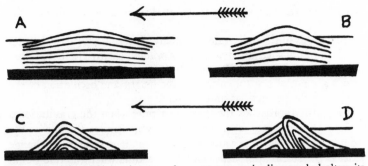

FIGURE 51. Wave (A) moving toward a coast over a shoaling sea bed alters its shape. The form becomes more abrupt (B), the crest more raised, the length decreased (C), and it finally changes from an undulation to a breaking wave (D). (After Wheeler.)

at the latter. In general, the larger the body of water, the longer will be the period of waves observed on its shores. Likewise, the more intense the storm at sea, the longer the period of the swells that break on shore.

The intermittent breaking of heavy swells on the shore when the wind is light is one of the signs of the hurricane. Ordinary waves of small period produce a more or less continuous noise.

### THE HURRICANE TIDE

As a precursory sign the tide is noteworthy. Ordinarily, a continuation of offshore winds will result in a tide below the normal and winds blowing for a considerable period toward the shore will cause a high tide. When a tropical storm approaches the coast, the tide rises even when winds are blowing offshore. The explanation of this phenomenon is that the winds locally may be offshore in the front of the cyclone but, farther at sea, the winds in the opposite side of the cyclone are blowing toward the shore. Currents are set up by the cyclonic winds which cause an accumulation of water along the coast.

At about the time that the winds at the outer limits of the hurricane are first felt, the tide begins to rise. The storm tide, however, is combined with the gravitational tide caused by the sun and moon. The gravitational tide comes generally in two oscillations daily, two high and two low tides. Along the Gulf of Mexico there are sometimes two oscillations daily and at other times there is only one. A knowledge of the gravitational tide is essential to an understanding of the storm tide.

Predictions of the daily tides for many places on the coast are prepared and published in advance for a whole year by the U.S. Coast and Geodetic Survey. When wind and atmospheric pressure conditions are not out of the ordinary, the height and oscillation of the tide follow the predictions quite closely.

If a storm approaches the coast at a time when the gravitational tide is due to go out, the storm tide may neutralize the ebb of the ordinary tide so that the water level will remain stationary or change little. If the storm approaches closely at a time when the tide would normally be rising anyway, the combined effect is a rise of water out of proportion to that which would otherwise be anticipated. If the storm center crosses the coast at approximately the time of high water from gravitational causes, the tide will be much higher than if the storm center should arrive at time of low water. The greater the ordinary daily oscillation of the gravitational tide, the more important is the predicted tide in relation to the rise of water that will be produced by the storm.

Ordinarily, the tide rises most rapidly at and to the immediate right of the point on the coast toward which the center of the storm is advancing.

If the predicted tide is subtracted, algebraically, from the observed tide, the difference is the rise of water caused by the storm.

As a precursory sign, the tide is of little value unless the normal daily oscillation due to gravitational forces is known and taken into account.

### BAROMETRIC PRESSURE PRECEDING THE CYCLONE

As a sign of the approach of a hurricane, the readings of the barometer at a single place are not often of great value until the storm center is so near that little time elapses before destructive winds occur. It has been asserted by some writers that a cessation of the diurnal variation of the barometer, which is most pronounced in the tropics, is an indication of the approach of a storm. There is little to support this view and, on the contrary, many barograph records show that the diurnal variation continues throughout the passage of the hurricane, though it is not conspicuous under such circumstances owing to the much larger oscillation of pressure in the storm. An example of a barograph trace during the passage of a hurricane, with the diurnal variation clearly shown, has been presented in Figure 47.

In the tropics, a fall of the barometer of 0.10 inch or more in three hours, exclusive of the diurnal change, is significant, e.g. if the normal diurnal change for the three hours is a fall of 0.04 inch, then a fall of 0.14 inch is significant, and, if the normal change is a rise of 0.04 inch in the three hours, then a fall of 0.06 inch in that three-hour period is significant. Outside the tropics, where irregular changes of greater magnitude are frequent, a much more rapid fall coupled with other precursory signs is necessary before the approach of a tropical storm reasonably may be suspected.

In the tropics, the temperature, barometric pressure and wind movement reproduce their daily changes with a regularity that verges upon monotony. Any disturbance of this daily regimen is immediately noticeable. While the hurricane is at a great distance, 1000 to 1500 miles as a rule, the barometer is likely to rise somewhat above the normal; the usual breezes fail and sometimes the wind sets in from an unaccustomed quarter. Night temperatures are a little lower than usual and day temperatures somewhat higher. These conditions are described as oppressive, largely because residents of the tropics accommodate their daily activities to the weather, particularly to the comfort of prevailing breezes, and when these are lacking or the wind comes from a strange quarter, they are not comfortable. These conditions are typical, and on the islands of the West Indies are the first indications of the storm's approach.

Farther northward, along the Gulf and South Atlantic coasts of the United States, these indications are not trustworthy. The weather there is more frequently dominated by anticyclonic conditions, often when no tropical disturbance exists, because of the more pronounced pressure variations of middle latitudes. Along these coasts, the observer who is in a position to view the open waters of the Gulf of Mexico or Atlantic Ocean will find the first reliable indication in the sea swell.

If he lacks this opportunity, he will find the first indications in the sky.

### CLOUDS AS PRECURSORY SIGNS

Father Viñes was of the opinion that the high clouds move outward in all directions from the center of the hurricane. Meteorologists now generally agree that the high clouds or cirrus types move forward with the general air stratum in which the storm is imbedded, coinciding roughly with the line of progression of the storm. In either case, the cirrus clouds extend forward to the limits of the advancing hurricane and sometimes beyond. They are among the first precursory signs. (Fig. 52.)

It has been stated by a number of writers that the center of the hurricane lies in the direction where the cirrus clouds seem to converge. However, it is not easy to determine whether or not the cirrus clouds are truly convergent at a point on the horizon. Clouds of the cirrus and cirro-stratus types are sometimes seen in bands or in parallel. Apparent convergence of parallel bands is an effect of perspective.

Shortly after the appearance of the precursory cirrus clouds, a veil appears, gradually increasing in density, so that the high clouds are indistinctly seen through it. Solar and lunar halos are sometimes observed after the appearance of the veil. At this stage the most brilliant sunsets are seen in tropical and subtropical latitudes. Of these Father Viñes says:

> The reddish colorations attending the sun's rising and setting are now of a most indescribable and threatening appearance, resembling the resplendence of a bright polar aurora. The ruby color is gradually turning into crimson as the sun is reaching the horizon, and shortly after its setting the whole sky has the appearance of an enormous conflagration.

### THE BAR OF THE HURRICANE

There next appears on the horizon, at about the point where the cirrus clouds diverge, an arc of dense clouds, which is the body of the hurricane itself. Its color is whitish or grayish at first, changing to dark gray, sometimes with a copperish hue. At this time low clouds appear in the direction from which the hurricane moves, gradually extending over the entire sky. They are broken clouds, moving swiftly at almost right angles to the cirrus clouds, so that the observer, directly facing the hurricane, sees the clouds move from his left to his right. The outlines of these low clouds, called fracto-stratus, or scud, are indistinct through the haze. If they appear early the observer may not be able to see the bar of the hurricane.

If the hurricane is moving directly toward the observer, the bar of the hurricane will remain at the same point on the horizon, gradually

FIGURE 52. Cirrus clouds with tufts.   —*F. Ellerman, Photo*

rising. If the hurricane is moving to his left or right, he will see the bar move slowly along the horizon.

### SHOWERS AND SQUALLS

At first the winds are light and blow from the observer's left to right as he faces the hurricane center. They have a peculiar gustiness which is ominous of the terrific squalls to come. As they increase, light showers attend the gusts. Father Viñes' observations are as follows:

Shortly after the bar is formed in the horizon the nimbus clouds of the hurricane begin to overrun the skies with inexhaustible succession and high speed. Showers of short duration begin, and the wind velocity increases from that moment. The barometer that has been falling slowly, now drops abruptly. . . . The rain at the beginning is of a showery nature, attended by squalls from 55 to 65 miles an hour, while the mean velocity of the wind is 35 to 40 miles. On the contrary, as the vortex approaches the rain is always continuous, although highly irregular, the showers succeeding each other at short intervals, and always attended by furious gusts of 100, 110, and sometimes 120 miles an hour.

# CHAPTER VIII

# UNUSUAL HURRICANE MOVEMENTS

WHILE there are no normal or average tracks of hurricanes in the sense in which those terms are ordinarily employed, nearly all of them pursue paths that have much in common. With few exceptions they move in a direction between west and north in the initial stages. Some continue a westerly course until they move inland. The majority, however, at some point in the line of progress, turn to the northward or northeastward. The prevalence of such tracks is apparent from the most casual inspection of any chart showing hurricane paths for a period of years.

The tracks of a few hurricanes have been quite unusual in that they have, in some stage or other of their progressive movements, pursued courses that have rarely, if ever, been followed by other hurricanes of which we have record. Five of these cases have been investigated in an effort to ascertain the causes of abnormal movements. (Fig. 53.) The dates are:

> September 9 to 25, 1900.
> October 11 to 23, 1910.
> September 7 to 14, 1919.
> October 21 to 30, 1921.
> October 14 to 21, 1922.

There have been other hurricanes whose paths were erratic and some of them have also been investigated, but the five listed are rather distinctive in type and were all of sufficient violence to be classed as fully developed tropical cyclones.

## HURRICANE OF SEPTEMBER 9 TO 25, 1900

This hurricane and two others were in progress at the same time. One of the others passed near Galveston, Tex., on September 8, 1900. The third, from September 13 to 20, 1900, moved from a point some distance east of Puerto Rico, recurved to the northward and then northeastward.

The hurricane of September 9 to 25, 1900, was first plotted a short distance south of the Cape Verde Islands. Its subsequent course and

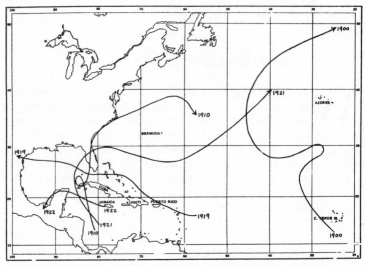

FIGURE 53. Tracks of centers of five hurricanes whose movements were quite unusual.

the conditions which influenced its movements have been carefully investigated by C. L. Mitchell. The tracks of this hurricane and of the four others discussed in this chapter will be found on the accompanying chart.

From September 9 to 13, this hurricane moved in a northwesterly direction. It then reached a region where the general drift above the surface was from the southwest, when it recurved to the northeast, moving with the air currents aloft. During the 15th and 16th, pressure increased materially over the region to the eastward and northeastward of the hurricane and the direction of its course changed to westerly on the 16th, evidently because the drift aloft had turned toward the west. During the 13th to 17th, an anticyclone moved rapidly east-southeastward from the Canadian northwest to the Atlantic, in latitude 40°N. and longitude 40°W. On the latter date the anticyclone was located a short distance northwest of the hurricane which evidently caused the winds aloft to blow toward the southwest, hence the hurricane moved to the southwestward.

The anticyclone then drifted eastward for two days, then slowly to the northwest and finally to the northeast. The track of the cyclone,

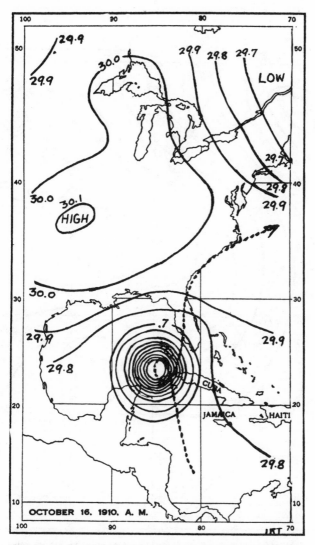

FIGURE 54. Location of the hurricane on the morning of October 16, 1910, at the western side of the loop, moving southward. Track of the center is shown by the dotted line. The anticyclone or "high" which influenced the movement of the hurricane is shown over the interior of the United States.

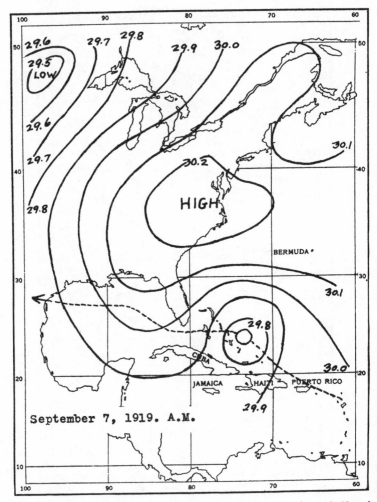

FIGURE 55. The hurricane on the morning of September 7, 1919, its track (dotted line), and the first of two anticyclones which deflected the hurricane to the westward.

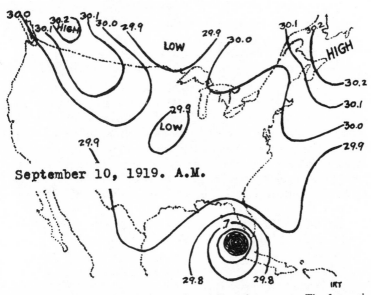

FIGURE 56. The hurricane on the morning of September 10, 1919. The first anti-cyclone is moving off in the northeast while a second one has appeared in the far northwest.

after it had moved southwestward for two days, was the usual broad, sweeping curve, as it skirted the western side of the anticyclone.

### LOOP HURRICANE OF OCTOBER 11 TO 23, 1910

This was a storm of great violence which described a loop in the southeastern Gulf of Mexico. (Fig. 54.) Its course at that time and since then has been the subject of considerable discussion. At the time the storm was in progress there were not enough observations to determine its actual path, hence it appeared that one hurricane had moved northwestward into the Gulf of Mexico and that another had developed over western Cuba or moved to that position, following shortly behind the first one. Later, some meteorologists were of the opinion that it was one and the same storm, but had remained stationary for several days in the vicinity of western Cuba and then moved rapidly north-northeastward.

Data assembled by the U.S. Weather Bureau and the Cuban Meteorological Service have convincingly shown that the hurricane actually described a loop.

C. L. Mitchell, in discussing the loop described by the center of this hurricane, says:

> When the track of a tropical cyclone describes a loop as in the case of the hurricane of October 12-21, 1910, the turning is always *to the left*.

The cyclone, when blocked by an anticyclone, will move southwestward or westward temporarily and then resume its movement to the northeastward when far enough from the anticyclone. If the anticyclone persists long enough, the cyclone will fill up, that is, diminish in intensity, the central pressure rising and the storm dissipating.

A cyclone will not describe a loop *to the right*, south of about 30°N., according to Mitchell, for the following reasons:

> In order to cause a cyclone to complete a loop to the right after being deflected to the southeast, it would be necessary for the anticyclone to outrun the cyclone and to move southeastward and southward after reaching a position northeast of the cyclone's center, thus causing the general drift aloft in the vicinity of the latter to change from the northwest through north, northeast, east and southeast to south. However, this, it is thought, can never occur south of about 30°N., inasmuch as the anticyclone that originally causes the deflection to the southeast is a slow-moving one, making it impossible for it to move in the manner indicated as necessary to cause a right-hand loop in the track of the cyclone.

This cyclone remained approximately in latitude 23°N. and longitude 85°W. for three days, while describing the loop, and its progressive motion during this period was extremely slow. Observations collected and plotted to determine the track of this hurricane were numerous on several days. The circulatory movement of the winds, uninfluenced by any appreciable progressive motion of the storm, and almost wholly over water areas, is shown clearly to be symmetrical with respect to the storm center, with an inclination inward to the center in all quadrants. There were no pronounced inequalities in wind force in the various quadrants, as observed in the case of hurricanes moving forward at usual speeds.

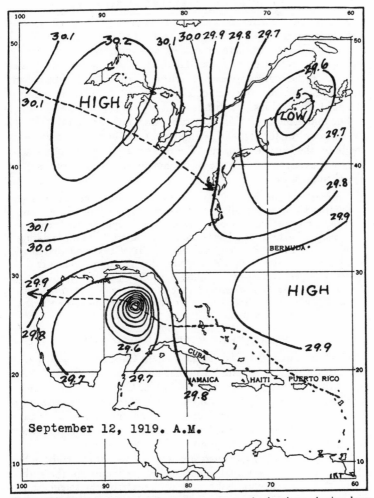

FIGURE 57. On the morning of September 12, 1919, the hurricane, having been deflected to the westward through the Florida Straits, has resumed a course more to the northwestward but is now turned again to the westward by the second anticyclone ("high"). Tracks of centers of the hurricane and anticyclone are shown by dotted lines.

### HURRICANE OF SEPTEMBER 7 TO 14, 1919

This hurricane attained great violence and pursued an unusual path in its later stages. It was first observed to the east of the Windward Islands; from there it moved west-northwestward until it reached a position east of the Bahamas, which is not an unusual course. It then turned westward through the Florida Straits and moved slowly across the Gulf of Mexico to the Texas coast, south of Corpus Christi. (Figs. 55, 56 and 57.)

The movement of this hurricane was investigated by R. H. Weightman, in the light of soundings of the upper air then being made by the Weather Bureau. The nearest sounding station was at Leesburg, Ga., some distance to the northward of the storm's path. Weightman says:

> A current from the east was then fully established at Leesburg at all altitudes up to probably 10 kilometers, at least, from the evening of the 5th to the morning of the 12th, a rather unusual occurrence, if we may judge by a casual inspection of the observations made during the two or three preceding months. . . . It will be seen that they [the wind direction at Leesburg and the direction of movement of the storm center] correspond in quite a marked degree, which would seem to indicate not necessarily that the storm was carried along in the drift of easterly winds but rather that the storm passed westward along the southern boundary of the great easterly current.

### HURRICANE OF OCTOBER 21 TO 30, 1921

This storm had its genesis in the western Caribbean Sea. It moved northwestward through the Yucatan Channel into the Gulf of Mexico and turned northeastward across Florida. Commonly, the western Caribbean storms, after the middle of October, move northward or northeastward and they rarely enter the Gulf of Mexico. After crossing Florida, this storm turned east-southeast and continued to move in a direction south of east for about three days.

During the birth of this hurricane over the western Caribbean Sea, the barometer in the Canal Zone steadily declined from the 13th to 18th. There were heavy daily rains, noticeably on the Pacific side of the Canal Zone. The cyclonic character of the storm was observed on the 20th. By the time it reached the Yucatan Channel it had developed marked violence. The master of the schooner *Virginia*, about that time, reported a minimum pressure of 27.80 inches in the cyclone center.

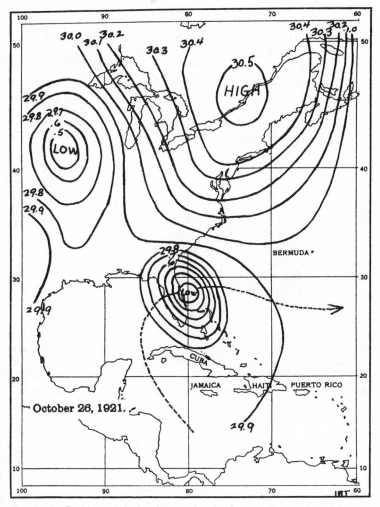

FIGURE 58. Positions of the hurricane and anticyclone on the morning of October 26, 1921. Dotted line shows track of the hurricane center.

At Tarpon Springs, the minimum barometer reading was 28.12 inches and a calm was experienced for more than an hour as the center crossed the coast line there on October 25.

From the 25th to the 28th, an extensive anticyclone moved southward from Hudson Bay and northerly winds extended over the region of the hurricane. (Fig. 58.) Of this movement, E. H. Bowie says:

> The southward-flowing air-stream controlled the movement of all pilot balloons released at pilot-balloon stations in the Atlantic States north of Florida during this period. This but confirms the opinion of the writer and others that the winds flowing out from and around anticyclones very largely determine the movement of tropical cyclones.

### SOUTHWESTWARD MOVEMENT OF THE HURRICANE OF OCTOBER 14 TO 21, 1922

This storm apparently originated a short distance south of Jamaica, on October 14 or thereabouts, and for four days moved slowly west-northwestward, when it reached the northeast coast of Yucatan. It then turned directly southwestward and passed into the interior in the neighborhood of Frontera. No storm of record had pursued a course similar to this in more than forty years.[1]

An anticyclone appeared in the far northwest on the 15th and spread rapidly southeastward, reaching the west Gulf coast on the morning of the 18th at which time the hurricane arrived at the northeast coast of Yucatan. (Fig. 59.) The wind circulation to a considerable height above the earth's surface was controlled by the anticyclone. Northeast winds set in aloft over the Gulf of Mexico. At Gulf coast stations, the movements of upper clouds indicated an exceptionally strong northeast current at high altitudes. Coincident with the establishment of this northeast current, the hurricane moved southwestward.

[1] Some remarkable hurricane movements occurred in 1934 and 1935, particularly the following: June and November 1934 (tracks I and X in Figure 111) and October and November 1935 (tracks IV and V in Figure 112).

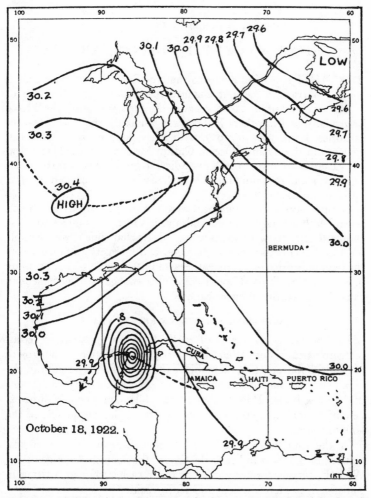

FIGURE 59. Positions of hurricane and anticyclone on the morning of October 18, 1922. Tracks followed by centers of hurricane and anticyclone ("high") shown by dotted lines.

# CHAPTER IX

# FREQUENCY OF WEST INDIAN HURRICANES

THERE is good evidence that the frequency of West Indian hurricanes has not changed materially since the days of Columbus. In some years of the present century there have been many and in others few, as was evidently the case in earlier centuries. From 1901 to 1937, with fairly good records of tropical cyclones in the Atlantic Ocean, Gulf of Mexico and Caribbean Sea, the variation from year to year is indicated by the maximum number, 21 in 1933, and the minimum, 2 in each of five years, 1911, 1914, 1917, 1929 and 1930. (Fig. 60.)

Comparatively small numbers were recorded in the sixteenth and seventeenth centuries but coastal and island areas subject to West Indian hurricanes were sparsely settled. At that time it was possible for a cyclone of considerable diameter and intensity to move across the Gulf of Mexico or Caribbean Sea and pass inland without coming in contact with ships at sea or going near enough to a settlement to cause winds worthy of historical note.

## INCREASING NUMBERS IN RECENT YEARS

The increasing frequency of tropical storms apparent in recent meteorological history (Fig. 61) is partially a reflection of the growth of facilities for reporting them. Since the Spanish-American War, the U.S. Weather Bureau has operated a network of observing stations in the West Indies. Prior to that time, public money could not be expended to maintain stations of the Weather Bureau outside of the United States.

Of the establishment of the Weather Bureau's meteorological stations in the West Indies at the time of the Spanish-American War, Willis L. Moore, formerly chief of the Weather Bureau, writing in *The American Mercury*, September 1927, said:

> It was the beginning of the hurricane season which begins in July and lasts until October. I knew that many armadas in olden days had been defeated, not by the enemy, but by the weather, and that probably as many ships had been sent to the bottom of the sea by storms as had been destroyed by the fire of enemy fleets. . . . I reported the

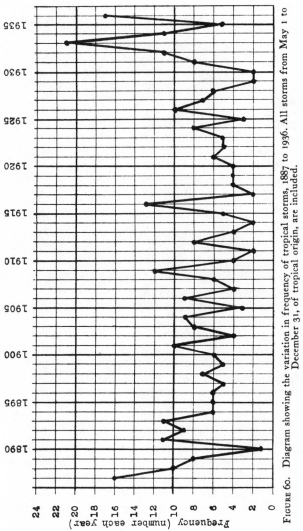

FIGURE 60.  Diagram showing the variation in frequency of tropical storms, 1887 to 1936. All storms from May 1 to December 31, of tropical origin, are included.

facts to Secretary of Agriculture James Wilson, under whom I served as chief of bureau and assistant secretary. He took me to President McKinley. I can see him now as he stood with one leg carelessly thrown across his desk, chin in hand and elbow on knee, studying the map I had spread before him. Suddenly he turned to the Secretary and said: "Wilson, I am more afraid of a West Indian hurricane than I am of the entire Spanish Navy." To me he said: "Get this service inaugurated at the earliest possible moment." When I told him I should need the authority of Congress, he directed me to report to Chairman Cannon of the Appropriations Committee, who would include the necessary authority in the bill that was then being held open for the purpose of giving to the President everything that he might need in the prosecution of war. . . . Thus was inaugurated as a war necessity the present West Indian weather service, which has been of such benefit to the shipping of our South Atlantic and Gulf waters, and to the commerce of the world in those regions.

### BEGINNINGS OF THE HURRICANE WARNING SERVICE

It is appropriate to note that the hurricane warning service which began in the West Indies as a result of this action, was not the first.

The observatory of the College of Belen (Havana) was founded in 1857 by Father Antonio Cabré. On March 1, 1858, meteorological observations were begun at the observatory. In 1870, Father Benito Viñes became the director. He set himself to discover ways and means of issuing timely warnings of hurricanes.

It is not certain when Father Viñes began his warning service. The earliest extant printed record of any forecast by him bears the date September 11, 1875. It is recorded that this forecast saved many lives during the storm which came on September 12. The Weather Bureau issued its first cautionary warning in connection with the hurricane of August 1873—the Nova Scotia storm.

### CHRONOLOGICAL LISTS OF POËY AND OTHERS

Andreas Poëy chronicled hurricanes of the West Indies from 1493 to 1855. During the first fifty-five years of the nineteenth century, Redfield, Reid and others carefully recorded the life histories of many hurricanes. During the next fifteen years, up to about 1870, no one seems to have assigned himself the task of keeping a complete record of West Indian hurricanes.[1]

---

[1] The chronological list in Chapter xv contains 24 tropical storms during the period from 1856 to 1870, inclusive.

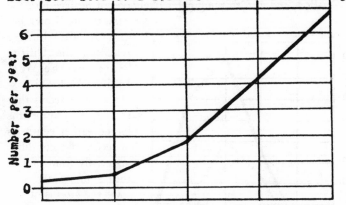

FIGURE 61. Average number of tropical storms per year in each century, 1501 to 1933. The storms included in these averages, approximately 900, are enumerated in the chronological lists of subsequent chapters. No storm which was first observed before June 1 or after November 30, has been included.

Frequency of hurricanes by months has been set forth by a number of writers. Mitchell's records for tropical cyclones of the Gulf, Caribbean and North Atlantic, from 1887 to 1932 are as follows:

| | May | June | July | Aug. | Sept. | Oct. | Nov. | Dec. | Total |
|---|---|---|---|---|---|---|---|---|---|
| Number of storms | 2 | 19 | 19 | 54 | 99 | 81 | 22 | 2 | 298 |
| Percentage | 1 | 6 | 6 | 18 | 33 | 27 | 8 | 1 | — |

### SEASONAL VARIATION IN INTENSITY

In the following table the number of storms in each month, 1887 to 1936, inclusive, and the number of known hurricane intensity are given.

| | May | June | July | Aug. | Sept. | Oct. | Nov. | Dec. | Total |
|---|---|---|---|---|---|---|---|---|---|
| Number of storms | 4 | 24 | 25 | 71 | 112 | 90 | 24 | 2 | 352 |
| Number of known hurricane intensity | 0 | 10 | 13 | 51 | 66 | 35 | 6 | 0 | 181 |

During August 72 per cent of tropical cyclones were of hurricane intensity; in September 59 per cent; and in October 39 per cent.

In the early years the greater frequency of August storms, as recorded, is apparently due to the fact that a higher percentage of them was of sufficient violence to justify a place in the historical writings of the period, and also to the greater likelihood of recurve into the Atlantic in September and October before reaching the United States or the West Indies. With this explanation it seems that the frequency by months in the earlier centuries of record did not differ materially from that of the last fifty years.

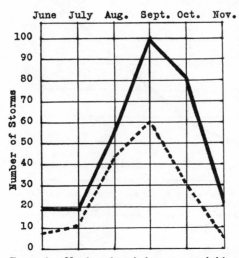

FIGURE 62. Number of tropical storms recorded in each month, 1887 to 1932, inclusive. Solid lines, storms of all intensities. Dotted lines, storms of hurricane intensity, as classified by Mitchell, i.e. central pressure 29.00 inches or lower and winds near center of more than 60 miles an hour.

Of the storms of full hurricane intensity, there appear to be two maxima, one in the first half of September, the other in the first half of October. Mitchell gives the following figures for half months, 1887 to 1923, inclusive:

|  | September | | October | |
|---|---|---|---|---|
|  | First Half | Second Half | First Half | Second Half |
| Number of storms | 34 | 12 | 22 | 4 |

A study of the charts of these storms leads to the conclusion that the second maximum is due to the increasing frequency and intensity of storms of the western Caribbean Sea during the first half of October, at which time the frequency of Cape Verde storms is rapidly diminishing. While it is admittedly impossible to determine the place of origin of many of these storms, I have divided those occurring in the period 1887 to 1932 into two classes, omitting some whose tracks gave no clue as to the place of origin.

|  | June | July | Aug. | Sept. | Oct. | Nov. | Total |
|---|---|---|---|---|---|---|---|
| Storms of the western Caribbean | 11 | 3 | 1 | 14 | 31 | 10 | 70 |
| Storms of the Cape Verde type | 2 | 11 | 44 | 64 | 29 | 5 | 155 |

The seasonal variation in frequency of these two classes of storms is quite distinct. The Cape Verde type reaches its greatest frequency in early September, but with average intensity diminishing. The western Caribbean type increases to a maximum frequency in October, but with a secondary maximum in June.

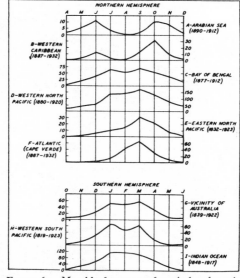

FIGURE 63.   Monthly frequency of tropical cyclones in various parts of the world.

## EFFECT OF TEMPERATURE ON FREQUENCY OF HURRICANES

At the equator the sun at noon is at the zenith twice each year, at the equinoxes. Two periods of maximum heat occur there, lagging somewhat behind the equinoxes but about six months apart. At 23½° latitude, the sun is at the zenith at noon once each year, at time of the summer solstice. From that latitude poleward in each hemisphere there is only one period of maximum heat, lagging somewhat behind the summer solstice. Between the equator and 23½° latitude there is a tendency toward the development of two periods of maximum temperature, lagging somewhat behind the dates when the sun is at the zenith. At about 10°N., for example, the sun is at the zenith at noon near the middle of April and again near the end of August. There is a tendency toward the development of two periods of maximum temperature lagging behind the sun so that the first comes in late May or June and the second in late September or early October.

Over large bodies of water in the tropics there is little effect from these two periods of maximum heat. The highest temperatures are found at some time after the summer solstice, there being only one maximum. This is explained by the transfer of water from higher latitudes. In more or less confined seas and bays in the tropics, the two maxima appear. In keeping with these annual temperature variations, there is usually only one period of maximum frequency of tropical cyclones which originate in the open oceans at some distance from the equator, while two periods are found in the frequency of tropical cyclones which have their genesis nearer the equator and in more or less confined seas like the western Caribbean. (Fig. 63.)

In the Arabian Sea there are maxima in June and October, as is the case in the western Caribbean. In the Bay of Bengal the two maxima come in July and September, while in the vicinity of Australia and over the western South Pacific, between 160°E. and 140°W., the two maxima come in January and March.

NUMBER OF TROPICAL CYCLONES BY MONTHS

| Place | Apr. | May | June | July | Aug. | Sep. | Oct. | Nov. | Dec. | Years of record |
|---|---|---|---|---|---|---|---|---|---|---|
| Arabian Sea | 2 | 5 | 11 | 3 | 0 | 2 | 10 | 8 | 2 | 1890-1912 |
| Bay of Bengal | 7 | 21 | 42 | 65 | 55 | 70 | 51 | 37 | 17 | 1877-1912 |
| | Oct. | Nov. | Dec. | Jan. | Feb. | Mar. | Apr. | May | June | |
| Australia | 4 | 10 | 22 | 54 | 49 | 58 | 29 | 7 | 7 | 1839-1922 |
| W.S. Pacific | 4 | 8 | 31 | 69 | 47 | 64 | 18 | 2 | 2 | 1819-1923 |

(From records of Visher and Newnham.)

In the North Pacific,[2] South Indian Ocean and the North Atlantic (exclusive of the western Caribbean), there is only one maximum, coming in September in the northern hemisphere and in January or February in the southern hemisphere.

NUMBER OF TROPICAL CYCLONES BY MONTHS

| Place | May | June | July | Aug. | Sep. | Oct. | Nov. | Dec. | Jan. | Years of record |
|---|---|---|---|---|---|---|---|---|---|---|
| E.N. Pacific | 1 | 5 | 10 | 14 | 31 | 22 | 7 | 3 | 1 | 1832-1923 |
| W.N. Pacific | 47 | 56 | 141 | 147 | 168 | 132 | 79 | 48 | 37 | 1880-1920 |
| Cape Verde type | 0 | 2 | 11 | 44 | 64 | 29 | 5 | 0 | 0 | 1887-1932 |
| | Oct. | Nov. | Dec. | Jan. | Feb. | Mar. | Apr. | May | June | |
| S. Indian | 7 | 33 | 58 | 113 | 115 | 98 | 68 | 25 | 3 | 1848-1917 |

(Pacific storms from records by Visher; South Indian Ocean storms from records by Newnham.)

[2] Typhoons of the Pacific originating in confined seas appear to have two maxima of frequency. Algué's record of typhoons which formed in the China Sea was: April 1, May 2, June 12, July 13, August 7, September 11, October 10, and November 2; other months, none.

In the "Cape Verde type" have been included all storms whose direction of movement and location at first observation definitely indicated that they did not originate in the western Caribbean Sea but in all probability came from the Cape Verde region or the Atlantic Ocean to the eastward of the West Indies.

### ADVANCE INDICATIONS OF FREQUENCY

C. L. Ray, meteorologist at San Juan, Puerto Rico, after investigating pressure conditions over the North Atlantic in spring and early summer in relation to the frequency of hurricanes in summer and autumn of the same year, says:

> Spring and summer pressure deviations in the North Atlantic, as indicated by the pressure at San Juan, have an inverse relation to tropical storm frequencies of the summer and autumn months. This is best indicated where pressure continues above normal from May through July, but is also related definitely to the July departure considered singly, and also as early as April-May. It is less well defined with respect to the west Caribbean, but has a 71 per cent probability of verification in relation to the May and June pressure deviation.

J. F. Brennan, meteorologist at Kingston, Jamaica, makes the following remarks in connection with a similar study:

> The island of Jamaica is near the southwestern limit of the zone exposed to the August and September hurricane tracks. If the observations during the three months of May, June, and July, as given in table 1 [not reproduced], be studied, it will be obvious that, in most cases, when the island mean rainfall is excessive, the mean surface wind below the daily normals, and the daily mean barometric pressure below the normal, there is much likelihood of the development of disturbed weather conditions in the eastern Caribbean, particularly during the ensuing months of August and September. Conversely, when during the same three months the island mean rainfall is deficient, the mean surface wind above the daily normals, and the daily mean barometric pressure consistently above the normal, there is little likelihood of disturbances occurring in the following months of August and September.

### FREQUENCY OF HURRICANES OF "GREAT" INTENSITY

Mitchell has determined the relative frequency of tropical cyclones of hurricane intensity at the coast line of each State along the South

Atlantic and Gulf coasts and Gray and Norton have shown the relative frequencies in various sections of Florida. These relative frequencies by months are readily determined from the track charts given in Chapter IV.

Concerning the frequency of West Indian hurricanes of great intensity, Mitchell (1928) says:

> In hurricanes of great diameter the central pressure usually falls nearly to, or below, 28.00 inches, and the diameter of the path of great damage from wind may range from 50 to 100 miles or more. In view of these foregoing facts, it is pertinent to state that of the 84 tropical cyclones of hurricane intensity that reached the coast of the United States during the last 50 years, only 16 can be classed as "great" hurricanes both as to intensity and diameter. They are enumerated below, showing the month and year of occurrence and the section of the coast at which the centers passed inland.

June: Apalachicola-Tallahassee, Fla., section, 1886.
July: Mobile, Ala.-Pensacola, Fla., section, 1916.
August: West Palm Beach-Lake Okeechobee, Fla., section, 1880.
 Eastern portion of the Carolinas, 1885.
 Indianola, Tex., 1886.
 Georgia and South Carolina coasts, 1893.
 Galveston, Tex., section, 1915.
 Between Corpus Christi and Brownsville, Tex., 1916.
September: Galveston, Tex., section, 1900.
 Alabama coast, 1906.
 Southeastern Louisiana, 1915.
 Key West, Fla.-Corpus Christi, Tex., 1919.
 Miami-West Palm Beach-Lake Okeechobee, Fla., section, 1926.
 From near Miami north to Jupiter and inland to Lake Okeechobee, Fla., 1928.
October: Key West-Fort Myers, Fla., 1910.
 Mobile, Ala.-Pensacola, Fla., section, 1916.

To the above list, prepared in 1928, may be added the following:

September 1929: Long Key-Panama City, Fla., sections.
August 1933: Norfolk, Va.-Chesapeake Bay section.
September 1933: Brownsville, Tex.
September 1933: Hatteras-New Bern, N. C., section.

One of the most destructive hurricanes of record was that of September 1935 on the Florida Keys with a barometer reading of

26.35 inches; this storm, however, was of small diameter when it crossed the Keys.

On the southern coasts of the United States as a whole, tropical cyclones of hurricane intensity have occurred with a frequency of about two a year, while those of "great" intensity have occurred somewhere in that region about once in three years.

### HURRICANE FREQUENCY BY STATES

The following table shows frequency of tropical storms of hurricane intensity by States from 1879 to 1936, this being an extension of data collected by Mitchell:

| State | Number of Storms of hurricane intensity 1879-1936 | Length of Coastline | Average per 100 miles of Coastline |
|---|---|---|---|
| Texas | 30 | 367 | 8.2 |
| Louisiana | 17 | 397 | 4.3 |
| Mississippi | 10 | 65 | 15.4 |
| Alabama | 7 | 53 | 13.2 |
| Gulf coast of Florida | 33 | 798 | 4.1 |
| Atlantic coast of Florida | 13 | 399 | 3.3 |
| Both coasts of Florida | 46 | 1197 | 3.8 |
| Georgia | 7 | 100 | 7.0 |
| South Carolina | 12 | 187 | 6.4 |
| North Carolina | 16 | 301 | 5.3 |
| All States | 145 | 2667 | 5.4 |

Discussing the frequency of Florida hurricanes in the fifty-year period ending with 1935, Gray and Norton found 56 tropical storms crossing the Florida coast line in that period, 41 of which were of hurricane intensity. Although this is an average of one tropical storm of hurricane force each year in Florida as a whole, the average for any given part of the State is much less and there is a marked difference in frequency in different parts of the State. Their table showing the chances of winds of hurricane force in any given year is as follows:

| City | Chances |
|---|---|
| Jacksonville | 1 in 50 |
| West Palm Beach | 1 in 20 |
| Miami | 1 in 20 |
| Key West | 1 in 10 |
| Fort Myers | 1 in 20 |
| Tampa | 1 in 30 |
| Pensacola | 1 in 10 |

The variation in frequency by months in the various sections is shown by the following table of occurrences from 1879 to 1936:

| | Texas | Louisiana | Florida Gulf | Florida Atlantic | North Carolina |
|---|---|---|---|---|---|
| June | 8 | 2 | 5 | 0 | 0 |
| July | 5 | 0 | 2 | 1 | 1 |
| August | 8 | 5 | 2 | 4 | 5 |
| September | 7 | 8 | 11 | 7 | 8 |
| October | 2 | 2 | 11 | 0 | 1 |

# CHAPTER X

# DESTRUCTIVE EFFECTS OF HURRICANES

W IND is air in motion. Despite its tenuity, air becomes, when moving at high velocities, a very destructive agent, partly because of the force exerted by the wind itself but also because of solid objects which are carried along with it. In tropical storms, water, both from the increased level of the sea and the torrential rainfall, becomes an additional and important agent of destruction. Buildings in coastal areas are sometimes subjected to all of these destructive forces when the hurricane strikes.

## PRESSURE EXERTED BY THE WIND

The pressure exerted upon a plane surface normal to the direction of the wind increases with the square of the wind velocity. When the wind velocity is 50 miles an hour, the perpendicular force is approximately 10 pounds on an area of one square foot; at 100 miles an hour it is about 40 pounds per square foot. Sir Isaac Newton was the first to give a theoretical treatment of the relation between pressure and velocity. William Ferrel showed that the force of the wind upon an object is the difference of pressure upon the two sides. Pressure is increased upon the side exposed to the wind and diminished upon the other side. While wind pressures are measured by instruments suitably exposed to the wind, such as pressure tube anemometers (Fig. 64), the reaction between the wind and buildings in its line of progress is extremely complicated.

From the velocity of the wind, the pressure in pounds per square foot may be computed from the formula $P = KV^2$, in which $P$ is pressure in pounds per square foot and $V$ is wind velocity in miles per hour. Pressure is considered to be that exerted when the wind is normal to a flat surface of appreciable size; it is the pressure on the front plus the suction in the rear. Many investigators have assigned values to $K$. According to Newton it is 0.0027. Others have adopted values ranging from 0.0025 to 0.0054. With a coefficient of 0.004[1], the

---

[1] Dryden and Hill concluded (1933) from measurements of wind pressure on a model of the Empire State Building at the U.S. Bureau of Standards that a reasonable value is 0.0038.

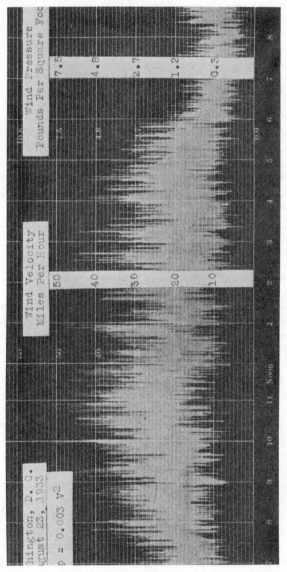

FIGURE 64. Record from Dines Pressure Tube Anemometer in Weather Bureau Observatory, Washington, D.C., during approach of hurricane of August 1933. It will be noted that the highest wind was recorded before noon of August 23, whereas the center of the storm did not pass Washington until after sundown. Decreasing wind was due to diminishing intensity of the storm as it passed inland.

pressure at a velocity of 150 miles an hour would be 90 pounds per square foot. However, the pressure varies somewhat with air density.

## DAMAGE TO BUILDINGS

During the Florida hurricane of 1926, two tall buildings in Miami suffered considerable damage, the Meyer-Kiser Building and the Realty Board Building. A small observation room, about 18 by 21 feet, was erected on top the Meyer-Kiser Building. It had four small columns in the corners supporting the roof. The walls were blown out and the four columns bent. A committee of the Structural Division, American Society of Engineers, estimated that a pressure of about 65 pounds per square foot would be required to produce the distortion which occurred. In the Realty Board Building the walls and partitions were much cracked but the steel framework was not badly distorted. Damage to these buildings was attributed to faulty design.

The general conclusion reached by engineers who studied damage to buildings in this hurricane and that of 1928 at West Palm Beach, was that the better-built buildings resisted the storm wholly or with minor damage.

In the official report of relief activities of the American National Red Cross in the Florida hurricane of 1926, there appears this statement:

> For the most part, though there were some notable exceptions, the large buildings of reinforced construction, the finer residences and the more sturdily built small buildings were not seriously damaged.

Doubtless the danger from collapse of buildings from wind pressure in hurricanes can be minimized by sturdy construction but, as stated in the report of the American National Red Cross, there are "notable exceptions."

In 1837 a very severe hurricane visited the Texas coast. At Galveston the Tremont Hotel had been newly built early in that year. It was blown down by the storm and was rebuilt and opened on April 22, 1839. No doubt the builders had learned a lesson in construction because the new Tremont Hotel survived a number of violent storms, including two really great hurricanes in 1900 and 1915, and after standing almost undamaged by storms for nearly one hundred years, was torn down to make way for more modern buildings. With its sturdily built buildings and its great seawall, Galveston is now more strongly fortified against the tropical cyclone than any other city in the world.

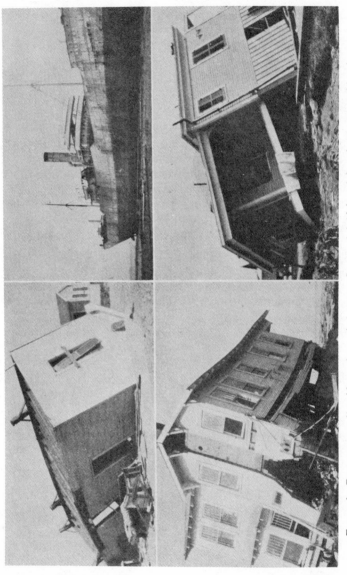

FIGURE 65. Damage to small residences in tropical storms. Steamer left high and dry after passage of hurricane.

In Miami there are several frame houses with shingle roofs which were erected in 1896 when the city was first laid out. There are also a number of frame buildings in Key West that have withstood, without serious damage, all the hurricanes of the last fifty-five years.

At many other places along the Gulf and South Atlantic coasts there are buildings that have survived a number of violent hurricanes. At Burrwood, La., buildings are sturdily constructed to withstand hurricane winds and along the Gulf Coast a sixtypenny nail is sometimes called a "Burrwood finishing nail."

### DESTRUCTIVE EFFECTS OF OBJECTS CARRIED BY THE WINDS

When sections of roofs, branches of trees, walls of buildings, and other objects are torn loose and carried along with hurricane winds, they strike with great force and are exceedingly destructive. Among the effects that certain hurricanes have produced there are some that would seem quite incredible were they not common results of the more violent tornado. On July 26, 1825, during a hurricane at Guadeloupe, it was reported that a gust of wind seized a plank an inch thick and sent it through the trunk of a palm tree sixteen inches thick. Photographs have been obtained of similar occurrences in the Havana hurricane of 1926 and the Puerto Rico hurricane of 1928. (Fig. 66.) Strips of weather boarding have been ripped from buildings and driven endways through porch columns.

Sir George Rodney, admiral in command of a squadron of ships and frigates, wrote to Lady Rodney on December 10, 1780, an account of the "Great Hurricane" of that year. The following extract of his letter is quoted from Colonel Reid's *Law of Storms*:

> You may easily conceive my surprise, concern and astonishment, when I saw the dreadful situation of the island [Barbados] and the destructive effects of the hurricane. The strongest buildings and the whole of the houses, most of which were of stone, and remarkable for their solidity, gave way to the fury of the wind, and were torn up to their foundation; all the forts destroyed, and many of the heavy cannon carried upwards of a hundred feet from the forts. Had I not been an eyewitness, nothing could have induced me to have believed it. More than six thousand persons perished and all the inhabitants were entirely ruined.

During the same hurricane at Barbados, Dr. Blane reported that the bodies of men and cattle were lifted from off the ground and carried several yards. Trees were torn up by the roots and stripped of

FIGURE 66.   Royal palm pierced by pine board (10 feet by 3 inches by 1 inch) in hurricane at Puerto Rico, September 13, 1928.

their bark. In the Antigua hurricane of 1837, "heavy tiles were flying about from the tops of shaking and trembling houses, killing and wounding many persons."

R. W. Gray, in charge of the Weather Bureau office at Miami, wrote of the hurricane of 1926:

> The intensity of the storm and the wreckage that it left can not be adequately described. The continuous roar of the wind; the crash of falling buildings, flying débris, and plate glass; the shriek of fire apparatus and ambulances that rendered assistance until the streets became impassable; the terrifically driven rain that came in sheets as dense as fog; the electric flashes from live wires have left the memory of a fearful night in the minds of the many thousands that were in the storm area.

P. McDonough, an observer of the Weather Bureau, who investigated records of the hurricane of 1831 at Barbados, reported that a piece of lead weighing 150 pounds was carried to a distance of more than 1,800 feet and another piece, 400 pounds in weight, was lifted up and carried 1,680 feet. There were many instances, according to McDonough, of shingles and pieces of tin being forced into trunks of hardwood trees.

Garriot quoted, in part, as follows from the *Nautical Magazine* of December 1867:

> The town of St. Thomas looked exactly as if an explosion had taken place; roofs, doors and windows having been blown away, and the streets were filled with tiles, trees and rubbish. The harbor was filled with wrecks. The wharfs which lined the shores were gone and every street was blocked up with broken rafters and débris of every conceivable description. Houses were even to be seen standing which had been lifted from their foundations many yards distant and dropped into some of the lanes running seaward out of the main street. A bombarded town could never have presented a worse picture of desolation and ruin. Plantations of whitened sticks covering the hills alone indicated that trees had at one time grown there.

### EARTHQUAKES ACCOMPANYING HURRICANES

In many of the hurricanes of early years there were reports of earthquakes but they are not well substantiated. Perhaps the inhabitants thought there was no other plausible way of accounting for the terrible destruction. Colonel Reid, who was employed two and

FIGURE 67.   Scene in the city of Santo Domingo after passage of the violent hurricane of small diameter in September 1930.

a half years in the islands of Barbados and St. Vincent, amidst the ruins caused by the hurricane of 1831, said:

> But after attentively listening to the opinions of different people on this point, and careful examination of the ruins with reference to it, I feel persuaded there are no sufficient reasons for believing that an earthquake occurred at this period.

However, one of the greatest disasters of modern times was the Japanese earthquake of September 1, 1923, to which a typhoon was a contributing factor. The typhoon was felt at Yokohama just before the earthquake began. It affected Tokio soon after, although there was high wind but no rain. Most of the loss of life was caused by fires which broke out after the earthquake. Many of the buildings were inflammable; it was the hour when meals were being prepared generally over the city; the flames were fanned by the winds of the typhoon and spread with great rapidity. Thousands in fleeing from the flames were trapped when the typhoon progressed to the point where the winds shifted in direction. Deaths by fire as well as by the earthquake were placed at 99,330, the injured at 103,700 and the missing at 43,500.

Some Japanese seismologists thought that the low barometric pressure attending the typhoon was one of the factors in starting the earthquake.

The coincidence of earthquakes and tropical cyclones has frequently been noted. C. F. Brooks attributes it to the unstable condition of the earth's crust and possible stresses set up by the cyclone. He calculates that a drop in barometric pressure of two inches removes a load of about two million tons from each square mile of surface, whereas a ten-foot rise of water would add about nine million tons to each square mile. The difference, nine million tons of water less two million tons of air pressure, is a possible net result. This effect upon the sea bottom might provide the necessary "trigger action" to set off the earthquake.

### ACTION OF CURRENTS, WAVES AND FLOATING DÉBRIS

When the sea rises and joins forces with the wind, destruction is complete. The foundations of buildings are undermined, the wind pushes the buildings over into the water and wave motion and currents, combined with the wind, completely demolish them. In this process, buildings moved by the water and wind act as battering rams and ruin other structures. The whole becomes a vast mass of floating wreckage which is carried on by the rising sea, sweeping everything before it. Ships, loosened from their anchorages, are carried over ground ordinarily above high tide and are left high and dry when the sea recedes. Other ships are driven against piers, bridges and wharves, where they lurch and pitch with the waves and batter solid structures to pieces.

Amidst the floating débris are many heavy objects such as telegraph and telephone poles, beams, and the trunks of trees more or less stripped of their branches. No structure will withstand the continued onslaught of such a mass thrown with terrific force by the monster waves and swells of the hurricane, as they pile up and spill over in shallow water. Much of the débris is pitched into the air by the waves and then carried by the winds.

The combined action of current and wave accounts for great rocks being washed loose at considerable depths and pitched on shore. In the hurricane at St. Thomas, in 1837, Reclus says, "the fortress which defends the entrance of the port was demolished as if it had been bombarded. Blocks of rock were torn from a depth of thirty or forty feet beneath the sea and flung on shore."

Of the Bermuda storm of 1839, Colonel Reid says:

> By examination of the south coasts of the islands, the sea was found to have risen fully eleven feet higher than the usual tides. It carried boats into fields above the usual high water mark, and removed several rocks, containing by measurement twenty cubic feet, some of them bearing evidence of having been broken off from the beds on which they rested, by the surge.

Usually the electric, telephone, and telegraph lines are thrown down. Communication to the stricken territory fails and, as night comes on, the inhabitants are left in darkness. In coastal areas, the source of the water supply—from wells and cisterns, or by pipe line from higher territory—fails, either by overflow of the sea which makes the water brackish or by severance of the pipe lines by the storm. Sanitary conditions become deplorable; there is a shortage of food; crops in the fields are laid waste and there is no prospect of food from that source; thousands are left shelterless, and disease almost inevitably follows.

### WORK OF THE AMERICAN NATIONAL RED CROSS

In recent years, the American National Red Cross, in close cooperation with the U.S. Weather Bureau, has perfected an organization which begins to concentrate its relief activities, even before the hurricane arrives. As the Weather Bureau tracks the storm from day to day, the Red Cross shifts its field workers and strengthens its organization in threatened areas. Then, when the hurricane arrives and the stricken section is cut off from communication with the outside world, relief is already at hand.

### TROPICAL STORMS THAT ARE BENEFICIAL

Not all tropical cyclones are destructive; in fact many of them are beneficial. Rains accompanying them revive crops and replenish supplies of storage water. Even in the most destructive hurricanes, areas at some distance from the storm center, where winds are not dangerous, receive beneficial rains.

Fassig found that 60 per cent of the storms that affected Puerto Rico from 1899 to 1928, inclusive, were beneficial. Only 10 per cent were overwhelmingly destructive, while 30 per cent were locally destructive but beneficial in some parts of the island. In the majority of

Puerto Rico hurricanes during this period, losses caused by the winds of the storm were insignificant compared with the great benefits to crops and municipal water supplies.[1]

Visher made a very thorough study of the effects of tropical cyclones, both direct and indirect. He says:

> The importance of tropical cyclones depends upon several factors besides the strength of the wind. They commonly yield rain, often very welcome rain, and produce a radical change in the weather. These weather changes and the fear aroused in those individuals who notice the approach of a cyclone of unknown severity, are the source of appreciable psychological effects. A disastrous storm may cause profound economic and social demoralization in the damaged tracts and associated areas. The effects of these cyclones upon the fauna and flora also are striking. Many of the storms travel for thousands of miles, carrying vast amounts of latent energy from the lower latitudes into somewhat higher latitudes. Sometimes débris and many living organisms are transported and weather conditions far from the tropics affected.

### HURRICANES THAT HAVE CHANGED THE COURSE OF HISTORY

The effect of some great storms has been so profound that they have been credited with changing the course of history. As has previously been stated, President McKinley is quoted as having remarked at the time of the Spanish-American War that more warships had gone to the bottom of the sea in storms than under the fire of enemy fleets. After the "Great Hurricane" of 1780, the governor of Martinique caused the English soldiers who had become his prisoners to be set free, though the French and English were then at war. He declared that in such a disaster all men should feel as brothers.

In March 1889, war was prevented between the United States and Germany by a tropical storm. Late in 1888 a German naval force carried the native chief of the Samoans away and set up another king in his stead. The natives rebelled and in one of the collisions twenty-two German soldiers were killed. The Germans retaliated by shelling a native village and incidentally destroying property of American citizens. An American flag raised by an American citizen to protect

---

[1] The destructive effects of torrential rains accompanying hurricanes are discussed in Chapter v.

Figure 68. Wreck of the German warship *Adler* at Apia, Samoa, March 16, 1889.

his property was torn down and burned. Secretary of State Bayard protested; American warships were ordered to Samoa to guard the rights of American citizens there.

On March 16, 1889, there were three American, three German and one British warship in the harbor at Apia, Samoa. With relations between the two countries in this state of strain, a vicious hurricane approached Apia.

The British warship *Calliope* steamed from the inner harbor in the teeth of the hurricane and survived. The remaining warships of the United States and Germany and also six merchant ships were dashed on the reefs, sent to the bottom or beached by the hurricane. (Fig. 68.) About one hundred fifty sailors lost their lives.

While the hurricane raged all the belligerents became friends and many acts of heroism were recorded. The natives came to the rescue of American and German sailors. The Navy Department expressed appreciation of the courage of the natives, especially to Chief Seumanu, a native leader, and suggested that he be presented with a double banked whaleboat with fittings and that his men be suitably rewarded. Thus the hurricane brought peace temporarily, but at a heavy cost.

The hurricane hastened action to settle differences in the congress and treaty of Berlin in 1889 and has been credited with being responsible, indirectly, for the founding of a modern navy of the United States.[2]

[2] In the words of Robert Louis Stevenson: "Thus in what seemed the very article of war, and within a single day, the sword arm of each of the two angry powers was broken; their formidable ships reduced to junk, the disciplined hundreds to a horde of castaways. The hurricane of March 16 made thus a marking epoch in world history; directly and at once it brought about the congress and treaty of Berlin; indirectly and by a process still continuing, it founded the modern navy of the United States."

# CHAPTER XI

# PRECAUTIONARY MEASURES

## REDUCTION OF LOSSES OF LIFE AND PROPERTY

IF taken in time, precautionary measures should eliminate practically all of the loss of life in hurricanes. Records fully bear out the statement that loss of life from this source has in recent years been very greatly reduced by the work of the U.S. Weather Bureau in locating tropical storms and issuing advices and warnings. In fact, the loss of life in the last fifteen years in coastal communities of Gulf and South Atlantic States has often been exceeded by fatalities in the interior, although hurricanes as a rule are much less severe after passing inland. This is doubtless due to the habit of people in coastal communities of heeding the warnings and taking proper precautionary measures, while those in the interior may pay less attention to them.

Losses in residential and business property can, to a great extent, be avoided by the slow process of building structures capable of withstanding the winds of the hurricane and placing buildings above the reach of storm tides. Movable property can be saved, but much of the losses caused by hurricanes, including damage to crops in the fields, cannot be averted.

The necessity for precautionary measures applies with equal force, though in different ways, to the mariner and the landsman.

To the landsman it is a question of safety of lives and property. The navigator is not only concerned with the safety of ship, cargo, passengers and crew, but with the necessity for an economical voyage, by the shortest route compatible with safety, so that his principals may survive in the highly competitive commerce of these times.

## PRECAUTIONARY MEASURES FOR SEAMEN

The student navigator is told how to judge the location of the storm center, how to maneuver his ship to avoid it, and how to anticipate changes in the progressive movement of the storm so that he may alter his course accordingly. Too often this is to be based upon his own observations, which is considerably better than guesswork but a poor substitute for definite and precise knowledge.[1] Instead of trusting solely to the inferences he draws from the winds, clouds, sea and barometer, he can secure through the ship's wireless station the latest report by a national meteorological service, giving what is known concerning the location, the direction and rate of progression, and the extent and intensity of the storm. If he should be in waters where no such service is provided, weather reports from other ships in his vicinity are his for the asking. He can obtain them by wireless at as frequent intervals as he desires, lay the reports out on a chart, and keep himself informed. Through his own observations he can know the weather and the state of the sea over a very limited area. Using the wireless station, he may greatly extend his horizon and in effect see the weather over a vast ocean area through the eyes of observers on other ships.

If the ship has no wireless station, or if it is not possible to secure official weather broadcasts or make contact with other ships in the region, a situation which rarely occurs, he must then depend entirely on his own observations.

At sea the precursory signs of the tropical storm, as described in Chapter VII, are much the same as on land. There is no satisfactory way of determining the distance of the storm center when the mariner has no observations except his own. The rule, based upon the law of Buys Ballot, that the observer in the northern hemisphere facing the wind will find the storm center to his right and somewhat to the rear, depending on the incurvature of winds, will be useful in getting the bearing of the center. The shift of wind as the storm progresses will serve to indicate the direction of its movement. In all of these observations the speed and direction of movement of the ship must be taken into account. For that reason, it is recommended, especially for sailing vessels, that they heave to for a while until the shifts of wind and change of the barometer indicate the direction of movement of the hurricane.

When the shipmaster has ascertained as best he can, from his own observations, from the weather chart, from the radio broadcast or from observations secured by wireless from other ships, the location, intensity, and direction and rate of progression of the hurricane, he is then faced with two problems. The first is how to maneuver his ship in accordance with the facts at hand so as to experience the least

[1] Nothing in these remarks should be construed to mean that the mariner should not utilize his own observations to the utmost in every emergency.

dangerous weather and sea conditions. The second problem is that of anticipating the future movements of the hurricane in relation to his own.

It is not within the scope of this volume to attempt a complete discussion of the navigational problem. The following illustration (Fig. 69) and rules are taken from the Pilot Chart of the U.S. Hydrographic Office.

The rules for maneuvering, so far as they may be generalized, are as follows:

### NORTHERN HEMISPHERE

*Right or dangerous semicircle.*—Steamers: Bring the wind on the starboard bow, make as much way as possible, and if obliged to heave to, do so head to sea. Sailing vessels: Keep close-hauled on the starboard tack, make as much way as possible, and if obliged to heave to, do so on the starboard tack.

*Left or navigable semicircle.*—Steam and sailing vessels: Bring the wind on the starboard quarter, note the course and hold it. If obliged to heave to, steamers may do so stern to sea; sailing vessels on the port tack.

*On the storm track in front of center.*—Steam and sailing vessels: Bring the wind two points on the starboard quarter, note the course and hold it, and run for the left semicircle, and when in that semicircle maneuver as above.

*On the storm track in rear of center.*—Avoid the center by the best practicable route, having due regard for the tendency of cyclones to recurve to the northward and eastward.

The winds of the hurricane, acting upon the water, set currents in motion about the center of the storm. While the speed of these currents is much less than that of the winds, it must be taken into account in reckoning the ship's position, if it is not possible to do so by observation or compass bearings. In general, they tend to drift the ship in the right semicircle into or in front of the storm center and in the left semicircle away and to the rear.

### PRECAUTIONARY MEASURES FOR THE LANDSMAN

Precautionary measures on land are for the most part obvious. In badly exposed locations it is the practice for the entire population to be removed to higher ground at some distance from the coast. In other places the public buildings are opened to those whose dwellings are not sturdy enough to protect them from the hurricane. It is necessary to remove livestock from places likely to be inundated. This

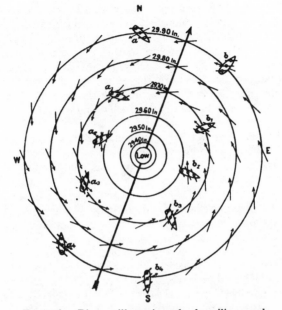

FIGURE 69. Diagram illustrating rules for sailing vessels,
for a tropical cyclone in the northern hemisphere after
recurving. The center is moving toward the NNE., in the
direction of the long arrow. The ship $a$ has the wind at
ENE.; she is to the left of the track, or in the navigable
semicircle. The ship $b$ has the wind at ESE. and is in the
dangerous semicircle. As the storm progresses these ships,
if lying-to, $a$ upon the port tack, $b$ upon the starboard
tack, as shown, take with regard to the storm center the
successive positions $a$, $a_1$, $a_2$, etc., and $b$, $b_1$, $b_2$, etc., the wind
of ship $a$ shifting to the left, of ship $b$ to the right, or in
both cases drawing aft, and thus diminishing the probability of either ship being struck aback, with possible serious
damage to spars and rigging, a danger to which a vessel
lying-to on the opposite tack (i.e. the starboard tack in the
left-hand semicircle or the port tack in the right-hand
semicircle) is constantly exposed, the wind in the latter
case tending constantly to draw forward. The ship $b$ is
constantly beaten by wind and sea toward the storm track.
The ship $a$ is drifted away from the track and should she
be able to carry sail would soon find better weather by
running off to the westward. (Reproduced by courtesy of
the U.S. Hydrographic Office.)

must be done early if the animals are to be driven in the direction from which the first winds of the hurricane are expected to come.

One who lives in a good house with a well anchored roof and a strong foundation, may elect to remain there throughout the storm. The house should have storm shutters; if not, the windows, at least those on the sides exposed to the most violent winds, should be boarded up. Window destruction is the first step toward demolition. Oil lanterns, food and drinking water should be provided. The water supply may fail or become brackish through overflow of the sea or spray. Most certainly the electric lighting will fail or will be cut off as a matter of public safety.

In this situation there may be many things to worry about. If there are tall trees in the yard, they may blow over on the house. The torrential rain, driven by powerful gusts, may come through at every crevice and may weaken the foundation. In coastal sections, the tide may come in rapidly. Then, if the house begins to give way, it is necessary to flee to a place of safety. At the height of the storm, flight is exceedingly dangerous. It is better to go to a place of assured safety before the storm arrives.

There are many places along the South Atlantic and Gulf coasts where there has not been, within the memory of the oldest inhabitant, a really great hurricane. Many have passed in the vicinity, perhaps, but the most destructive winds of a fully developed hurricane have not visited them. Too often, disaster has come because the inhabitants concluded that the place was somehow favorably situated so that it was to some extent immune. A disaster must come before such communities are convinced that the things that happen in other places, can occur in their own localities. Tides fifteen to twenty feet above mean sea-level have occurred in some places on the South Atlantic and Gulf coasts, and, in the future, will certainly occur at other places. The probability of such an event cannot be determined by the records of a comparatively short period of years, not even in the span of the average life. Within one year or one short period of consecutive years, a number of violent storms may visit one community; it may be many years before another storm of consequence occurs at that place. As an example, during the 1933 hurricane season seven tropical storms reached the Gulf coast at and south of Brownsville. An examination of records prior to 1933 will show that storms of hurricane force reach that region only about once in four years as an average.

Warnings and advices issued by the Weather Bureau in connection with a tropical disturbance, regardless of its intensity, are given an immediate and extensive distribution. They are disseminated from Weather Bureau offices and numerous storm warning display stations along the Gulf and South Atlantic coasts, from which further distribution is made by telephone, telegraph, publication in newspapers, radio broadcasts and by posting bulletins in public places. The information is given to press associations, which distribute it to member newspapers in the regions affected. Commercial and Government radio-telegraph stations broadcast the information on stated schedules for the benefit of mariners and others equipped to receive such broadcasts. Radio broadcasts by voice are made from numerous radio stations in South Atlantic and Gulf coast areas.

The first messages issued when the center of the disturbance is a long distance away, are headed "advisory." They give the location, intensity, and direction and speed of movement of the disturbance, so far as is known, but they are not intended as warnings to persons living in the areas in which advisory messages are distributed. However, it is a notice that a tropical disturbance exists and all persons in areas likely to be affected, should obtain by telephone, radio, printed bulletins, or from the newspapers, the latest official information issued by the Weather Bureau and keep in touch with the situation until all possibility of danger has passed.

The first warnings issued in connection with a tropical disturbance are usually storm warnings. They contain the same information as advisory messages and in addition direct the hoist of warning signals at display stations of the Bureau. They indicate that persons in the areas in which storm warnings are ordered to be displayed, are likely to experience at least winds of considerable force on the outer edges of the storm. As long as the disturbance is still some distance at sea, display of storm warnings indicates that there is a *possibility* that the storm center may later approach closely to any part of the area covered by the storm warning display, with resultant winds of great violence.

As soon as it becomes evident that the storm center will reach a certain section of the coast line, hurricane warnings are hoisted over a comparatively restricted area in which winds of hurricane force are expected to prevail. Hurricane warnings are given immediate distribution by every means available to the Weather Bureau and through numerous agencies that assist the Bureau in such emergencies.

Even with ample observations it is impossible on first appearance of a disturbance, to say exactly where the storm will strike on the coast or when it will arrive. Tropical storms progress rather slowly. Therefore, an interval of some hours is required for the disturbance to make sufficient progress so that the direction and speed of its movement can be determined.

When the storm center is well out at sea, advisory messages are as a rule issued every six hours. As it approaches the coast, the Weather Bureau secures special observations at intervening hours and issues more frequent advices when conditions justify. The Bureau aims to give the residents of every locality the fullest possible information needed by them in the protection of their interests, and, on the other hand, to avoid needless alarm and anxiety which would result from the dissemination of premature advices and warnings based on insufficient information.

To indicate the approach of storm or hurricane winds, the Weather Bureau displays, at many coastal points, flags by day and lanterns by night, as a warning. Descriptions of these displays and their meanings are as follows:

*The Northeast Storm Warning.*—A red pennant *above* a square red flag with black center, displayed by day, or two red lanterns, one above the other, displayed by night, indicate the approach of a storm of marked violence with winds beginning from the *northeast*.

*The Southeast Storm Warning.*—A red pennant *below* a square red flag with black center, displayed by day, or one red lantern, displayed by night, indicate the approach of a storm of marked violence with winds beginning from the *southeast*.

*The Southwest Storm Warning.*—A white pennant *below* a square red flag with black center, displayed by day, or a white lantern *below* a red lantern, displayed by night, indicate the approach of a storm of marked violence with winds beginning from the *southwest*.

*The Northwest Storm Warning.*—A white pennant *above* a square red flag with black center, displayed by day, or a white lantern *above* a red lantern, displayed by night, indicate the approach of a storm of marked violence with winds beginning from the *northwest*.

*Hurricane Warning.*—Two square red flags with black centers, one above the other, displayed by day, or two red lanterns, with a white lantern between, displayed by night, indicate the approach of a tropical hurricane, or of one of the extremely severe and dangerous storms which occasionally occur.

# CHAPTER XII

# EARLY HISTORY OF WEST INDIAN HURRICANES

## TROPICAL STORMS EXPERIENCED BY COLUMBUS

THE earliest West Indian hurricanes, of which we have record, occurred during the voyages of Christopher Columbus to America. Andreas Poëy gives the earliest date of a hurricane on February 12, 1493. True hurricanes do not occur in that region in February. The storm to which Poëy referred, was encountered by Columbus on the return from his first voyage to the West Indies. He left Spain on his first voyage on Friday, August 3, 1492, and arrived at San Salvador on October 12, 1492.

Washington Irving, in his *Life and Voyages of Christopher Columbus*, gives this account of the storm mentioned by Poëy:

> By February 12, 1493, they had made much progress toward Spain on returning home and began to flatter themselves with hope of soon beholding land. The wind now came on to blow violently. On the following evening there were three flashes of lightning in the north-northeast—the storm soon burst upon them in great violence. All night they were obliged to scud under bare poles. As morning dawned there was a lull but the wind then rose with redoubled fury from the south. On the morning of February 15 they came in sight of land which proved to be the Azores.

Columbus sailed on his second voyage from Cadiz on September 25, 1493, and arrived in the West Indies on November 3 of that year. The second storm listed by Poëy occurred on May 19 to 21, 1494, in Cuba. Hurricanes very rarely occur in May and it is doubtful whether this record should be accepted. W. H. Alexander, who collected records of West Indian hurricanes, mentions stormy weather experienced by Columbus in 1492 but does not give the date.

Alexander states that Columbus anchored at Cape Santa Cruz and while there, on July 16, 1494, a violent hurricane occasioned the Admiral to declare that "nothing but the service of God and the extension of the monarchy should induce him to expose himself to such dangers." According to Irving, Columbus, during his explorations, left the eastern extremity of Jamaica on August 19, 1494, and on the following morning "made that long peninsula of Hayti since called

Cape Tiburon." He coasted the whole of the south side of the island and had to take refuge in the channel of Saona from a violent storm which raged for several days. Poëy lists a storm in June of 1494, but does not mention the storms of July and August of that year.

In 1495 Columbus undoubtedly experienced a hurricane. Juan de Aguado set sail from Spain toward the end of August 1495, and arrived at Santo Domingo, probably in October. Columbus then determined to return to Spain. When the ships were ready to depart a terrible storm swept the island of Santo Domingo. Three ships at anchor in the harbor were sunk and others were dashed against each other and driven mere wrecks against the shore. Poëy does not give the date of the hurricane of 1495, but it likely occurred in October. Irving says the Indians were overwhelmed with astonishment at the violence of this storm for never in their memory or traditions had they known so tremendous a storm.

### EARLY SIXTEENTH CENTURY HURRICANES

By 1502 Columbus had apparently acquired a knowledge of the precursory signs of the hurricane, either through observation or by conversation with the natives. On June 29, 1502, Columbus arrived at Santo Domingo on his last voyage. He sent an officer ashore and requested permission to shelter his squadron in the river as he apprehended an approaching storm. His request was refused. Columbus then sent a second message entreating that the sailing of the fleet of Bobadilla for Spain be delayed as there were indubitable signs of an approaching tempest. This request was as fruitless as the preceding. The weather, as is often the case just before the arrival of a hurricane, was fair and tranquil. The predictions of Columbus were verified. Bobadilla set out confidently to sea, headed for Spain, and his fleet was all lost except one ship. Columbus' ships passed through the storm with more or less injury.

Again, on the third day of August 1508, a severe hurricane visited Santo Domingo. All the thatched houses and several built of stone, and every house in Bonaventura, were destroyed. Twenty sailing vessels were wrecked. At first the gale blew from the north, according to accounts, then shifted suddenly to the south.

On July 29, 1509, almost the entire city of Santo Domingo was destroyed by a hurricane.

In all, Poëy lists sixteen hurricanes in the sixteenth century. Of these, two were probably not true tropical cyclones. Seven of them occurred at Santo Domingo. During the forty-six years from 1887 to 1932, Mitchell accounted for 298 tropical cyclones and probably his list is incomplete. There is reason to believe that the number of hurricanes that occurred in the Atlantic, Gulf of Mexico and Caribbean Sea in the sixteenth century was in the neighborhood of 600, unless the frequency of these storms was materially different than from what it is today.

## PRINCIPAL STORMS OF THE SEVENTEENTH CENTURY

In the seventeenth century, Poëy lists thirty-three tropical storms of the West Indies and adjacent areas. This list is of course fragmentary but it contains a number of notable storms.

In 1642 there were three hurricanes. The second devastated St. Kitts, wrecking twenty-three fully laden vessels, and destroying all the houses and the cotton and tobacco crops.

A fearful hurricane desolated the island of Guadeloupe in 1656. There was another violent hurricane at Guadeloupe in 1664. On August 4, 1666, an intense hurricane struck the islands of St. Christopher, Guadeloupe, and Martinique. Every vessel and boat on the coasts of Guadeloupe was dashed to pieces. A fleet of seventeen sail with two thousand troops went down in the hurricane and only two were heard of afterwards. The sea rose and was driven to an unusual height. All the batteries, with walls of six feet in thickness, were destroyed and the guns, 14-pounders, were washed away.

On September 1, 1667, a tremendous hurricane devastated the island of St. Kitts. All the houses and buildings were thrown down and the inhabitants sought shelter by throwing themselves on the ground in the fields. M. Laurent, the governor, said it was the most violent hurricane ever known.

In 1674 at Barbados, on August 10, a hurricane blew down three hundred houses, killed two hundred persons and wrecked eight ships. In 1675 Barbados was again devastated by a hurricane which came in August of that year.

There was a tremendous hurricane on the Island of Antigua in 1681. In that same year there were two hurricanes at St. Kitts.

## HURRICANES OF THE EIGHTEENTH CENTURY

The town of Port Royal, Jamaica, was visited by a severe hurricane on August 28, 1722. Twenty-six merchant vessels were wrecked and four hundred persons lost their lives.

Alexander quotes from a report of the storm of 1759, a story credited to a Wm. Gerard de Brahm, which smacks of Münchhausen:

> A heavy gale of wind from the northeast so greatly impeded the current of the Gulf Stream that the water forced, at the same time, in the Gulf of Mexico by the trade winds, rose to such a height that not only the Tortugas and other islands disappeared, but the highest trees were covered on the Peninsula of Larga, and at this time (so says Wm. Gerard de Brahm, Esq.), the *Litbury*, John Lorrain, master, being caught in the gale, came to an anchor, as the master supposed, in Hawke Channel, but to his great surprise found his vessel the next day high and dry on Elliott's Island and his anchor suspended in the boughs of a tree.

Anyone who has seen modern ocean-going steamers sitting high and dry some distance from shore after a hurricane, would be inclined to accept as truth the statement that the master of a sailing vessel cast his anchor in a tree rather than this explanation of how it happened to the *Litbury*.

In 1768, on October 25, a hurricane of great violence but short duration occurred at Havana. In the same year, a ship carrying convicts to Maryland was forced by stress of weather to seek shelter at Antigua. It was stated that there was much distress among the convicts. Eleven died and the survivors had to eat their shoes and the like to sustain life.

During the last days of August and the first days of September, in 1772, a hurricane passed over the West Indies, causing frightful havoc among the Leeward Islands. At Dominica eighteen vessels were driven ashore and lost. Several warships were driven ashore at Antigua. At Montserrat and Nevis nearly every house was blown down.

This hurricane passed over St. Kitts on August 31, beginning at daylight. At noon the storm abated to such an extent that people thought it was over, but the wind suddenly shifted to the southeast (from northeast) and blew with increased violence, destroying almost every house, sugar mill, tree and plant, killing several and wounding many persons. The same storm was felt forcibly at Santa Cruz, where the account cited by Alexander says the sea rose 72 feet above its usual height, carrying every ship on shore, some as much as three hundred feet inland. Large stones were brought down from the

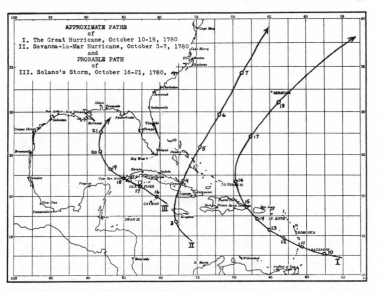

FIGURE 70. Paths of the hurricanes that occurred in the year 1780. Courses of the "Great Hurricane" and the "Savanna-la-Mar Hurricane," as determined by Colonel Reid. Probable path of "Solano's Storm" as deduced from observations on ships of the Spanish fleet en route from Havana to attack Pensacola.

mountains and there was a terrific electrical display. Piddington quoted from the *Annual Register* to the effect that the water in this storm rose 70 feet at Santa Cruz and indicated that he doubted the accuracy of the statement.

### THE THREE FAMOUS HURRICANES OF 1780

The year 1780 is noted as that of "The Great Hurricane." It was undoubtedly the most violent of the eighteenth century. Poëy listed five storms as occurring in that year. Colonel Reid says: "Three great storms occurred nearly at the same time; and these have been confounded together, and considered but as one. The first destroyed the town of Savanna-la-Mar, on the 3rd of October, 1780. The second, by far the greater one, passed over Barbados on the 10th and 11th of the same month and year. The third dispersed and disabled the Spanish fleet, under Solano, in the Gulf of Mexico, after it had sailed from Havannah, to attack Pensacola." (Fig. 70.)

Concerning the hurricane at Savanna-la-Mar, the following is quoted from Southey's *West Indies*:

> Upon the 3rd of October, the inhabitants of Savanna-la-Mar were gazing in astonishment at the sea swelling as it had never before; on a sudden, bursting through all bounds and surmounting all obstacles, it overwhelmed the town and swept everything away so completely upon its retreat as not to leave the smallest vestige of man, beast or habitation behind. The sea flowed half a mile beyond its usual limits, and so sudden and unavoidable was the destruction, although it took place at noonday, that of the inhabitants of one gentleman's house, consisting of 2 whites and 40 negroes, not a soul escaped.

The "Great Hurricane" was first felt at Barbados on October 10, 1780. The following account is taken from *The Ocean*, by Élisée Reclus, published in 1874. Alexander quotes from *The Atmosphere*, by Flammarion, an account which contains much of the same language as that of Reclus. No doubt they both came from the same original source.

> The most terrible cyclone of modern times is probably that of the 10th of October, 1780, which has been specially named the "great hurricane." Starting from Barbados, where neither trees nor dwellings were left standing, it caused an English fleet anchored off St. Lucia to disappear, and completely ravaged this island, where 6,000 persons were crushed under the ruins. After this, the whirlwind, tending toward Martinique, enveloped a convoy of French transports, and sunk more than 40 ships carrying 4,000 soldiers; on land the towns of St. Pierre and other places were completely razed by the wind, and 9,000 persons perished there. More to the north, Dominique, St. Eustatius, St. Vincent and Porto Rico were likewise devastated, and most of the vessels which were on the path of the cyclone foundered with all their crews. Beyond Porto Rico the tempest bent to the northeast, toward the Bermudas, and though its violence had gradually diminished, it sunk several English warships returning to Europe. At Barbados, where the cyclone had commenced its terrible spiral, the wind was unchained with such fury, that the inhabitants hiding in their cellars did not hear their houses falling above their heads; they did not feel the shocks of earthquake which, according to Rodney, accompanied the storm.

### THE HURRICANE AT TOBAGO, 1790

Among the accounts collected by Alexander was that of a hurricane at the little island of Tobago, in August 1790. Twenty vessels were wrecked on the coast. As illustrating some of the marvellous things that happen in a hurricane, he reproduces this account of what happened on the estate of a gentleman named Hamilton in the Tobago storm of 1790:

His new mansion, which had been built upon pillars, was lifted by the tempest and removed to some distance, but being well made did not go to pieces. Mrs. Hamilton, two ladies, and five children, were in the house and suffered little or no harm. Mr. Hamilton, being absent from home, knew not what had happened, but returning in the night, which was excessively dark, and groping for his door, fell over the rubbish left on the spot, and so far hurt himself that he was confined for a week.

# CHAPTER XIII

# MEMORABLE HURRICANES
# OF THE NINETEENTH CENTURY

### RECORDS OF REDFIELD AND REID

FOR records of West Indian hurricanes during the early part of the nineteenth century we are indebted chiefly to W. C. Redfield. The first of his memoirs on the subject appeared in the *American Journal of Science* in April 1831. Redfield explained the rotary and progressive movements of tropical storms, which had been described independently by Dove in 1828.

Redfield and Reid both collected reports of weather conditions from the logs of a considerable number of ships and were able to determine with accuracy the tracks of a number of West Indian hurricanes.

### THE ANTIGUA-CHARLESTON HURRICANE OF 1804

The Antigua-Charleston hurricane was the first great West Indian storm of the century. It occurred in 1804. At Antigua and St. Kitts on the 3rd of September and at Puerto Rico on the 4th, it was a very severe storm. On the 7th it reached the South Atlantic coast. Houses were blown down and wharves destroyed at Charleston. There was immense damage on the coasts of South Carolina and Georgia.

It is reported that, after this gale, fruit trees flowered and bore fruit a second time. After the destructive hurricane in southern Louisiana, August 31 to September 3, 1772, it is recorded that mulberry trees blossomed and bore the second crop of fruit. Similarly, after the hurricane at Charleston on September 15, 1752, trees which were stripped of their leaves again blossomed and bore fruit in the late autumn. These cases were cited by Blodgett from the historical writings of Ramsay and Gayarre.

### FOUR DESTRUCTIVE STORMS AT DOMINICA

The next great hurricane of the century occurred in 1806. It was especially severe at Dominica. There were four very destructive hurricanes at Dominica during the nineteenth century, 1806, 1813, 1834, and 1883. The storm of 1834 is generally accepted as the most violent of the four at Dominica. The hurricane of 1806 occurred on September 9. The *Dominica Journal* of September 20, 1806, described the horrors of the hurricane, in the midst of which the river Roseau overflowed its banks and inundated the town from every direction.

There were 131 known dead and many missing at the time of the *Journal* account, from which the following is taken:

> The spectacle which presented itself on the return of daylight was horrid beyond every power of description. Heaps of mud and sand (in some places 5 or 6 feet deep) through all parts of the town; the form of a street hardly to be discerned; two large streams, or rather torrents, running through the midst of the town; ruins of houses blown down and others brought down by the flood, obstructing every passage; the carcasses of several of the unfortunate victims of this event drawn out from the ruins and lying in the streets, while numbers almost distracted were searching for some near relation or friend who had perished in the storm . . . and, in general, the whole island offers a scene of devastation and ruin.

### OTHER HURRICANES OF THE EARLY NINETEENTH CENTURY

In 1807, the Bahama Islands were so devastated by a hurricane that the inhabitants suffered great hardships in securing the necessities of life. This is possibly the storm listed by Poëy as occurring on September 5, although there was a severe hurricane in Puerto Rico and the Virgin Islands on August 17, 18 and 19, 1807.

Hurricanes described as "big storms" occurred in Cuba in 1812, 1819 and 1821. The storm of October 14, 1812, wrecked five hundred houses in Trinidad, Cuba, damaged the Pope's Convent and the hospitals, and sank a number of ships.

In 1813, two hurricanes succeeded each other in a short time at Dominica, causing great suffering on the island. One of the storms occurred on July 22 and 23. The date of the other storm is not known. There were three severe hurricanes in 1815; one in the Leeward Islands on August 31 and September 1; another at Turks Island on September 20; and a third at Jamaica on October 18.

### THE LONG ISLAND HURRICANE OF 1821

A remarkable hurricane occurred in 1821. It appeared near Turks Island on September 1, pursued a west-northwest course toward the Bahamas, turned to the northward and crossed the eastern portion of North Carolina. On September 3, it followed the New Jersey coast line and the center crossed Long Island. (Fig. 71.) At New York the gale came from the northeast and east, became very violent at 5 p.m. and continued with great fury for three hours. More damage was sustained in two hours than ever before witnessed in the city, according to accounts. The wharves were overflowed and it is said that the tide rose thirteen feet in one hour.

The center of this hurricane was felt at Cape May, N.J., and at Cape Henlopen, Del. At the former place, there was a fifteen-minute lull, after which the wind blew with renewed violence. At Cape Henlopen, the calm occurred about 1 p.m. and lasted about half an hour. The wind then shifted to west-northwest and blew with what seemed to be greater violence than before the calm. From Long Island, the hurricane center passed again into the interior and on the night of September 3-4 crossed the New England States with diminishing force.

### HURRICANES OVER AND NEAR PUERTO RICO

A hurricane which swept over Guadeloupe and reached Puerto Rico on July 26, 1825, was an exceptionally violent one. It is customary in Puerto Rico to name a hurricane after the particular saint's day on which it happens to occur. Seven hurricanes of Puerto Rico are historic because of their violence:

Santa Ana.......................................July 26, 1825.
Los Angeles....................................August 2, 1837.
Santa Elena....................................August 18, 1851.
San Narciso....................................October 29, 1867.
San Felipe (the first)........................September 13, 1876.
San Ciriaco....................................August 8, 1899.
San Felipe (the second)......................September 13, 1928.

In 1825, the devastations in Puerto Rico were extraordinary. Nearly 7,000 houses were blown down; 374 lives were lost and 1,210 persons were injured. The storm was very severe in Guadeloupe where the barometer fell 1.86 inches.

The hurricane of August 17-28, 1827, was very destructive at St. Kitts and was declared the most violent in more than fifty years. Great loss of crops was reported in Puerto Rico. It recurved after passing Haiti and its path lay midway between Bermuda and Charleston.

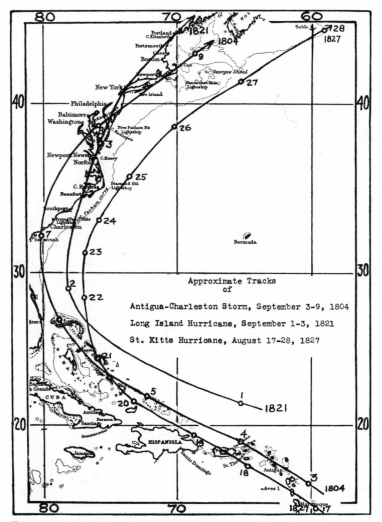

FIGURE 71. Paths followed by centers of three noteworthy hurricanes early in the nineteenth century, 1804, 1821 and 1827.

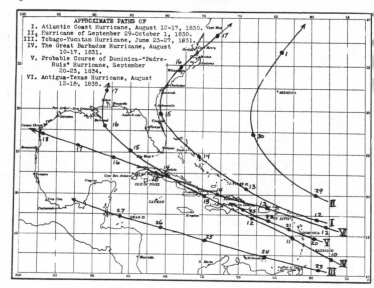

FIGURE 72. Path followed by center of the Great Barbados hurricane of 1831, and five other hurricanes of the same period.

### THE BARBADOS HURRICANE OF 1831

In 1831 a hurricane of tremendous force struck the island of Barbados. (Fig. 72.) Colonel Reid was employed in reestablishing the government buildings blown down in this hurricane and its great violence, plentiful evidence of which he found on all sides, induced him to undertake a study of hurricanes.

Calamitous as were the numerous hurricanes from which Barbados had suffered up to that time, the aggregate destruction caused by all of them combined was considered unequal to that effected by the hurricane of 1831. The hurricane of 1780, fearfully tremendous though it was, is admitted to have been inferior in force and less destructive to property at Barbados. More than fifteen hundred lives were lost and property damage was estimated at $7,397,532.

Redfield traced this storm from Barbados to Haiti and thence across Cuba where it reached Havana on the 14th. It continued to move northwestward from Cuba across the Gulf of Mexico until it passed inland on the Gulf coast east of New Orleans on the 16th. In

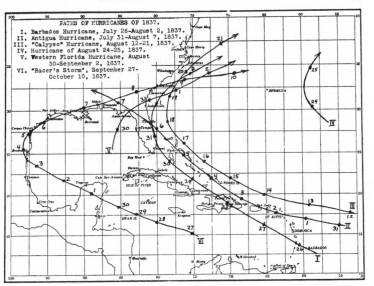

FIGURE 73. Track of "Racer's Storm" and five other hurricanes of 1837.

this storm, as in many others that have devastated islands of the West Indies, it was said that the surface of the ground was denuded of vegetation, appearing as if a fire had passed over it.

### THE DOMINICA HURRICANE, 1834

The island of Dominica was visited by a hurricane on September 20, 1834, which destroyed houses and crops and took over two hundred lives. The storm of 1834 was considered the most destructive that ever visited the island.

This hurricane apparently moved west-northwestward, because there is a record of a severe storm at Santo Domingo on September 23 of that year, about sixty hours later than the storm at Dominica. At Santo Domingo it is known as the "Padre Ruiz Hurricane" because it began when funeral services were being held over the body of a priest of that name in the church at Santa Barbara. According to an account in the *Historia de Santo Domingo*, the loss of life and property at Santo Domingo was appalling. Everything was laid waste before its fury. Large tracts of timber on both sides of the Ozama River were torn up by the roots; many vessels were lost and the "suffering of the people was something terrible."

"RACER'S STORM," "ANTJE'S HURRICANE"
AND THE CUBAN HURRICANES

In 1837 there were a number of hurricanes, there being authentic records of at least eight in the West Indies. It appears that the most violent was that of August 2, 1837, known in Puerto Rico as the "Los Angeles" hurricane. It was soon followed by another of great diameter and exceptional fury which passed near Turks Island on August 15. Both of these hurricanes were traced by Reid; also a hurricane in late September and early October in the western Caribbean Sea and Gulf of Mexico, which is known as the "Racer's Storm," because the *Racer*, a British sloop of war, encountered the storm in the Yucatan Channel on October 1. This storm reached the Mexican Gulf coast south of Brownsville, recurved, followed the coast line, and passed near Galveston on October 5. (Fig. 73.) It then crossed the Louisiana coast and passed into the Atlantic near Charleston.

Five tropical storms were in progress during the month of August 1837. Fairly complete courses of three of these and of the "Racer's Storm" and partial tracks of the other two August storms have been reconstructed from Colonel Reid's tracks and notes. (Fig. 73.)

"Racer's Storm" was first located to the southeast of Jamaica. On September 27 and 28 it caused severe gales on the island and the streets of Kingston were continually inundated for two days. On the 29th, the sloop *Racer* was approaching Yucatan Channel and experienced the full force of the hurricane. On September 3 and 4, the center of the storm passed near Matamoras, destroyed the town of Brazos Santiago, and inundated the coast for many miles inland.

The Bermuda hurricane of 1839 came from the Atlantic far east of the Windward Islands. (Fig. 74.) The barque *Euterpe* was dismasted by the storm on the evening of September 8, at approximately 20°N. and 46°W. On the 9th, while the storm was six hundred miles from Bermuda, a swell began to break on the south side of the islands with a loud noise. Colonel Reid says that on the 11th in the afternoon the surf broke on the south side of the island with great grandeur. At 5 a.m. of the 12th, the barometer was lowest, 28.30 inches. Passing northward from Bermuda, the hurricane turned somewhat to the eastward and crossed Nova Scotia where it was quite severe.

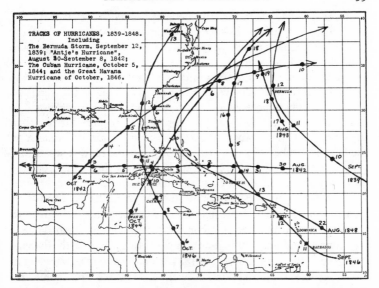

TRACKS OF HURRICANES, 1839-1848.
Including
The Bermuda Storm, September 12, 1839; "Antje's Hurricane", August 30-September 8, 1842; The Cuban Hurricane, October 5, 1844; and the Great Havana Hurricane of October, 1846.

FIGURE 74. Tracks of eight hurricanes during the ten-year period, 1839 to 1848, including the Bermuda Storm, Antje's hurricane, and the Cuban and Great Havana hurricanes.

Although the course is considered an abnormal one, there have been a considerable number of hurricanes which have moved almost due westward in the closing days of August or the first week in September, from the Atlantic to the eastward of the Bahamas through the Florida Straits or over Cuba or Florida, to the coasts of Texas or Mexico. Such a storm, known as "Antje's Hurricane," was traced by Redfield. It dismasted the schooner *Antje* at about 26°N. and 63°W. and later crossed the Mexican coast near Tampico.

It was encountered by the *Antje* on August 30, 1842. Passing Havana on September 4, lowest barometer 28.93 inches, the storm continued westward into the Gulf. Center of the hurricane reached the town of Victoria, Mexico, on September 8, 1842, at 1 p.m. There was a calm of five or six minutes after which the wind came from the south with renewed fury. The coast was inundated northward to the mouth of the Rio Grande.

The Cuban hurricane of 1844 passed to the eastward of Florida. Center of the hurricane on October 5 was a short distance east of

Matanzas, Cuba. There the barometer fell to 28.00 inches and there was great destruction. Between Havana and Cardenas all of the villages were almost totally destroyed. At Havana the lowest pressure was 28.84 inches. Seventy-two ships were either upset or driven ashore at Havana; all the trees in the city were blown down. At Key West the storm was very violent but the center passed to the eastward. Lowest barometer reading at Key West was 29.13 inches.

The hurricane of 1846 was perhaps somewhat more intense than the storm of 1844. It was first observed to the south of Jamaica on the 6th of October. On the 11th the storm came on at Havana. At 4 a.m. the barometer read 29.24 and it blew a hurricane from the northeast and north. At noon the barometer was 28.35, wind northwest and west-northwest. At 2 p.m. the barometer had risen to 28.91 inches, wind west and west-northwest. Lowest pressure is given as 27.06 inches but the exact time is not recorded. Very great damage was done to buildings throughout Havana. In the harbor the damage was greater than in the storm of 1844. Hundreds of lives were lost in Cuba. At Key West and Sand Key the lighthouses were swept into the sea and twenty vessels were lost on the reef.

### PRINCIPAL HURRICANES IN THE LATTER HALF OF THE CENTURY

The Cape Verde and Hatteras Hurricane of August 30 to September 11, 1853, was said to be the most extensive on record but this probably refers to the length of its track which was traced by Redfield from the coast of Africa. (Fig. 75.)

Another hurricane, frequently mentioned because of its great violence, occurred in September 1854. It approached Florida on the 6th, passed near Savannah on the 8th, Norfolk on the 9th, and reached Boston on the 10th and 11th. The center appears to have been a short distance inside the coast line, having passed inland between Jacksonville and Savannah. It was very destructive at Savannah, Charleston and Philadelphia. There were extraordinarily high tides at Charleston and Savannah.

The celebrated hurricane at Isle Dernière, or Last Island, occurred on August 10 and 11, 1856. It was a pleasure resort on the extreme point of land south-southwest of New Orleans. A high northeast wind set in at Isle Dernière on the 9th and on the 10th, when the storm

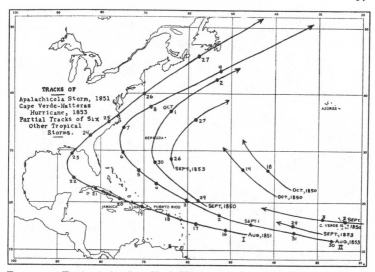

FIGURE 75. Track of the Cape Verde-Hatteras hurricane, the first to be traced from the region of the Cape Verde Islands to the vicinity of the Atlantic coast, also of the Apalachicola Storm, and six other hurricanes of the same period.

was at its height, the wind shifted to the southeast, flooding the island and destroying everything on it. This storm appears to have dissipated near the coasts of Louisiana and Mississippi. Thirteen inches of rain fell at New Orleans.

On August 27 and 28, 1856, a violent hurricane moved westward across Cuba, barometer 28.62 at Havana. It recurved in the north-central Gulf and passed inland in the vicinity of Mobile on August 30. The ship *Daniel Webster* was involved in the storm for two days near latitude 26° 30′N. and longitude 87°W. Lowest barometer reading on the *Daniel Webster* was 28.60 inches. By some it was considered the most disastrous hurricane since 1846.

During the next ten years, 1857 to 1866, there appears to have been a remarkable scarcity of violent hurricanes. There is a record of a hurricane of some force in Cuba in October 1865. In September 1865, a hurricane struck the Louisiana coast near the town of Calcasieu. The place was inundated and several persons perished.

The "Great Bahama Hurricane" of September and October 1866 was of wide extent and great severity. At 8 p.m. of October 1 the

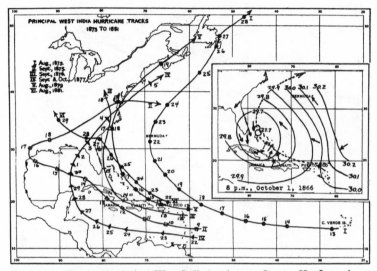

FIGURE 76. Tracks of principal West India hurricanes, 1873 to 1881. Inset shows wind direction and pressure map of "Great Bahama Hurricane" at 8 p.m., October 1, 1866, and the probable path of the storm. (After Buchan.)

vortex was over Nassau, barometer 27.7 inches. (Fig. 76.) The calm lasted from 7:20 to 8:50 p.m. from which it was concluded that its diameter was 23 miles. At first the clouds in the zenith seemed to revolve rapidly, then the stars appeared but banks of clouds remained all around the horizon in dense masses. Alexander Buchan said of this storm that "the long black list of wrecks recorded, bears testimony only too emphatic to the devouring energy of the hurricane."

On the night of October 2 and 3, 1867, a severe hurricane passed near Galveston. Much of the city was flooded and the damage to property was placed at $1,000,000. It appears that this storm followed a course somewhat like that of the "Racer's Storm" of 1837 and the Indianola hurricane of 1875. It is recorded that the towns of Bagdad and Clarksville, situated opposite each other at the mouth of the Rio Grande, were destroyed by this hurricane. At Galveston the gale began from the eastward, turned to northeast and then backed to northwest as the center passed, indicating that the storm recurved from the southward.

One of the really great hurricanes of the century was that of October 29, 1867, in the Virgin Islands and Puerto Rico. At St. Thomas the barometer fell as low as 27.95 inches just prior to the calm which occurred shortly after noon. More than six hundred persons were drowned at St. Thomas and many more were killed on shore by falling houses. In Puerto Rico this storm is known as "San Narciso." It is considered the most violent ever experienced in many parts of the island. The center passed over the town of Caguas, where there was a calm lasting ten to twelve minutes. Accounts of this storm, both in Puerto Rico and the Virgin Islands, indicate that it was a storm of rather small diameter and fairly rapid movement, though of terrific violence.

In August 1873 a hurricane, pursuing a rather ordinary course, from the position in which it was first observed in latitude 14°N. and longitude 27°W., westward and northward between Hatteras and Bermuda, finally reached the coast line of Nova Scotia. It was very destructive there and in Newfoundland, New Brunswick, Labrador, and Prince Edward Island. More than twelve hundred vessels were lost in this storm. It was unusual in that few storms at that time were traced so far to the eastward and because the destructive effects of the storm were felt so far from the tropical region in which it originated.

The hurricane of 1875, in September, followed a course somewhat similar to the "Racer's Storm" of 1837; it recurved on reaching the west Gulf coast and then turned northeastward from Louisiana, passing into the Atlantic near Norfolk. This storm was very destructive at Indianola, Tex.

In August 1879, a hurricane swept the Atlantic seaboard and exceptionally high wind velocities were recorded. At nearly every point in its line of progress, wind recording apparatus failed before the height of the storm was reached.

Hurricanes were particularly numerous and severe in Texas in 1886. In June a hurricane passed inland near Sabine, Tex., causing an inundation extending several miles inland. In August the destruction of Indianola, Tex., occurred. This storm first appeared over the eastern Caribbean Sea, moved north of west across Cuba into the Gulf of Mexico, and reached the Texas coast early on the 20th. From Indianola, it moved a little north of west and passed over San Antonio at 2:40 p.m. of the same day; barometer 29.03 inches and wind estimated at 80 miles. In September, a hurricane which had previously passed near Martinique and Jamaica, crossed the coast near Brownsville. In October, another hurricane passed over Sabine, Tex. The inundation extended twenty miles inland. Nearly every house in the vicinity was moved from its foundation; one hundred fifty lives were lost.

While there were many tropical storms in 1887, none of them appears worthy of special reference.

The great Cuban cyclone of 1888 was in progress in the first week of September and took a westward and then southwestward course. The majority of Cuban storms of great severity come in October or November from the western Caribbean Sea. Occasionally, however, they come from the eastward, generally late in August or early in September. The storm of 1888 was one of the latter class. (Fig. 77.)

On September 1, the center was north of the western end of Puerto Rico; on the 2nd it was over Turks Island; by noon of the 3rd it was just north of Great Inagua, barometer 28.70; on the 4th and 5th it crossed Cuba and thereafter took a very unusual course to the west-southwestward, over northern Yucatan on the 6th and struck the Mexican coast south of Vera Cruz on the night of the 7th-8th. The hurricane was destructive at Turks Island; 250 houses were destroyed and twenty-one lives lost. In Cuba the property losses ran into many millions of dollars and more than six hundred persons perished in the storm. The principal buildings in the cities were destroyed and whole towns near the seaboard were swept out of existence by gigantic seas. There was also great damage in Mexico.

The Martinique hurricane of August 18, 1891, was one of the most disastrous of West Indian hurricanes. Seven hundred lives were lost at Martinique and property damage was estimated at $10,000,000. It was of small diameter but of great intensity. At Martinique the storm lasted only four hours, from 6 to 10 p.m. of August 18.

A very destructive hurricane devastated the coasts of Georgia and South Carolina in August 1893. This storm followed a westward course somewhat farther north than is usual. It struck the islands in the vicinity of Charleston and Savannah on the 27th. It was accompanied by a tremendous wave which submerged the islands; at least one thousand lives were lost; property damage approximated $10,000,000.

The ravage at Charleston was reported in the press as terrific. "Hundreds of corpses were strewn among the farms, unknown except to the vultures which flocked about them. Whole families are wiped

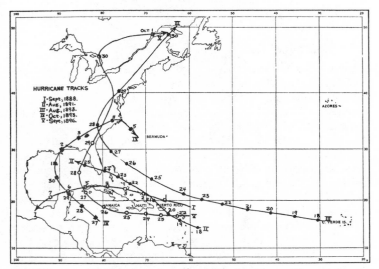

FIGURE 77.   Tracks of principal West Indian hurricanes, 1888 to 1896.

out in some places. The coroner has sworn in an army of deputies and
these are hunting for the dead."

In October 1893, a storm of small diameter but great violence
moved from the Gulf across southeastern States. Violent winds,
heavy rains and local storms attended its passage through South
Atlantic States, but the greatest damage was in southern Louisiana.
It passed between New Orleans and Port Eads on October 1. The
storm was accompanied by what was reported to be a tidal wave
which engulfed everything before it and caused a loss of life which was
given in one account at two thousand persons. There was immense
destruction of shipping and in the aggregate property losses ran into
the millions.

The hurricane of September 22-October 1, 1896, was an exceptionally severe one and was unusual in that it retained much of its
force after passing inland. After crossing Florida and Georgia, in the
interior, it increased rapidly in intensity on the 29th, and was central
over the District of Columbia late that night. The greatest violence
was manifested in Florida on first moving inland. A second period of
violence began in Virginia and continued into Pennsylvania. More

than one hundred lives were lost and property damage was reported at $7,000,000.

### THE PUERTO RICO HURRICANE OF 1899 (SAN CIRIACO)

"San Ciriaco," one of the greatest of Puerto Rican hurricanes, occurred in 1899. On August 8 of that year, one of the most destructive hurricanes in history passed directly across the entire length of the island. The center entered Arroyo on the southeast coast at about 8 a.m. At Arroyo there was a calm lasting about fifteen minutes, barometer 27.75 inches. A tidal wave destroyed almost all the houses at the port of Humacao. More than eighty lives were lost there. Property damage at Arroyo and Humacao exceeded $2,000,000. Between 1 and 2 p.m. the center left the island in the vicinity of Aguadilla on the west coast. Destructive winds and torrential rains accompanied the hurricane in its progress across the island. In all, more than 3,000 lives were lost in Puerto Rico, mostly from drowning. Total property loss on the island was finally placed at $20,000,000.

In its passage over the Bahamas the storm was quite severe. By the morning of August 13 it was off the Florida coast; from there it moved along the coast, some distance at sea. From the 16th to 18th it attained great violence off Hatteras, minimum pressure 28.60 inches. It is said that this storm was the most severe within the recollection of the oldest inhabitants at Hatteras.

"San Ciriaco" was not exceptionally severe at San Juan as the center passed some distance to the southward. The maximum wind there was estimated at 90 miles an hour.

### THE GALVESTON HURRICANE OF 1900

In September 1900, a hurricane of moderate intensity moved west-northwestward across the Greater Antilles and into the Gulf of Mexico on the 6th. It had apparently originated near the Cape Verde Islands on August 31. On passing into the Gulf of Mexico it developed destructive energy and on reaching the Texas coast on September 8, it was a hurricane of tremendous fury. The center passed near Galveston, Tex., where the winds and the storm wave accompanying the hurricane, resulted in a loss of life in excess of six thousand and property damage exceeding $20,000,000. After passing inland the storm lost force rapidly but again attained marked intensity on approaching the Great Lakes where it was attended by gales of great violence.

# CHAPTER XIV

# CHRONOLOGICAL ACCOUNT OF
# HURRICANES OF THE TWENTIETH CENTURY

## 1901

T HE hurricane season of the year 1901 was an unusually active one from the standpoint of storm frequency. (Fig. 78.) The first disturbance apparently originated in the Caribbean Sea; it crossed western Cuba on the 12th of June and passed inland near Mobile on the 13th.

The second storm was of greater intensity but does not seem to have been a fully developed hurricane. It appeared in the vicinity of Barbados on July 2, where the Barbados lightship *Flummense* encountered high winds. On the 4th there were severe wind and rain storms on the south coast of Haiti. It passed through the Yucatan Channel on the 7th and reached the Texas coast on the 10th. It was not severe in Texas.

On the 6th of July another storm appeared over the eastern Caribbean, passed south of Puerto Rico on the 7th (wind 56 miles an hour at San Juan), skirted the Bahamas and passed near Hatteras on the 10th (wind 64 miles an hour).

There were two storms in August, both of full hurricane intensity. The course of one lay entirely in the Atlantic. The other was first charted far to the northeastward of Puerto Rico, whence it moved in a direction slightly south of west, reaching southern Florida on the 10th. It passed into the Gulf south of Tampa on the early morning of the 11th and moved slowly through the northeastern Gulf. In Florida the storm was of slight intensity; it increased in fury while crossing the Gulf and was attended by hurricane winds on the Louisiana coast. At Port Eads the wind reached a velocity of 72 miles an hour. The anemometer cups were blown away and the anemometer support was thrown down. High tides accompanied the storm. The storm-warning displayman at Pilottown, La., reported that the tide on the 14th rose four feet in about ten minutes. Damage to property in southern Louisiana, exclusive of growing crops, was estimated at $1,000,000.

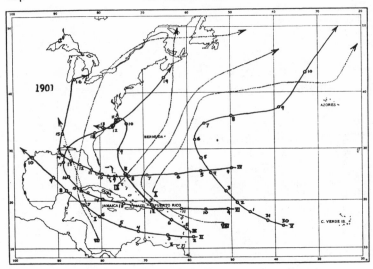

FIGURE 78.   Tracks of tropical storms of 1901. I. June 10 to 13; II. July 2 to 10;
III. July 5 to 13; IV. August 4 to 16; V. August 30 to September 10; VI. September
9 to 19; VII. September 20 to 30; VIII. October 7 to 14; IX. October 16 to 18; and
X. October 31 to November 10. On this and succeeding maps, noteworthy storms are
tracked by solid lines with open circles to indicate approximate positions at 8 a.m.
(75th meridian time) on date given near circle. Other storms are tracked by dotted
lines *without* position circles and dates. Arrow indicates final direction of movement, but not always the end of the track, as it has extended in many cases beyond
the limits of this map.

In September a storm approached St. Kitts on the 11th and passed
inland on the Gulf coast near Pensacola on the 17th. It lacked the
energy of a full-fledged hurricane. Four other tropical disturbances
occurred later in the season; none of them was of marked energy.

### 1902

Four tropical disturbances were recorded in 1902. Three of them
were of hurricane intensity at some point in the line of progress but
none of them was of exceptional severity. (Fig. 79.)

### 1903

Eight tropical storms were charted during the hurricane season of
1903 and all but two of them were of known hurricane intensity at
some points in their paths. (Fig. 80.)

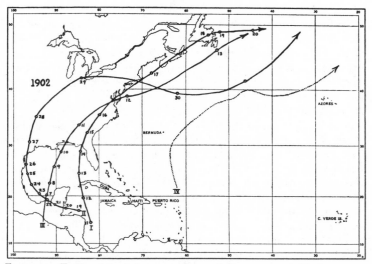

FIGURE 79. Tracks of tropical storms of 1902. I. June 11 to 20; II. June 19 to July 1; III. October 7 to 13; IV. November 1 to 9.

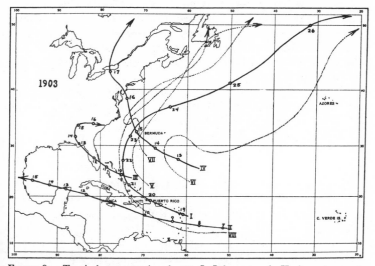

FIGURE 80. Tropical storm tracks of 1903. I. July 19 to 26; II. August 7 to 15; III. September 10 to 16; IV. September 13 to 17; V. September 22 to 25; VI. October 1 to 10; VII. October 7 to 14; VIII. October 18 to 27.

On September 10 the center of a tropical disturbance was located over the eastern Bahamas. By that evening it had advanced to the vicinity of Nassau. The barometer reading at 7 p.m. was 29.20 and between 6 and 7 p.m. the wind at Nassau reached 60 miles an hour when the anemometer cups blew away. The wind then went to southerly and increased to an estimated maximum of 90 miles an hour. At Cat Bay, Bahamas, the minimum reading of the barometer was 28.82 inches. On the 11th the storm approached the Florida coast. The center passed about 50 miles south of Jupiter with barometer 29.63 and wind 78 miles an hour at 6:45 p.m. of the 11th. For one minute it blew at a rate of 84 miles an hour. During the 12th the storm moved across Florida into the Gulf and passed inland near St. Andrews, Fla., on the 13th. At 4:15 p.m. of the 13th the barometer at St. Andrews had fallen to 29.08 inches and the wind was estimated at 75 to 80 miles. The storm then dissipated over the East Gulf and South Atlantic States.

Another storm, moving from the middle Atlantic, passed south-westward of Bermuda and crossed the middle Atlantic coast on September 16. Winds exceeding 60 miles an hour occurred along the coasts of New Jersey, New York and southern New England.

On the 28th a severe storm recurved northeastward in the vicinity of Bermuda. Winds of hurricane force uprooted trees, damaged houses and destroyed crops. The barometer fell to 29.18 inches. History of this storm before and after it reached Bermuda is not known and no track is given.

There were three tropical storms in October, two of hurricane force. One followed an erratic path and at one time approached the North Carolina coast. Neither of them was of particular interest. The third was of slight intensity. It passed near Haiti and to the westward of Bermuda.

### 1904

While there were more than the average number of tropical storms during 1904, the season was quite late in beginning. (Fig. 81.) None occurred until September. There were three in September, five in October and one in November.

The only important storm in September first attained marked intensity when in the subtropical regions north of the West Indies. It moved to the South Atlantic coast from where it recurved to the northeastward and progressed rapidly to New England, attaining

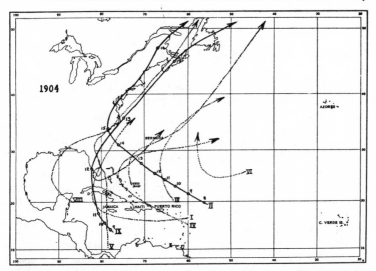

FIGURE 81.    Tracks of tropical storms of 1904. I. September 3 to 9; II. September 8 to 16; III. September 24 to 30; IV. October 10 to 16; V. October 10 to 23; VI. October 19 to 23; VII. October 28 to November 2; VIII. October 29 to November 6; IX. November 9 to 14.

hurricane force at points along the Atlantic coast. A number of lives were lost and there was much damage to seaside property and many vessels were wrecked.

Center of the storm passed near Delaware Breakwater where a wind of 100 miles an hour from the northwest was recorded at 2:30 p.m. of September 15.

The other two storms in September were of slight intensity; one crossed southern Florida and the other moved northward and northeastward in the Atlantic, passing slightly east of Bermuda.

There were no storms in October of hurricane intensity, though five of tropical origin were charted. One is worthy of note. A shallow depression formed over the Caribbean Sea early in the month of October. It moved slowly northward during the 11th and 12th, crossed western Cuba, and caused high winds over southern Florida on the 14th. On the evening of the 16th it had attained considerable force and communication to southeast Florida failed. The wind at Jupiter, Fla., increased to 68 miles an hour on the 17th. Thereafter the storm diminished rapidly in intensity, described a loop over Florida and then moved into the Atlantic.

On the 20th a new center appeared to form a short distance off the Carolina coast. It moved rapidly north-northeastward, causing gales and heavy rains in the Carolinas, Virginia, Maryland, eastern Pennsylvania, eastern New York and New England States.

The November storm also moved from the Caribbean Sea northward along the Atlantic seaboard, but was unusual in that it was attended by snow as far south as the Carolinas.

It originated as a shallow depression on the 9th of November, south of the Isle of Pines. Progressing slowly northward, the storm increased in intensity and on the night of the 12th to 13th moved from Jacksonville to Hatteras, the central pressure falling to 29.08 inches. On November 13 the barometer at Norfolk fell to 29.00 inches and at New York to 28.74 inches. At 8 a.m. of the 14th the storm was over Nova Scotia, barometer 28.60 inches.

There were heavy rains along the Atlantic coast and in many places precipitation was in the form of snow; gales occurred along the coast; at Block Island the wind reached 78 miles an hour.

## 1905

The season of 1905 was an exceptionally quiet one. Only three tropical storms were recorded and they came late in the season. (Fig. 82.)

In October a tropical disturbance of marked intensity developed over the western Caribbean Sea and moved northeastward. It was first observed to the southwestward of Santo Domingo on the 3rd of the month. It passed between Haiti and Cuba on the 5th, west of Turks Island on the 6th, and to the south and east of Bermuda on the 8th. At Hamilton, Bermuda, at 8 p.m. of the 8th, the barometer read 29.66 inches. However, it increased greatly in force after passing Bermuda. The S.S. *La Savoie* was caught in the storm and at 45°N. and 45°W., recorded the pressure at 27.92 inches.

The other storm of that year occurred in the latter half of September. It originated in the western Caribbean, crossed Yucatan and passed inland on the middle Gulf coast. It was not of hurricane force.

## 1906

The year 1906 was memorable because of the active hurricane season and the intense storm which crossed the middle Gulf coast in

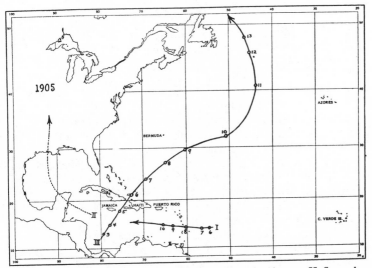

FIGURE 82. Tracks of tropical storms of 1905. I. September 6 to 10; II. September 24 to 30; III. October 3 to 13.

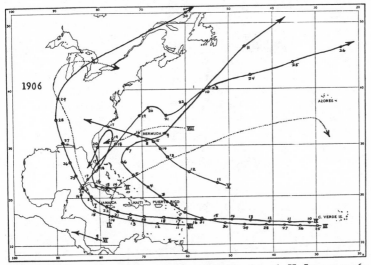

FIGURE 83. Tracks of tropical storms of 1906. I. June 8 to 16; II. June 14 to 26; III. August 25 to September 11; IV. September 10 to 30; V. September 11 to 17; VI. October 9; VII. October 11 to 20; VIII. October 13 to 17; IX. November 6 to 13.

the vicinity of Mobile and Pensacola. There were nine charted storms; two in June, one in August, two in September, three in October and one in November. (Fig. 83.)

Of the June storms, one passed inland near Apalachicola on the 12th, attended by heavy rains but no winds of extraordinary force.

Crossing southeast Florida on the 17th, the second June storm was of greater intensity; winds reaching a velocity of 70 miles an hour from the northeast at Sand Key on the 16th and 49 miles northeast at Jupiter on the 17th. It was attended by heavy rains.

In August a storm originated near the Cape Verde Islands, moved westward, recurved near Haiti and Puerto Rico and passed near Bermuda. At St. Kitts the wind reached an extreme velocity of 70 miles an hour. The S.S. *Koenigin Luise*, in latitude 39°N. and longitude 55°W., recorded a barometer reading of 28.06 inches.

Considerable damage to shipping resulted from the first September storm, between Charleston and Wilmington. It crossed the Carolina coast on the 17th with winds about 50 miles an hour at outlying stations. No reports were received from the immediate storm center as it moved inland.

The second September storm was one of great violence. It was first observed in the western Caribbean Sea on the 22nd, although its course has been traced to the Cape Verde Islands. On the 27th it reached the middle Gulf coast. Destructive winds and unprecedented tides accompanied the storm.

At Pensacola the height of the storm was reached between 3 and 4 a.m. of the 27th. Trees were uprooted, houses unroofed and vessels dragged their anchors. The tide was ten feet above normal. Thirty-two lives were lost in Pensacola and damage in that vicinity amounted to more than $2,000,000. It was said to have been the most violent storm there in one hundred seventy years. Wind velocities at Pensacola were extremely high; the maximum was 83 miles an hour from the east.

At Mobile the barometer fell to 28.84 inches. Damage to property there was severe. The tide was 9.9 feet above normal. At 7 a.m. of the 27th, the U.S. Revenue Steamer *Winona*, at Scranton, Miss., recorded a pressure of 28.50 inches. There was an extraordinary tide at Burrwood, approximately eight feet above normal.

Three tropical storms occurred in October. One appeared over the western Caribbean and moved westward into Honduras. It crossed the coast north of Bluefields attended by destructive winds and a

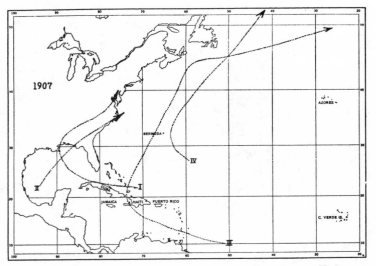

FIGURE 84. Tracks of tropical storms of 1907. I. September 16 to 23; II. September 27 to 29; III. October 3 to 17; IV. October 17 to 20.

very high tide on the coast from Bluefields northward for about 90 miles. The highest tide was fifteen feet and it was reported to have come in the form of a tidal wave. Barometer at Bluefields, when the center crossed the coast about 9:30 p.m. of October 9, was 29.57 inches.

An unusual course, and one which illustrates the effect of pressure from higher latitudes, was taken by another hurricane of that month. Center of the storm passed near to Havana on the 17th at 11:30 a.m., barometer 28.86 inches. It was reported in Cuba to have been of small diameter but of great intensity. It passed Key West at 3 a.m. of the 18th, wind 54 miles an hour, barometer 29.30 inches. Its northeastward course in the Atlantic was blocked by high pressure on the North Atlantic coast and on the 20th it turned westward, then southward across Florida where it dissipated. At Sand Key the wind reached 75 miles an hour northwest on the 18th; at Jupiter 60 miles northeast on the same date. Laborers building the Florida East Coast Railroad were quartered in houseboats; one hundred twenty-four of them lost their lives, also four or five of the natives.

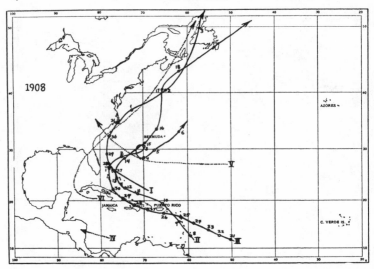

FIGURE 85. Tracks of tropical storms of 1908. I. July 27 to August 4; II. September 8 to 18; III. September 21 to October 6; IV. October 17; V. October 18 to 23; VI. October 25 to 31.

## 1907

Two slight tropical disturbances were recorded in September 1907. (Fig. 84.) One moved from the Bay of Campeche to Hatteras and did not develop great intensity. The other appeared north of Haiti, moved westward across northern Cuba, thence to the middle Gulf coast. At Pensacola the wind reached 46 miles northeast, the highest recorded along the coast.

## 1908

Six disturbances, identified as tropical cyclones, were charted during the hurricane season of 1908. (Fig. 85.)

A shallow barometric depression (not charted) advanced from the Caribbean Sea into the Gulf of Mexico from the 21st to the 23rd of July. Pressure continued low over the Gulf until the 25th when the center drifted slowly northward and crossed the coast line without developing marked intensity. At the same time a storm moved northwestward through the Bahamas, skirted the east Florida coast and on the 30th was a storm of marked intensity, central off the North Carolina coast. At 4:20 p.m. the barometer reading at Wilmington

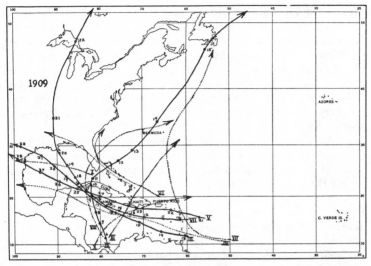

FIGURE 86.   Tracks of tropical storms of 1909. I. June 25 to 30; II. June 26 to July 1; III. July 13 to 22; IV. July 27 to August 10; V. August 21 to 28; VI. August 27 to 31; VII. September 10 to 22; VIII. September 22 to 30; IX. October 6 to 15; X. November 8 to 14; XI. November 22 to 25; XII. November 25 to December 2.

was 29.18, and wind there reached 48 miles northeast. It moved northward on the 31st; with wind reaching 58 miles northwest at Hatteras.

In the absence of ship reports at the time these storms were in progress, it was thought that the Gulf disturbance had developed two centers, one of which moved into the Atlantic. Subsequently it appeared that they were separate and distinct storms, but no data are available to determine the track of the earlier of the two.

### 1909

During the hurricane season of 1909 there was unusual storm activity; twelve disturbances of tropical origin with definite cyclonic characteristics were charted. Of these four were of full hurricane intensity and two were storms of tremendous force. (Fig. 86.)

Of the two July storms, one first appeared at about 10°N. and 50°W. It progressed westward through the Caribbean Sea, crossed Yucatan into the Gulf and entered Mexico. The other was first

observed in the Yucatan Channel on the 18th, though its course has
since been traced as far eastward as the Windward Islands. From the
Yucatan Channel it moved northwestward and the center passed
over Velasco, Tex. It had by that time attained full hurricane force.
One-half the town of Velasco was destroyed. There was a calm at
Velasco lasting forty-five minutes. At Bay City the barometer fell to
29.00 at 2:30 p.m. of the 21st. In Texas, 41 lives were lost and
property damage was estimated at $2,000,000. The tide at Galveston
was ten feet above normal.

In August a slight disturbance moved from a position north of
Puerto Rico through the Bahamas and approached the east Florida
coast. It then turned northward and dissipated off the Carolina coast,
during the night of August 31.

A very violent hurricane of the latter half of August was first
located in the Atlantic to the east of the Windward Islands, on
August 20. When south of Puerto Rico on the 22nd, it was a storm of
marked intensity. On the 23rd many houses were wrecked at Mole
St. Nicholas, Haiti, by high easterly gales as the storm passed to the
southward. Havana experienced winds of 60 miles an hour from the
northeast on the 24th and heavy winds and rains visited western
Cuba as the storm progressed. It reached the Yucatan Channel on
the 25th. On that day the S.S. *Cartago*, in the Channel, was caught in
the storm and the master estimated the winds at 100 miles an hour.
On the 26th the captain sent a wireless message to New Orleans,
giving an account of the storm. This was the first wireless report of a
tropical storm from a ship at sea, received in time to be used in forecasting.

As the storm center approached the Mexican coast, it caused gales
and tremendous seas along the Texas coast with the highest tides
along the south Texas coast for many years. On the 27th it passed
inland, causing an enormous loss of life and property in northeastern
Mexico. The unofficial estimates were that fifteen hundred persons
perished as a result of floods caused by the storm.

On September 10, the barometer began to fall over the Leeward
Islands; a disturbance moved westward over the Caribbean Sea. It
reached extreme western Cuba on the 17th. The barometer at Pinar
del Rio fell to 29.44 inches with highest wind 60 miles from the northeast. Damage in the province was estimated at $1,000,000. It crossed
the middle Gulf coast on September 20 and passed about fifty miles
west of New Orleans at 8 p.m. of that day. The wind there reached

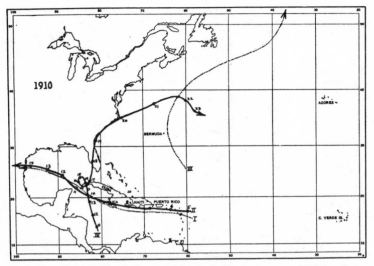

FIGURE 87. Tracks of tropical storms of 1910. I. August 23 to 31; II. September 5 to 14; III. September 23 to October 1; IV. October 11 to 23.

an extreme velocity of 68 miles, minimum pressure 29.22 inches. Property damage in Louisiana and Mississippi was estimated at $5,000,000. Three hundred and fifty lives were lost.

Another disturbance, apparently of slight intensity throughout its course, originated in the western Caribbean, reached the Florida Straits on the 25th and was lost in the vicinity of Bermuda.

The hurricane of October 1909, was one of exceptional intensity. It formed over the extreme southern portion of the western Caribbean Sea, moved north-northwestward and on the 11th approached the Florida Straits. First evidence of the storm was noted on October 2. It was destructive over the Yucatan Peninsula and in western Cuba and a number of lives were lost. It recurved over the extreme southern tip of Florida, at which time it had attained tremendous force.

At that time the Weather Bureau had a station at Sand Key, Fla. The station was abandoned at 8:30 a.m. and supplies and instruments were carried to the lighthouse. The wind was then 75 miles an hour; shortly thereafter the anemometer cups were carried away and the wind was estimated at 100 miles an hour. All the trees were blown down and at 9:35 a.m. heavy seas swept over the island. At 10:30

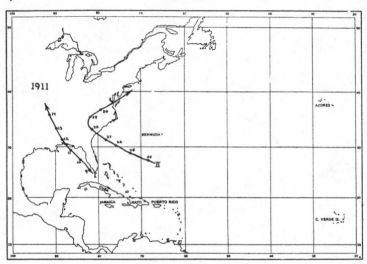

FIGURE 88. Tropical storm tracks of 1911. I. August 9 to 14; II. August 24 to 30.

a.m. the Weather Bureau building went over and was swept out to sea. The lowest barometer reading was 28.37 inches.

At Key West the barometer fell to 28.50 inches and the extreme wind velocity was 94 miles. Property damage there amounted to $1,000,000. About four hundred buildings collapsed.

1910

In October 1910, a hurricane, now famous because of the loop (Fig. 87) in its track which puzzled the forecasters at the time, developed exceptional violence in the vicinity of western Cuba and southern Florida. It has been described in a previous chapter. At Sand Key the barometer fell to 28.40 inches at 1:50 p.m. on the 17th and the wind was estimated at 125 miles an hour.

1911

The hurricane season of 1911 was a mild one; only two storms were definitely charted, both in August. (Fig. 88.) One of them appears to have developed near the Florida Straits; it moved northwestward across the Gulf and passed inland near Pensacola on August 11. It

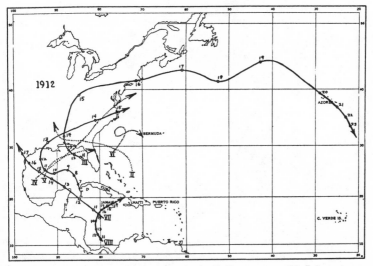

FIGURE 89.   Tracks of tropical storms of 1912. I. June 7 to 15; II. July 12 to 17; III. September 11 to 23; IV. September 21 to 25; V. October 2 to 4; VI. October 4 to 9; VII. October 11 to 17; VIII. November 11 to 19.

was of small diameter but of considerable intensity; the wind reached 80 miles an hour from the southeast at Pensacola.

The other was of hurricane intensity also. First observations of this storm were at about 27°N. and 66°W. Pursuing a west-northwest course, it passed inland between Savannah and Charleston on the 28th. There was great damage from winds and high tides between those cities. At Charleston, the barometer fell to 29.30 inches and the wind reached 106 miles an hour from the northeast at 11:50 p.m. of the 27th. On the 28th, at 3:10 a.m. the center was closest to Savannah, barometer 29.02 inches, wind 88 miles northwest.

### 1912

Beginning early in June and continuing until after the middle of November, storm activity was above the normal in 1912. There were eight tropical storms, five of them of full hurricane force. (Fig. 89.)

The Jamaica hurricane of 1912 was one of the most violent of record. A description of its passage over Black River, Jamaica, has been given in Chapter I. At Negril Point on the 18th of November at

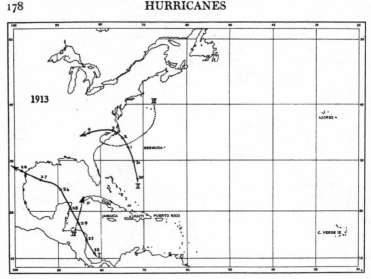

FIGURE 90.    Tracks of tropical storms of 1913. I. June 22 to 28; II. August 30 to
September 4; III. October 3 to 9; IV. October 27 to 29.

6 a.m., the barometer fell to 28.48 inches and the wind reached 120
miles northeast, when two anemometer cups were wrenched off.
There was great damage in Jamaica from winds and tidal waves
caused by the storm. One hundred lives were lost in Jamaica. At
Savanna-la-Mar the tide was the highest in a century. The storm lost
intensity rapidly after passing Jamaica and was not traced beyond
extreme eastern Cuba.

1913

In June 1913, a disturbance formed over the extreme southwestern
Caribbean Sea, and from the 24th to the 27th progressed north-
northwestward, then west-northwestward to the Texas coast. (Fig.
90.) It passed to the interior near the mouth of the Rio Grande during
the night of the 27th to 28th, with full hurricane force. This storm
caused what was, up to that time, a record rainfall in Texas. At Mon-
tell, in Uvalde County, 20.60 inches of rain fell between 2:30 p.m. of
the 28th and 9 a.m. of the 29th.

On August 29, there was a slight pressure fall over the Windward
Islands, indicating the formation of a slight disturbance. It probably
drifted slowly northwestward; at any rate it was charted from a point

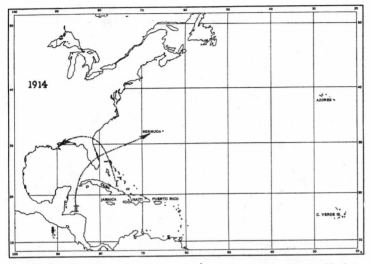

FIGURE 91. Tracks of tropical storms of 1914. I. September 14 to 18; II. October 24 to 27.

northeast of the Bahamas to the North Carolina coast where it turned westward into the interior. Five lives were lost and property damage was estimated at four or five million dollars. On September 3, on passing inland it caused a wind of 74 miles southeast at Hatteras.

## 1914

The hurricane season of 1914 was an abnormally quiet one. There were only two disturbances of tropical origin and both were of slight intensity. (Fig. 91.) One was first sighted east of the Bahamas and went inland in Georgia; the other formed over the western Caribbean and lost its identity in the vicinity of Bermuda.

Activity in the Cape Verde region was at a minimum during the years 1912, 1913 and 1914. There is no definite indication that any tropical storm originated east of longitude 70°W. during those three years.

## 1915

In 1915 the formation of hurricanes in the Cape Verde region was resumed and in 1916 hurricane activity reached a record for the century until the great year of 1933.

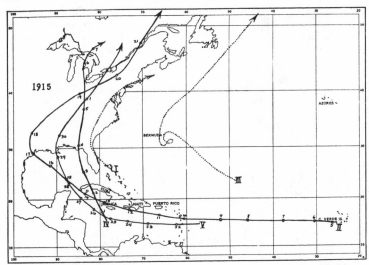

FIGURE 92. Tracks of tropical storms of 1915. I. July 31 to August 5; II. August 5 to 24; III. August 28 to September 13; IV. September 1 to 7; V. September 22 to October 2.

What was probably the greatest hurricane of the century, up to that time, in diameter and intensity, formed in the Cape Verde region and moved westward across the Atlantic during the early part of August. (Fig. 92.)

It appeared between Guadeloupe and Dominica on August 10, already a severe storm. Passing south of San Juan where the wind reached 60 miles from the northeast, it continued on a westward course. Gales occurred on the 12th in southern Haiti. The storm center passed slightly north of the island of Jamaica on the night of the 12th to 13th with a whole gale at Kingston. Its passage over Cape San Antonio, Cuba, has been described in Chapter iv. It was then a hurricane of tremendous force.

By the time it reached the Texas coast, where it passed inland on the 16th and 17th, it was of great diameter and fearful violence. Though ample warnings had been issued nearly 24 hours in advance by the Weather Bureau, 275 lives were lost and damage was estimated as high as $50,000,000. The tide at Galveston was twelve feet above normal, inundating the business district to a depth of five or six feet. The extreme wind velocity was 120 miles an hour.

The third storm was first charted midway between Bermuda and the Cape Verde Islands. It moved northwestward to the vicinity of Bermuda, described an irregular path, including a loop, and continued northeastward. It remained in the vicinity of Bermuda from the 2nd to the 8th of September.

Another hurricane was in progress at the same time. It was first noted south of the Isle of Pines on September 2. The storm center struck the coast near the mouth of the Apalachicola River on September 4, barometric minimum 29.32 inches and wind about 70 miles an hour.

Another violent hurricane, equal in intensity to that of August 10 to 17, 1915, occurred in September. The point of origin was probably the Cape Verde region, though it was first detected near the Windward Islands on September 22. Its course through the Caribbean was somewhat farther south than the great August hurricane so that its effects on the islands were less pronounced. After passing through Yucatan Channel, the storm turned northwestward and reached the Louisiana coast on September 29.

Property losses on the middle Gulf coast exceeded $13,000,000. Loss of life was placed at 275.

At New Orleans the lowest barometer reading, 28.11 inches, was recorded at 6:50 p.m. of the 29th, the lowest of record in the United States at that time. The extreme wind velocity was 130 miles an hour from the east.

At Burrwood, La., a perfect anemometer registration was secured showing a maximum five-minute velocity of 124 miles an hour and an extreme wind of 140 miles an hour.

Destruction of buildings was very great. Of the one hundred houses in Leeville, only one was left standing. At several places on the Mississippi River below New Orleans and on Lake Ponchartrain 90 per cent of the buildings were completely destroyed. It is a remarkable testimony to the warnings of the Weather Bureau that in such a vast storm-swept territory, less than three hundred lives were lost.

## 1916

The hurricane season of 1916 was one of the most active of record. As is usual in active seasons it began early, continued into November, and movement of storms from the eastward into the Caribbean began in July. (Fig. 93.)

The first officially recorded tropical storm of the season originated in the western Caribbean Sea in late June, progressed north-north-westward through the Yucatan Channel and inland near Mobile, Ala., July 5 and 6.

Within the city limits of Mobile it was the most destructive storm of record. The tide was 11.6 feet above normal; the barometer fell to 28.92 inches at 3:45 p.m. of the 5th; the highest wind at Mobile was 107 miles an hour from the east. At Pensacola it was 104. Four lives were lost and property damage approached $3,000,000.

In July a hurricane originated northeast of the Bahamas and passed inland on the South Carolina coast on July 13 and 14. Highest wind recorded was 64 miles north at Charleston. The storm was of small diameter; property damage was not great and no lives were lost.

The second hurricane of the month was already in progress. It approached and crossed the Windward Islands from the southeast, continued on a broad recurve and passed near Hatteras on the 19th and Nantucket on the 21st. Winds of about 50 miles an hour attended its passage along the middle and north Atlantic coasts.

Three tropical storms of full hurricane force occurred in August. All of them were of small diameter but great intensity. The first originated east of the Windward Islands, crossed over the Caribbean Sea, passed through the Yucatan Channel and moved across the Gulf to Corpus Christi with an unusually rapid progressive movement. It reached the Windward Islands on the 12th of August and the Texas coast on the 18th.

Winds were very destructive but the storm moved too rapidly to produce an excessive tide. At 6:30 p.m. of the 18th, the wind instruments at Corpus Christi were wrecked; the five-minute maximum wind was estimated at 90 miles an hour; lowest barometer reading 29.07 inches. Fifteen lives were lost and damage was placed at $1,800,000.

The second hurricane of the month was of exceptionally small diameter. About all that is known of this storm is what occurred during its passage over Puerto Rico. Destructive winds extended over an area about fifty miles wide. At San Juan the wind blew 92 miles an hour for ten minutes at the height of the storm; pressure fell to 29.44 inches. This was at about 7 a.m. of August 22. Damage was estimated at $1,000,000. Apparently the storm dissipated off the Florida coast

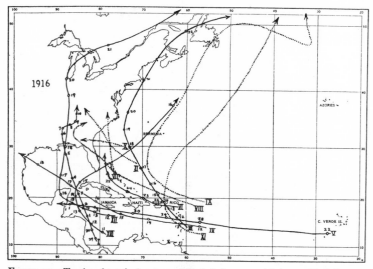

FIGURE 93.  Tracks of tropical storms of 1916. I. June 29 to July 10; II. July 11 to 15; III. July 12 to 22; IV. August 12 to 18; V. August 22 to September 1; VI. August 22 to 25; VII. September 4 to 7; VIII. September 9 to 14; IX. September 21 to October 2; X. October 3 to 5; XI. October 6 to 14; XII. October 12 to 21; XIII. November 11 to 16.

on the 25th or 26th. It was not felt at any of the islands of the Bahamas.

Point of origin of the third storm of October is uncertain. First definite indications of cyclonic circulation were south of Jamaica on the 11th. It was not severe on the 13th, though twenty-four hours later the center passed near Swan Island, barometer 28.94 inches, wind of hurricane force from the north, estimated at 100 miles an hour. The storm then crossed the Yucatan Peninsula and turned abruptly northward to the middle Gulf coast. On the 18th the vortex passed almost directly over the city of Pensacola. At 10:12 a.m., the wind reached a five-minute maximum velocity of 114 miles an hour and an extreme of 120 miles an hour from the southeast. Lowest pressure was 28.76 inches. At Mobile the pressure was not so low, 29.22 inches, but the wind was as high, 115 miles for five minutes, extreme 128 miles. The storm moved rapidly, the tide was not excessive and there was little damage.

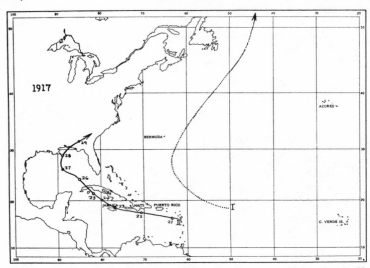

Figure 94. Tracks of tropical storms of ·1917. I. August 31 to September 6; II.
September 21 to 29.

The tropical disturbance of November 1916 made its appearance
on the 12th east of Honduras, recurved over the eastern Gulf and
moved rapidly northeastward over southern Florida on the 15th.
Considerable damage to property was reported on the coasts of Honduras and Yucatan. Maximum wind was 71 miles north at Sand Key,
Fla.

## 1917

Only two tropical storms were charted during the season of 1917.
Both were of hurricane intensity. (Fig. 94.)

The September hurricane caused heavy south and southeast sea
swells on the Leeward Islands on September 21. On the 22nd the
storm was south of Santo Domingo; on the 23rd it was of great intensity, central north of Jamaica, pressure at Kingston, 29.14 inches
at 4:45 p.m. There was great damage in the northern part of the
island of Jamaica. It recurved sharply over the northern Gulf and
turned northeastward over Pensacola, having reached the coast line
late on the 28th. At Mobile the barometer fell to 29.16 inches and the
maximum wind was 98 miles from the north. At Pensacola, pressure
was 28.51 inches, wind 103 miles southeast, extreme 125 miles. Five

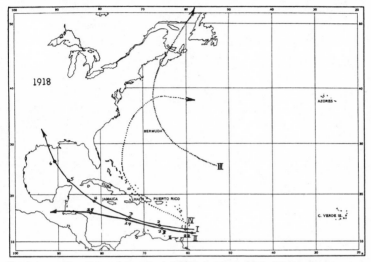

FIGURE 95.   Tropical storm tracks, 1918. I. August 1 to 6; II. August 21 to 25; III. September 4 to 8; IV. September 9 to 16.

lives were lost at Crestview, Fla. Damage at Pensacola was placed at $170,000.

### 1918

In 1918 there were two hurricanes in August and two storms, one of hurricane intensity, in September. (Fig. 95.)

The first was a rapidly moving storm of small diameter but great intensity. First evidence of its existence came in cable reports from Barbados on August 1. It passed south of Jamaica on the 3rd and moved inland over Louisiana on the 6th. The area of destruction was about twenty-five miles wide. There were estimates of damage running to $5,000,000. Wind velocity at Lake Charles reached an estimated velocity of 100 miles an hour. Thirty-four lives were lost in Louisiana. Severe damage was reported from Gerstner Field which was in the storm's path.

### 1919

In July a slight disturbance developed in the Gulf not far from western Cuba and moved north-northwestward to the vicinity of Pensacola. Wind there reached 58 miles northeast as the storm moved inland on the 4th.

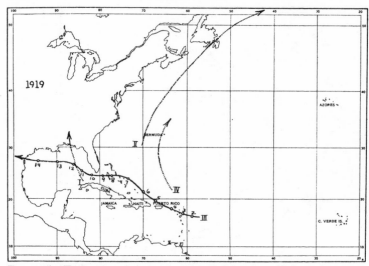

FIGURE 96. Tracks of tropical storms of 1919. I. July 2 to 4; II. September 1 to 4; III. September 2 to 14; IV. November 11 to 14.

Of the two September storms, one was possibly the greatest of the present century. As a minor disturbance, it made its appearance on September 2, at about 17° or 18°N. and 63°W. Its progressive movement was very slow. (Fig. 96.) Passing north of Santo Domingo and over the central Bahamas, it began to increase rapidly in force. At Nassau on the evening of the 7th, barometer reading was 29.46 inches, wind 56 miles northeast.

By the time it reached the Florida Straits it was a storm of terrific force. It passed near Key West on September 9 and 10, moving slowly, the most violent storm there since the beginning of available records. The anemometer cups were blown away at about 80 miles of wind velocity. Minimum pressure there was 28.81 inches. Gales endured from 7 a.m. of the 9th until 9:30 p.m. of the 10th. Rainfall was 13.39 inches.

At Sand Key the Weather Bureau station was abandoned at 1 p.m. of the 9th. The anemometer cups were blown away at 84 miles. At midnight the barometer was lowest, 28.35 inches.

At Key West the property damage was estimated at $2,000,000.

Center of the storm passed over Dry Tortugas, 65 miles west of Key West, where the barometer fell to 27.51 inches. On the S.S. *Fred*

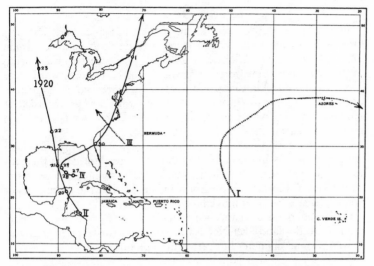

FIGURE 97.  Tracks of tropical storms of 1920. I. September 10 to 18; II. September
19 to 23; III. September 22 to 23; IV. September 27 to October 1.

*W. Weller*, in the vicinity of Dry Tortugas on September 9, the
barometer fell to 27.36 inches. Ten vessels were listed as lost; among
them the Spanish S.S. *Valbanera*, not far from Dry Tortugas,
foundered with 400 passengers and a crew of 88.

The hurricane continued slowly westward, causing gales along the
Gulf coast, and kept the people in a state of anxiety for several days.
Few ship reports were received and the Weather Bureau had diffi-
culty in keeping track of the storm, despite its great diameter and
tremendous force. On September 12, at latitude 26° 30′N. and
longitude 90° 30′W., the S.S. *Berwyn* was caught in the storm,
barometer 27.50 inches. Tide at Galveston was 8.8 feet above normal.

On September 14, the center went inland south of Corpus Christi,
still moving on a westward course, slowly. The tide rose 16 feet above
normal; 284 lives were lost; property damage was placed at $20,-
000,000. Minimum pressure was 28.65 inches and maximum recorded wind 72 miles at Corpus Christi. At Brownsville the barometer fell to 29.16 inches and at Miami, Burrwood, and Galveston the
wind reached a velocity of approximately 60 miles an hour, which
indicates the diameter of the circle of destructive winds.

## 1920

Four tropical storms occurred in 1920, all in September. (Fig. 97.) One of hurricane force moved from latitude 20°N. and longitude 48°W., far out in the Atlantic. Originating in the western Caribbean, a storm of hurricane force progressed north-northwestward over Yucatan and into Louisiana on the 21st. Its center did not pass near any Weather Bureau station so there are very meagre records. At Houma, La., at 10:15 p.m. of the 21st the barometer fell to 28.99 inches. Damage in Louisiana was $1,500,000.

From the 25th to 28th a disturbance of great energy remained almost stationary in the Gulf, then moved across Florida on the 29th to 30th with greatly diminished force. There was some damage on the west coast of Florida. Ship reports indicated that the storm was of great intensity before it moved inland.

On the 22nd a disturbance which had originated southwest of Bermuda moved inland over North Carolina near the Cape Fear River. It was of small diameter but rather intense.

## 1921

Five storms of definite tropical cyclone character were charted in 1921. There were a number of minor disturbances. (Fig. 98.)

On June 16 a storm of moderate intensity appeared near the coast of Honduras and on the 18th passed inland over British Honduras, not far from Belize. On the 19th it passed into the Gulf. There were no further reports from the vicinity of the storm until the evening of June 21 when it approached the mouth of the Rio Grande. On the night of the 21st and 22nd it passed to the east of Corpus Christi where the wind rose to 68 miles from the north. The center passed directly over Palacios, Wharton, and Wallis, Tex., and to the westward of Houston. Lowest pressure at Houston was 29.37 inches. Wind at Galveston and Houston reached 60 miles. It was of small diameter and of moderate intensity.

There were three storms in September of tropical origin. One originated in the Bay of Campeche, progressed northwestward into Mexico and northward across the Rio Grande into Texas. The torrential rains in Texas resulting from this storm were described in Chapter v.

The October storm was a full-fledged hurricane to which reference has been made in Chapter viii. The tide at Tampa was 10.5 feet, the

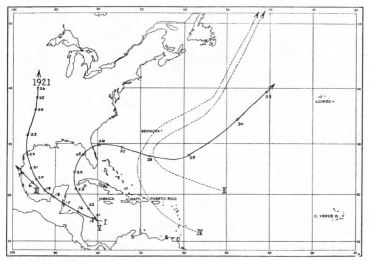

FIGURE 98. Tracks of tropical storms of 1921. I. June 15 to 26; II. September 5 to 14; III. September 6 to 7; IV. September 8 to 17; V. October 21 to 31.

highest since 1848. Only five or six lives were lost but property damage was placed at $3,000,000 in Florida.

At Tampa the barometer fell to 28.81 inches, the lowest of record. Wind, extreme velocity, was 72 miles from the south.

### 1922

In June a disturbance originated over the western Caribbean and went inland not far from Tampico. This storm caused torrential rains in the vicinity of Swan Island on the 12th and 13th, later over British Honduras and Yucatan where there were unprecedented floods, and in Mexico and southern Texas on passing inland there on the 16th. The floods in the Rio Grande resulting from this rainfall were the highest of record.

In September a disturbance moved from the Gulf into Florida near Tampa on the 17th and into the Atlantic. It was of slight force.

The second September storm originated in latitude 11°N., longitude 50°W., and recurved east of Bermuda on the 21st, where it was the most severe hurricane experienced in many years. Lowest pressure was 28.57 inches at Bermuda. The master of the S.S.

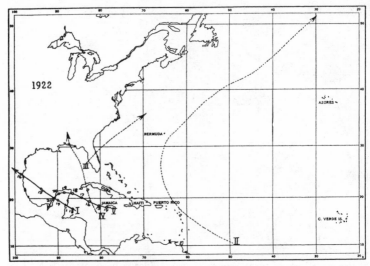

FIGURE 99.  Tracks of tropical storms of 1922. I. June 13 to 16; II. September 13
to 24; III. September 17 to 22; IV. October 12 to 17; V. October 14 to 21.

*Aquitania*, caught in this storm, reported that he had never seen
higher seas or known the wind to blow harder. Ten ports on the "B"
deck, fifty feet above the water line, were smashed in by the seas.

A slight disturbance formed on the 12th of October east of Swan
Island and struck inland between Pensacola and Mobile on the 17th.

As already described in Chapter VIII, the course of the other
October storm of 1922 was unusual. (Fig. 99.) There was much
damage to property on the east coast of Yucatan.

### 1923

In August a storm of slight intensity came into the field of observation east of Puerto Rico, moved northwestward and recurved near
Bermuda. It developed later and was a storm of considerable severity
south of Newfoundland.

The September storm began northwest of Haiti on the 25th,
reached the vicinity of Nassau and turned to the north and northeast.
One vessel reported a minimum pressure of 28.50 inches.

There were three storms in October. (Fig. 100.) One developed
northeast of Puerto Rico and turned northwest in latitude 30°N.,

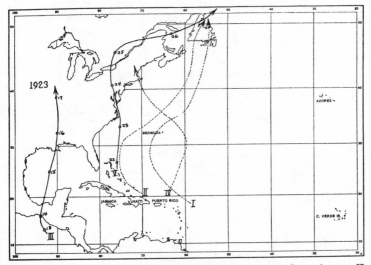

FIGURE 100.    Tracks of tropical storms of 1923. I. August 29 to September 10; II. September 24 to October 2; III. October 13 to 17; IV. October 14 to 19; V. October 22 to 26.

passing to the interior near Boston on the 19th. It was of slight energy. During the 9th to 14th of October, pressure was low over Mexico, the southwest Gulf and western Caribbean. On the 15th, two ships in the Gulf reported pressures about 29.20 inches and high winds. It crossed the Louisiana coast line early on the 16th, barometer at Morgan City 29.25 inches. It was of small diameter and there were no reports to indicate exceptional intensity. The third storm was slight; it moved from the Bahamas to Hatteras and went inland over Chesapeake Bay on the 23rd, having developed considerable force in its northward movement. Highest wind recorded was 82 miles northeast at Atlantic City.

## 1924

Eight tropical storms occurred in 1924, five of hurricane intensity. (Fig. 101.)

First sighted between Dominica and St. Lucia, the first August storm on the 17th was moving northwest. As it approached the Atlantic coast it moved slowly and was attended by hurricane winds

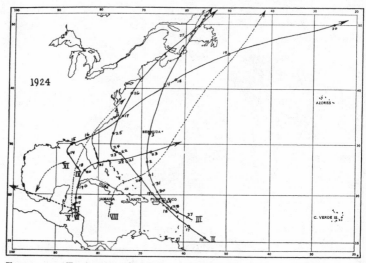

FIGURE 101.   Tracks of tropical storms of 1924. I. June 18 to 21; II. August 16 to 27; III. August 27 to September 5; IV. September 13 to 20; V. September 27 to 30; VI. October 12 to 14; VII. October 16 to 23; VIII. November 7 to 15.

and mountainous seas. Highest wind reported from a land station was 72 miles northwest at Hatteras on the 25th.

The second August storm developed farther to the east, apparently, because it was already a storm of much force when it appeared near Dominica on the 27th. By the time it reached the Virgin Islands on the 29th it was a very destructive storm. A number of lives were lost there and hundreds of houses were destroyed and thousands damaged. Highest wind was estimated at 110 miles an hour. On the eastern end of the island of St. John, minimum pressure was 28.56 inches. It passed to the westward of Bermuda.

There were indications of a disturbance over the southeast Gulf on September 13 which moved northwestward, then recurved sharply to the northeast and struck the western Florida coast near Port St. Joe, during the 15th. Wind on the Florida coast blew about 75 to 80 miles an hour near the storm center.

A very deep depression with hurricane winds was located west of Swan Island on the 18th. On the U.S.S. *Denver*, the barometer fell to 28.92 inches. It was the worst storm ever known in western Cuba which it crossed on the 19th. At Jutias City the barometer fell to

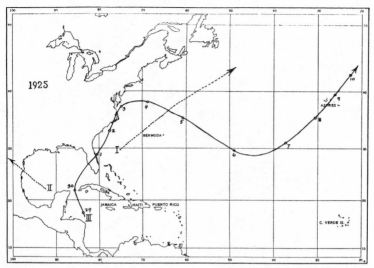

FIGURE 102.   Tracks of tropical storms of 1925. I. August 18 to 21; II. September 6 to 7; III. November 29 to December 10.

27.22 inches. This record was secured from the S.S. *Toledo* near that place at 3:30 p.m. of the 19th. At Los Arroyos, pressure at the lowest was 27.52 inches. It passed inland over Florida near Cape Romano. No wind records were obtained near the storm center.

## 1925

Only three disturbances that might be classed as tropical cyclones occurred in 1925. (Fig. 102.)

In September a storm, its genesis probably over the southwestern Gulf, moved northwestward to the Texas-Mexican coast, near Brownsville. It caused heavy rains and moderate gales in the lower Rio Grande valley.

Only one storm in 1925 seriously affected the coasts of the United States. It came very late in the season, originating over the western Caribbean Sea on November 29. Crossing the Florida Peninsula on the night of November 30-December 1, it turned north-northeastward through eastern North Carolina and then out into the Atlantic. It was not of great force in Florida but increased in intensity as it moved northward. A report from the U.S.S. *Patoka*, one hundred miles south-

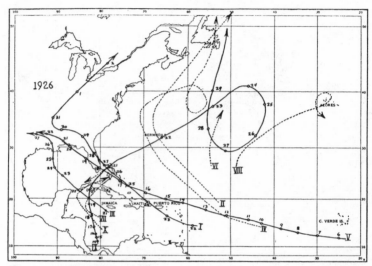

Figure 103.    Tracks of tropical storms of 1926. I. July 22 to August 2; II. August
1 to 9; III. August 21 to 27; IV. September 2 to 23; V. September 6 to 22; VI.
September 11 to 14; VII. September 11 to 17; VIII. September 22 to 29; IX. October 14 to 29; X. November 13 to 16.

southeast of Wilmington on December 2, gave a barometer reading of
28.90 inches.

Highest wind recorded at a coastal station was 64 miles northeast
at Atlantic City.

This storm has been recorded as of hurricane intensity and is unusual because tropical storms of such force rarely occur after November 1.

### 1926

Of the ten tropical storms recorded in 1926, eight were of hurricane
intensity. (Fig. 103.)

In July a storm appeared east of the Leeward Islands on the 22nd.
Intensity of the storm gradually increased as it followed the usual
west-northwestward course, passing south of Puerto Rico, over northeastern Haiti, then northwestward through the Bahamas to Florida.
At Nassau it was more fearful and devastating than any storm in
recent years. The center passed in the early morning of the 26th.

On the 27th and 28th the storm center moved north-northwestward
along the east Florida coast line, passed very close to Jacksonville,

then turned west-northwestward over Gulf States. Damage in Florida probably amounted to about $2,500,000.

On August 20 and 21 conditions became unsettled between Jamaica and Yucatan. The disturbance moved northwestward to the northern Gulf, increasing in intensity, and passed inland over southern Louisiana on the 25th. Lowest barometer readings were 28.31 inches at Houma, La., and 28.80 inches at Morgan City. Twenty-five lives were lost and damage to property, exclusive of crops in the field, was estimated between $3,000,000 and $4,000,000.

Of the five tropical storms in September, three were of full hurricane force but their tracks lay well out in the Atlantic, at a considerable distance from the coast of the United States. Four hurricanes were in progress at the same time; the only other similar occurrence up to that time was in 1893.

A slight disturbance originated in the Caribbean on the 11th, crossed Cuba moving northeastward to the Bahamas, then turned southwestward to the Florida Straits and dissipated. At that time a hurricane was moving west-northwestward toward the Bahamas. It had originated near the Cape Verde Islands and passed north of Puerto Rico on September 15.

This latter storm was one of the most destructive of the century. Its calm center passed directly over Miami on the morning of September 18. Instrumental records of this storm have been previously discussed. The barometer fell to 27.61 inches at Miami and the wind velocity for two minutes reached 138 miles an hour. On the water front south of the Miami River the tide was 11.7 feet above mean low water. The storm continued across Florida and through the northeastern Gulf, maintaining great energy and crossed the coast near Mobile and Pensacola after which it died out in the interior.

At Pensacola pressure fell to 28.56 inches on September 20; at Perdido Beach, Baldwin County, Ala., the lowest was 28.20 inches. At 9:30 p.m. of the same day the center passed a short distance south of Mobile, pressure 28.76 inches. Maximum wind velocity at Pensacola was 116 miles an hour from the east, at Mobile 94 from the north.

Damage resulting from the storm in Florida was estimated at $100,000,000. More than one hundred lives were lost in the city of Miami.

There were a number of minor disturbances in October. Beginning on the 14th and continuing for several days pressure fell slowly over the southwest Caribbean Sea. Definite cyclonic circulation appeared on the 16th. The disturbance moved north-northwestward with rapidly increasing intensity, passing near and east of Swan Island on the 18th-19th.

By the night of the 19th the storm had developed terrific force at which time it turned due north and the center passed over Nueva Gerona at 3 a.m. of the 20th, with a calm lasting thirty minutes. The storm then approached Havana where the lowest pressure, 28.07 inches, was recorded at 11:10 a.m. Wind at Havana reached 110 miles an hour at Belen College when the anemometer was blown away and 99 miles an hour at the National Observatory when the tower supporting the anemometers was blown down. Twenty inches of rain fell in Havana on the 20th. Damage was enormous on the Isle of Pines and in the Province of Havana. The center passed south of the southern tip of Florida where the wind blew 60 to 70 miles an hour. On the 22nd, moving rapidly, it crossed Bermuda where there was a calm lasting nearly an hour with lowest pressure 28.45 inches and maximum wind 128 miles an hour. The origin of this storm is discussed in Chapter III.

### 1927

There were seven tropical disturbances in 1927 but none of them was of any particular interest. (Fig. 104.)

### 1928

On August 3, 1928, a storm passed near Trinidad, headed north-westward and continued over Haiti and middle Florida. (Fig. 105.) It was not of great energy. There were moderate to strong gales on the Florida coast.

Another passed near Trinidad on August 7, following somewhat the same course but, after crossing Haiti, it lay somewhat to the westward across central Cuba through the eastern Gulf and entered Florida near Apalachicola on the 14th. It had no great force in Florida.

There were three hurricanes in September. Two were not of hurricane force. One of them moved westward from Puerto Rico on the 1st and reached Mexico a week later. The other recurved far out in the Atlantic.

The third September storm was perhaps the most violent and destructive of the century.

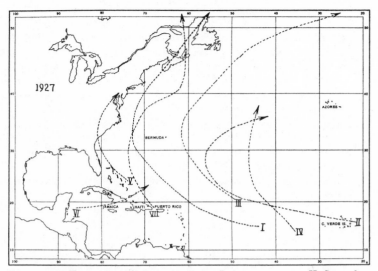

FIGURE 104. Tracks of tropical storms of 1927. I. August 19 to 27; II. September 3 to 11; III. September 23 to 30; IV. September 25 to 29; V. October 1 to 3; VI. October 17 to 19; VII. November 1 to 6.

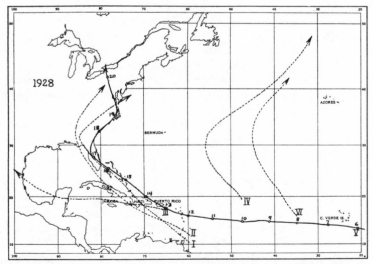

FIGURE 105. Tracks of tropical storms of 1928. I. August 3 to 12; II. August 7 to 17; III. September 1 to 7; IV. September 8 to 12; V. September 6 to 20; VI. October 10 to 14.

No doubt it originated near the Cape Verde Islands, though it was first reported by the S.S. *Commack* in latitude 17°N. and longitude 48°W. This was the most easterly vessel report received by radio in the Atlantic in connection with a hurricane up to that time.

Center of the hurricane, fully developed, passed over Pointe à Pitre, Guadeloupe, about noon of the 12th, pressure 27.76 inches. There was great destruction in Guadeloupe, and at St. Kitts and Montserrat. About 11 a.m. of the 13th, the S.S. *Matura* was near the center when southwest of St. Croix, barometer 27.50 inches. The wind reached 90 miles an hour on the island of St. Thomas and there was much destruction in the Virgin Islands.

This hurricane, now known as "San Felipe," was then a storm of tremendous force. On the 13th it crossed Puerto Rico, wind there was the highest, rainfall the heaviest and destruction the greatest of record in recent years. These records have been previously cited.

At Nassau the barometer fell to 28.08 inches and the anemometer cups blew away after the wind reached 100 miles an hour. The center moved over the Florida coast line near Palm Beach early in the night of September 16, crossed the Lake Okeechobee region and turned northward with diminishing force.

The minimum barometer reading at West Palm Beach, 27.43 inches, was at that time the lowest of record in the United States.

Property loss in Puerto Rico was said to be $50,000,000. Three hundred lives were lost there.

In Florida damage was placed at approximately $25,000,000. The Red Cross found the number of dead in Florida to be 1,836 and the injured 1,870. Nearly all the loss of life occurred in the Lake Okeechobee area.

A hurricane in October originated near the Cape Verde Islands on the 10th and recurved far out in the Atlantic.

## 1929

Cyclonic activity was at a low ebb in 1929 and 1930; there were only two well defined tropical storms in each of those years. (Fig. 106.)

In 1929 the first storm was of very small diameter with winds 75 to 80 miles near the center. It developed in the western Gulf, was first observed on June 28 and passed inland at Port O'Connor about 4:30 p.m. of the same day. The area of destruction was only about twenty miles wide. Lowest pressure was 29.12 inches at Port O'Connor.

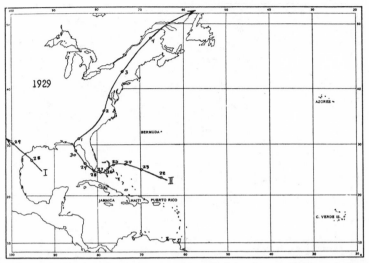

Figure 106.  Tracks of tropical storms of 1929. I. June 28 to 29; II. September 22
to October 4.

A disturbed condition was noted in the vicinity of the Cape Verdes
about September 11. On the 17th it was a slight disturbance northeast
of Puerto Rico. When over the Bahamas it turned to the south of
west and passed through the Florida Straits, moving slowly. It had
developed great intensity on reaching the Bahamas.

On the 25th, when the storm center was fifteen miles west of Abaco
Island, a vessel reported a barometer reading as low as 27.30 inches
(uncorrected). At Nassau it was 27.64 the same day. The center
passed over Key Largo on the 28th, barometer about 28 inches and
wind estimated at 150 miles an hour. There was a ten-minute lull as
the center passed. At Long Key the barometer fell to 28.18 inches.
At Everglades the wind was estimated at 100 miles an hour, barometer 28.95 inches. The storm reached Panama City on the 30th,
barometer 28.80 inches.

Although there was enormous damage at Nassau and many lives
were lost there, its course in Florida was such that damage probably
did not exceed $500,000 and only three lives were lost. The population
had been thoroughly warned by the Weather Bureau and there had
been ample time for all possible precautions.

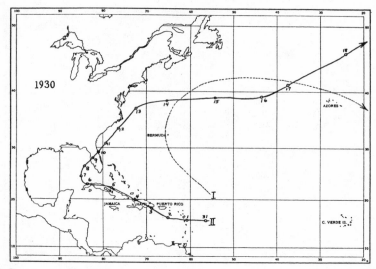

FIGURE 107.   Tracks of tropical storms of 1930. I. August 22 to 31; II. August 31
to September 18.

1930

The storm of August originated at about latitude 21°N. and
longitude 55°W. It recurved in the Atlantic and did not approach
closely to the coasts of the United States. (Fig. 107.)

The September storm originated or was first observed east of the
Windward Islands, on August 31. It passed Dominica on September
1, wind estimated at 80 to 100 miles. Though of small diameter, it
developed exceptionally high winds before reaching Santo Domingo.
The center passed over the city of Santo Domingo on September 3.

Because of its small diameter, the barometer fell with great rapidity
and the wind increased at an alarming rate. The Weather Bureau
observer, A. Ortori, recorded a minimum pressure reading of 27.56
inches. By experienced observers the wind was estimated at 150 to
200 miles an hour. In Santo Domingo two thousand lives were lost
and eight thousand persons were injured, with a property loss of
$15,000,000. Losses were negligible outside of the city of Santo
Domingo. After leaving Santo Domingo, the storm skirted the
northern coast of Cuba, recurved over the east Gulf and crossed

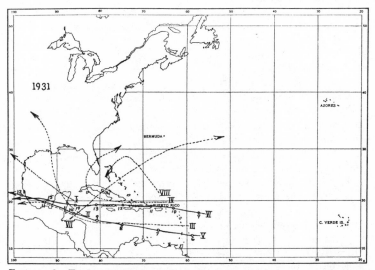

FIGURE 108.   Tracks of tropical storms of 1931. I. June 25 to 28; II. July 11 to 15; III. August 10 to 18; IV. September 2 to 9; V. September 6 to 12; VI. September 9 to 15; VII. October 18 to 21; VIII. November 22 to 25.

central Florida, moving northeastward. It was of small force after passing Santo Domingo.

1931

After 1930 storm activity in the Caribbean Sea increased. In 1931, eight storms were charted (Fig. 108); in 1932 there were eleven; in 1933, a new high record was established so far as is revealed by historical records from the time of Columbus.

In June 1931, a disturbance originated east of Yucatan on the 25th and moved northwestward to the Texas coast between Brownsville and Corpus Christi. No high winds were recorded.

The disturbance which was first observed in the Caribbean Sea on July 11 and subsequently went inland on the Louisiana coast, was also of slight force.

The first September storm was located north of Puerto Rico on the 2nd. It moved westward, recurved over western Cuba and southern Florida. It was mild in character; no gales attended its passage except in the vicinity of Haiti.

On the 6th a hurricane appeared east of Barbados. It was of small diameter but considerable force as it moved west-northwestward over the southern Caribbean. Late on September 10 this storm ravaged Belize, Honduras. Center of the storm passed Belize about 3:30 p.m. For ten minutes the wind blew 132 miles an hour, 2:50 to 3:00 p.m. At 3:44 p.m., the anemometer gave way. In the storm center the wind blew only 12 miles an hour. Hurricane winds followed, driving the sea forward over the environs of the port, choking the Belize River with the wreckage of small boats and with the wreckage as a battering ram, smashed into the structures of the town itself. The result was a disaster of major proportions. Fifteen hundred lives were reported lost and property damage was said to reach $7,500,000.

Another hurricane was already in progress, starting east of Antigua on the 9th, and on the 10th raked the northern coast of Puerto Rico. "San Nicolas" is the name given this storm in Puerto Rico. Destruction extended over an area ten to twelve miles wide.

Without any further destructive effects of a serious nature, the storm continued on a course almost due westward until it reached Vera Cruz about 4 a.m. of September 16. Wind at Vera Cruz rose to 95 miles an hour at the height of the storm; lowest pressure was 29.43 inches.

## 1932

The season of 1932 was an active one and began early. (Fig. 109.) A disturbance developed in the extreme southwestern Caribbean about May 15 and followed an irregular course northeastward, without attaining much force.

There was a slightly disturbed condition between Belize and Tela in Honduras on August 10. This condition progressed northwestward to the west central Gulf and because of its very slight nature was difficult to trace on the weather chart. During the 12th and 13th it developed with great rapidity and crossed the Texas coast line near Freeport on the latter date.

On the morning of the 13th the S.S. *J. C. Donnel*, latitude 27°N. and longitude 93°W., became involved in the storm and sent a radio report, barometer reading 28.88 inches. This was the first intimation of the storm's sudden increase in force. Center of the hurricane passed slightly east of Freeport and directly over East Columbia where the wind was estimated at 100 miles an hour with minimum pressure, 27.83 inches. It was of small diameter.

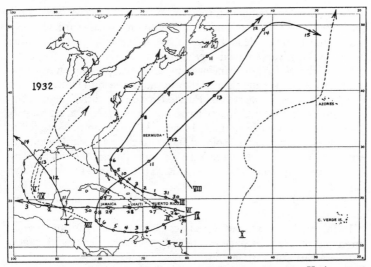

FIGURE 109.   Tracks of tropical storms of 1932. I. August 11 to 14; II. August 24
to September 4; III. August 30 to September 12; IV. September 9 to 17; V. September 18 to 21; VI. September 26 to October 3; VII. October 7 to 17; VIII. October
9 to 12; IX. October 31 to November 15; X. November 3 to 11.

A tropical disturbance of very slight intensity appeared southeast
of Puerto Rico on August 24. While passing over southwestern Puerto
Rico, the disturbance was not destructive. On the evening of the 29th
the center was about fifty miles south-southwest of Miami; on the
night of August 31 the storm center was a short distance west of
Mobile. Its diameter was small and hurricane winds were confined to
a small area.

A storm of minor intensity was first noted north of the Virgin
Islands on August 30. Moving slowly west-northwestward the intensity of the storm gradually increased as it passed through the
Bahamas. As it recurved to the north and northeast, the center
passed over Great Abaco Island, having attained tremendous fury.
There was great damage on the island. By an experienced observer
the wind was estimated at more than 200 miles an hour. Two
churches, both built of heavy stone with walls almost three feet in
thickness, were demolished. Some of the heavy stone blocks were
carried nearly half a mile.

Of the three September storms, two were of minor character. Both originated in the Gulf and moved, roughly, northeastward. One was first noted on the 6th and crossed the Louisiana coast; the other began on the 9th and moved over northern Florida.

When the third hurricane was in progress, pressure was extraordinarily high over the entire Atlantic and the eastern United States. Center of the hurricane crossed Puerto Rico on the 26th of September, entering the island at Ceiba at 10:00 p.m., pressure 27.70 on the S.S. *Jean* in the harbor of Ensenada Honda. At San Juan pressure fell to 28.95 as the center passed some distance to the southward; wind was estimated at not less than 120 miles an hour, though the wind-instrument tower was wrecked. In Puerto Rico the storm is known as "San Ciprian."

Due to high pressure to the northward, the storm moved almost due westward into Mexico.

In Puerto Rico 225 lives were lost, 3,000 or more persons were injured and property damage was near $30,000,000. Persons left homeless were variously estimated from 75,000 up to 250,000.

In October a disturbance came from the western Caribbean on October 7, moving west-northwestward, and recurved over the Gulf into Louisiana. Another started far northeast of Puerto Rico and recurved in the Atlantic. Neither was of hurricane force within the field of observation.

The third storm of October was first located on October 30 two hundred miles east of Guadeloupe. In the early stages it moved southwestward, a very unusual course for that season; then it recurved very slowly in the central Caribbean Sea and turned northeastward across Cuba. At the point of recurve, to the south and southwestward of Jamaica, it was one of the most intense tropical cyclones ever recorded anywhere in the world. It maintained this intensity in its passage across Cuba.

The S.S. *Phemius*, on voyage from Savannah to Colon, became involved in the center of the storm on November 5, was severely damaged, and was carried in an unmanageable condition along with the hurricane during the four succeeding days, or until the storm reached Cuba. Captain D. L. C. Evans was master of the ship. The observing officer, Mr. H. Nicholas, secured readings from a standard mercurial barometer placed on the ship by the British Meteorological Service. The following are extracts from the ship's meteorological log:

At 2 p.m. [November 5, 1932] the wind shifted to N.E. blowing with hurricane force accompanied by blinding squalls and a very high sea. The barometer was then falling rapidly reaching the low point of 914.6 mb. [27.01 inches] by 8 p.m. A fierce hurricane was blowing and a very high sea running. The ship was enveloped in spindrift, reducing the visibility to Nil, the No. 1 hatch not being visible from the bridge. The vessel was rolling heavily, the helm being of little use. So great was the force of the wind that shortly before 8 p.m. the funnel was blown overboard. The ship was rendered helpless and from then on was carried with the hurricane in an unmanageable state. It would not be overestimating to put the wind force at 200 miles per hour. Hatches were blown overboard like matchwood, derricks and lifeboats wrecked, upper and lower bridges blown in.

The weather conditions remained unchanged throughout the night. At 2 a.m. on November 6 there was a temporary lull wind being E. force 4. The sea was high and confused. This lasted about one hour, when the wind shifted to S.S.E. and blew with renewed vigour.

At 4 a.m. barometer 927.9 mb. [27.40 inches], wind S.S.E. force 12. Precipitous sea. The ship lay heading southwest labouring heavily and rolling through an arc of 70°.

8 a.m. barometer 938.0 mb. [27.70 inches], wind S.E. 12. Conditions remained unchanged. Shortly after 8 a.m. the barometer commenced to fall and at 9:30 a.m. was reading 921.1 mb. the wind remaining steady in force and direction.

At noon on the 6th November the wind had decreased to storm force. The sea still running very high. A heavy confused swell was also to be seen.

4 p.m. the same day a lull occurred. The sea was confused and the wind variable in direction force 4. Sky completely overcast, visibility about half a mile.

During this period the ship was besieged by hundreds of birds, the majority being of the swallow type with a sprinkling of larger birds about the size of a seagull. They took refuge in every part of the ship but lived only a few hours.

The statement in the log that the ship was carried along with the hurricane is evidently correct for the following conditions were noted at noon of the 7th and 8th:

By noon [7th] the barometer had again fallen. The reading being 951.6 mb. [28.10 inches], wind S.S.E., hurricane force. Precipitous sea.

Noon November 8th, barometer 951.6 mb. [28.10 inches], wind south 12, mountainous sea and heavy confused swell.

The vessel was taken in tow by a salvage steamer.

The subsequent passage of this hurricane over Cuba has been described in Chapter II.

At Nuevitas an experienced observer of the Pan American Airways estimated the wind velocity at 210 miles an hour which agrees closely with the statement in the log of the S.S. *Phemius* that it was not over-estimating to put the wind force at two hundred miles an hour.

## 1933

In at least two respects the hurricane season of 1933 was remarkable. First, the number of tropical disturbances charted was the greatest within the known history of the New World. (Fig. 110.) Second, there was a strong westward drift in the movements of the majority of the twenty-one disturbances of the season. Only four of them moved northward in the Atlantic to the eastward of New York. Five of them moved in a direction to the south of west in their final stages. To a certain extent this westward drift may have contributed to the number of storms charted; otherwise some of them might have moved on a more northerly course, or even to the northeastward, far out in the Atlantic where ship reports are less numerous so that at least some of the minor ones might not have been charted at all.

The second disturbance of the season was first reported by the Brazilian S.S. *Jaboatao* on the morning of June 27 in about latitude 9°N. and longitude 59°W. An easterly gale with barometer 29.27 inches was reported in the message from the *Jaboatao*. This is one of the earliest storms ever recorded in that region. Its course from the Atlantic into the eastern Caribbean Sea is paralleled by the hurricane of June 23 to 27, 1831. The storm of June 1933 passed farther to the southward but occurred four days later in the month in the vicinity of Trinidad. The track of the hurricane of June 1831 is given in Chapter XIII.

It is the only hurricane in the entire record the center of which passed to the southward of the island of Trinidad. However, a hurricane in September 1877 passed to the southward of the island of Curaçao, moving from the southeast. This storm's path before it reached Curaçao is not known. At Willemstad the barometer fell to 29.45 inches and the wind began at northeast, backed to north, then shifted to east and southeast. The captain of a small sailing vessel reported a barometer reading of 29.20 inches at some distance south of Curaçao. Many houses in Willemstad were totally destroyed by the wind and waves. The course of the center of the Trinidad storm

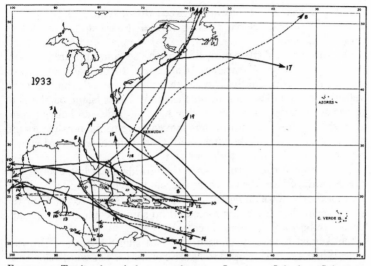

FIGURE 110. Tracks of tropical storms of 1933. 1. June 27 to July 6; 2. July 14 to 19; 3. July 21 to 27; 4. July 25 to August 4; 5. August 12 to 20; 6. August 16 to 21; 7. August 17 to 23; 8. August 24 to 28; 9. August 27 to 29; 10. August 28 to September 5; 11. August 31 to September 7; 12. September 10 to 16; 13. September 10 to 15; 14. September 16 to 24; 15. September 27 to October 4; 16. September 28 to 30; 17. October 1 to 7; 18. October 27 to 30; 19. October 28 to November 7; 20. November 16.

of June 1933 and the Tobago storm of June 1831 lay to the north of Curaçao; thus the storm of 1877 may have crossed the northeast corner of Venezuela in even a lower latitude than the 1933 storm. Such paths are exceedingly rare.

In June 1933 the hurricane at Trinidad caused the death of thirteen persons; one thousand were rendered homeless and property damage, practically all in the southern portion of the island, was placed at $3,000,000. The towns of Carupano and Rio Caribe in northeast Venezuela suffered severely. Many business houses and private dwellings were destroyed, several boats were sunk and a number of lives were lost.

At 8 p.m. of June 27, the American tanker *E. J. Bullock*, in the Gulf of Paria, experienced a wind of force 11, barometer 29.12.

The hurricane turned westward across the Gulf of Mexico and finally southwestward into Mexico, thus completing a course which was very abnormal throughout, considering the season. The storm entered Mexico about midway between Brownsville and Tampico in a sparsely settled region, causing several deaths and considerable property damage.

On July 26, a disturbance, fifth of the season, appeared a short distance southeast of Antigua. It advanced to the west-northwestward, passing south of St. Thomas that night where the highest wind velocity was 60 miles from the northeast. At Turks Island on the 27th it was accompanied by winds estimated at 85 miles an hour, barometer 29.37 inches. The storm then moved more to the northwestward across the northern Bahamas and then turned westward across southern Florida on the 30th and 31st.

The center of the storm crossed the Florida coast line a short distance south of Fort Pierce where the wind reached 60 miles an hour. In Florida there was no great damage. On passing into the Gulf the storm seemed to have lost force and no ship encountered what appeared to be a well developed center.

On August 5, when it crossed the coast slightly south of Brownsville, it had again developed full hurricane force. The wind velocity at Brownsville was 72 miles an hour. There was considerable damage in the vicinity of Brownsville and westward to Monterey, chiefly caused by torrential rains.

The third August storm was one of major intensity. Ships' observations are not available to trace it farther to the eastward than 51°W. though it had considerable force when first observed and probably had originated some distance from the Windward Islands. This storm travelled northwestward in somewhat higher latitudes than is usual and reached the coast at Cape Hatteras on the night of August 22 to 23. The center passed about one hundred miles to the southwestward of Bermuda, where the wind reached 64 miles an hour, at the maximum velocity. It had already attained great intensity, as is indicated by reports of ships which encountered the storm to the southeastward of Bermuda.

On the 18th, the Norwegian S.S. *Tana* became involved in the storm. In latitude 23°N. and longitude 54° 50'W., an aneroid barometer on the *Tana* indicated a minimum pressure of 27.98 inches, uncorrected.

At Cape Hatteras the lowest barometer reading was 28.67 inches and highest wind 64 miles an hour from the northeast. The center passed slightly to the eastward of Hatteras. On the morning of August 23, the center was a few miles south of Norfolk. Lowest pressure there was 28.68 inches and highest wind 56 miles an hour. At Cape Henry the maximum wind velocity was 68 miles an hour.

These velocities seem rather low by comparison with similar storms but they are true winds, a correction having been applied as explained in Chapter 1.

The tide at Norfolk rose seven feet above the normal, flooding the downtown business section as never before known. There was a great deal of damage to resorts on the Maryland, Delaware and New Jersey coasts. There was great damage in northeastern North Carolina. At 8 p.m. of the 23rd, the storm was central near Washington, D.C., with much diminished intensity.

In Maryland the damage to property of all kinds, including crops, was estimated at $17,000,000.

On the afternoon of August 23, at Washington, the wind velocity decreased while the storm center was approaching, owing to its rapidly diminishing intensity.

On August 29 another tropical storm was moving westward to the north of Puerto Rico, having been first observed on the 28th at about 19°N. and 55°W. The path it followed is quite uncommon and closely parallels the course of "Antje's Hurricane" of August and September 1842, as shown in Figure 74.

On the 30th, as it passed Turks Island, the storm was of marked intensity, though apparently of rather small diameter. The S.S. *Jamaica Pioneer* on August 30 was very near but slightly to the north and west of Turks Island with minimum pressure 27.47 inches. The ship was in the center of the storm but clear skies were not observed. Three days later, the S.S. *Harvester* recorded 27.99 inches in this same storm, at approximately 25°N. and 86°W. Hurricane winds attended the storm as it passed along the northern coast of Cuba where there was considerable loss of life and much property damage.

During the late afternoon of September 1 the barometer at Havana read 28.92 inches as the storm center passed a short distance north of the city. The highest wind velocity at Havana was 94 miles an hour from the south.

The center passed inland a short distance north of Brownsville during the night of September 4 to 5. At 1:30 a.m., the barometer reading 28.02 inches and wind estimated at 80 miles an hour, the height of the storm was reached. According to estimates at the time, there were twenty-two known dead in that general area and property damage amounting to millions of dollars.

This storm had not reached Cuba, however, before another appeared to the northeastward of Puerto Rico and followed it, travelling somewhat more to the northward. It arrived off Turks Island on the evening of September 1 where the S.S. *Gulf Wing* reported a barometer reading of 28.98 inches and wind 80 miles an hour. Thus it appears to have already developed full hurricane intensity. During the morning of September 3, the center passed over Harbour Island, Bahamas, and there was a calm lasting thirty minutes, preceded by hurricane winds estimated at 140 miles an hour. At midnight of the 3rd and 4th, the calm center passed over Jupiter Inlet, barometer 27.98 inches, the calm lasting forty minutes. Wind at Jupiter was estimated at 125 miles an hour. There was considerable property damage in Florida, principally in the area between Jupiter and Fort Pierce.

Recurving slowly, the storm dissipated over Georgia.

The first September hurricane, thirteenth storm of the season, was definitely located on the 10th at about 20°N. and 59°W. Disturbed conditions had been previously reported to the eastward of the Leeward Islands from the 7th to 9th of September. A report from the S.S. *Washington* gave minimum pressure in the storm, on September 11, at 23° 15′ N. and 61° 40′ W., at 27.96 inches.

At Cape Hatteras the lowest barometer reading was approximately 28.25 inches about 7 a.m. of September 16, when the center passed a short distance west of the Weather Bureau station. Preceding the arrival of the center, the maximum wind was 68 miles an hour; after the center passed it rose to an estimated velocity of 76 miles, one of the anemometer cups having been blown away.

Up to this time the storm had followed a path similar to the Hatteras-Norfolk hurricane of August, but it recurved to the north and northeast off the Atlantic coast. At Norfolk and Cape Henry the wind was high, maximum 68 miles northeast at Cape Henry, but there was considerably less damage in that section than in the August storm. South of the Virginia Capes to New Bern, N.C., the hurricane was very severe. Old residents of Beaufort, N.C., declared it the worst storm they had ever experienced. Twenty-one lives were lost and property damage along the North Carolina coast was estimated at more than $1,000,000.

On the following day, September 16, a storm was located to the southeastward of Barbados. This storm also crossed the Mexican coast at Tampico. Its early history from the 16th, southeast of Barbados, through the Caribbean Sea is uncertain. It was traced as a disturbed condition without definite center or winds of storm velocity until the 20th. On that day the S.S. *Virginia* went through the center of the storm. Observations on the *Virginia* show that it was a hurricane of extremely small diameter and great violence. The account from the *Virginia* was received later by mail.

The barometer readings in this account have been corrected so that they represent true pressures as verified by comparison with a standard mercurial instrument. At 8 p.m. the reading was 28.74 inches; at 8:20 it was 27.40; this represents a most remarkable fall of an inch and a third in twenty minutes. The rise was nearly as rapid, from 27.40 to 28.60 at 9:00 p.m. A fall of an inch an hour has been considered remarkable in other storms.

The report of the *Virginia* shows that the diameter of the circle of pressure of 29.50 inches was only about fifty miles and that the calm center was about ten or twelve miles in diameter.

The hurricane thereafter moved west by north, entering the Yucatan Peninsula about forty miles south of Cozumel Island near midnight of the 21st and thence across the southwestern Gulf of Mexico and inland just south of Tampico on the 24th. Storm damage in the city of Tampico was very great and many lives were lost.

Unsettled conditions continued over the southwestern Caribbean Sea and on the 1st of October a shallow depression appeared and started northward. On the 2nd and 3rd it moved due northward between Jamaica and Swan Island. During October 4 the center moved over Havana, with a calm alternating with light winds from 10 a.m. until noon. The lowest reading at Havana was 28.81 inches.

There were two other tropical storms in October. One originated northeast of the Bahamas about the 26th or 27th and attained considerable force after moving northward into the Atlantic. The other was first detected over the Caribbean Sea south of Jamaica where it probably existed for several days as a slight barometric depression. By the morning of October 28, it had developed considerable force. From October 28 to November 4 it moved slowly along an irregular course across Jamaica, eastern Cuba and the Bahamas, from where it turned northeastward into the Atlantic.

In extreme western Jamaica on October 29 it attained great force. The wind was estimated at 100 to 120 miles an hour. Large trees were uprooted along the track of the storm center. Many buildings were destroyed and ten lives were lost. The calm center reached Savanna-la-Mar at about 2:30 p.m. of the 29th, lowest barometer reading about 29.00 inches.

## 1934

Eleven tropical disturbances were reported from the Atlantic, Caribbean and Gulf during 1934. Of these, six were of hurricane force or very near it, but no tropical storm of more than ordinary intensity reached the coasts of the United States. The tracks of four of them were quite unusual.

The May disturbance appeared to the westward of the Florida Straits on the 27th, crossed southern Florida into the Atlantic and then turned north-northwestward into the interior between Savannah and Charleston on the 29th. At Charleston the maximum wind was 53 miles an hour from the southeast.

The June storm seems to have developed over the Bay of Honduras. Records indicate that it described two loops counter-clockwise, as shown in the track chart. (Fig. 111.) It attained marked strength by the 15th in the central Gulf. On the 16th it crossed the Louisiana coast, moving at the unusually rapid rate of about 27 miles an hour. At Morgan City the lowest barometer reading was 28.90 and the highest wind 68 miles, southeast. At Jeanerette the lowest was 28.52 inches. Six persons were killed in Louisiana and damage was placed at $2,605,000.

The track of the July storm was most unusual. It appears to have developed off the coast of the Carolinas on July 21. It then moved south and southwest as a very mild disturbance, across Florida and then westward through the Gulf. To the southward of Louisiana on the 24th it developed rapidly in strength and crossed the Texas coast a short distance north of Corpus Christi on the 25th, with lowest pressure 29.12 and highest wind 52 miles, south. Higher winds were undoubtedly experienced to the northward of Corpus Christi. Damage was variously estimated from $1,000,000 to $2,000,000. Eleven deaths were directly or indirectly attributed to the storm in Texas.

Early in September a storm of full hurricane force appeared east of the Bahamas, skirted the Atlantic coast, passed over Cape Hatteras, crossed Long Island Sound and went inland. It was first observed on the 5th and disappeared on the 9th. Many ships in its path experienced hurricane winds. Lowest barometer reading reported was 28.56 inches on the *Albert Watts*. The rescue of passengers from the *Morro*

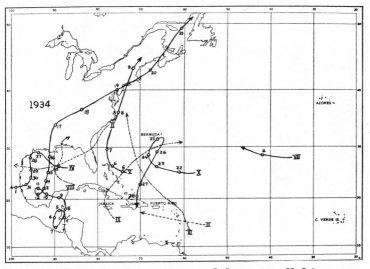

FIGURE 111.   Tracks of tropical storms of 1934. I. June 4 to 21; II. July 21 to 25; III. August 20 to 22; IV. August 26 to September 1; V. September 5 to 9; VI. September 15 to 21; VII. October 1 to 2; VIII. October 3 to 5; IX. October 19 to 23; X. November 21 to 28.

*Castle*, then burning off the New Jersey coast, was hampered by the winds of this hurricane.

On October 1 a hurricane was reported in the Atlantic at about 29°N., 42°W. It was charted on a very short course north-northwestward to about 30°N., 45°W. Two other disturbances in October were of minor character. One reached the coast near Pensacola on the 5th where it was attended by a record rainfall of 15.29 inches in 24 hours.

In November another tropical storm with a very unusual track was first observed southeast of Bermuda on the 21st. It described a clockwise loop to the southwest of Bermuda and then progressed south-southwestward to Haiti. Lowest pressure was 28.20 inches on the S.S. *Malacca*. This storm was of full hurricane force.

## 1935

Hurricane activity in 1935 was late in beginning but the season was rather remarkable for the violence of its storms. Five occurred, all of hurricane intensity. (Fig. 112.)

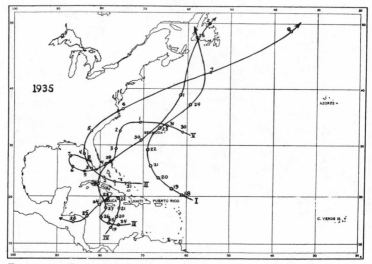

FIGURE 112. Tracks of tropical storms of 1935. I. August 18 to 25; II. August 31 to September 8; III. September 23 to October 2; IV. October 19 to 26; V. October 30 to November 8.

The first appeared on August 18 near 20°N., 60°W., recurved in the Atlantic southwestward of Bermuda, and finally dissipated over Newfoundland. The lowest barometer reading, 28.20 inches, was recorded on the S.S. *Angelina* at 5 a.m. of August 21 at about 27°N., 68½°W. On striking Newfoundland on the 25th, it caused much damage to the fishing fleets and considerable loss of life on the Grand Banks and on the coasts of Newfoundland and Labrador. In many respects this storm was quite similar to the famous "Nova Scotia hurricane" of August 1873.

As one of the most violent of record in the world, the second storm of 1935 is known as the "Labor Day hurricane." It was first sighted east and north of Turks Island, from whence it travelled toward the Florida Straits, but with a broad recurve which brought it to the Florida Keys late on September 2. By that time it was of small diameter but of tremendous force.

At Long and Matecumbe Keys it was attended by a storm wave which reached a height variously estimated at 15 to 20 feet above mean low water. (See Chapter 11.) The lowest barometer reading,

26.35 inches near the north end of Long Key, is a record for the western hemisphere. (See Chapter VI.)

About seven hundred World War veterans were located at relief camps at the point where the hurricane crossed the Keys. Acting upon warnings from the Weather Bureau, the Florida East Coast Railroad, at the request of camp officials, dispatched a rescue train on September 2 to remove the veterans and native civilians. The train was delayed, reaching the camps at about 8:30 p.m., approximately an hour before the center of the storm arrived. The wind and sea were then so violent that the train, with the exception of locomotive and tender, was swept from the tracks. (Fig. 20.) The loss of life among veterans was 121, with 90 missing and about 100 that were injured more or less seriously. About 165 civilians lost their lives, making a total of identified dead, missing and unaccounted for, nearly 400.

The S.S. *Dixie* endeavored to run through the Florida Straits ahead of the hurricane but its broad recurve brought the center somewhat to the northward and the vessel was caught in high winds and heavy seas and went on French Reef on September 2 but was refloated on September 19. The American tanker *Pueblo* drifted helplessly in the storm from 2 to 10 p.m. of the 2nd and was carried completely around the storm center, arriving within twenty-five miles of her original position after eight hours.

There was a calm of forty minutes on Lower Matecumbe Key and about fifty-five minutes at the Long Key fishing camp, 9:20 to 10:15 p.m. The rate of progress of the hurricane was about ten miles an hour and the calm center must have been nine or ten miles in diameter.

After leaving the Keys, the storm skirted the Florida Gulf coast on a broad recurve, passed inland at Cedar Keys and finally left the continent near Cape Henry. The damage occasioned by this hurricane was estimated to be somewhat in excess of $6,000,000, practically all of which occurred in Florida.

On September 23, a disturbance formed over the Caribbean Sea southwest of Haiti from where it moved westward, then northward across Cuba on the 28th and reached Newfoundland on October 2. There was heavy property damage in Cuba during its passage on the 28th, barometer 28.31 at Cienfuegos. Casualties in Cuba were estimated at 35 deaths and a possible 500 injured. At Bimini, very early on the 29th, the barometer read 27.90 inches an hour before the center passed. Wind there was estimated at 120 miles an hour. The tide at Bimini was reported to have risen fifteen feet. More than half the dwellings on the island were damaged and fourteen persons were killed.

The fourth storm of 1935 has been called the "hairpin hurricane" because of the shape of its track. It formed in the western Caribbean Sea between October 17 and 19 and moved over an unprecedented track. It first went eastward past Jamaica, then to the south coast of extreme eastern Cuba, after which it turned southwestward and passed inland over Honduras as a destructive storm and then dissipated.

It produced one of the major disasters of West Indian history; the losses and damage occurred almost wholly on land areas where the hurricane winds impinged on mountainous territory and caused torrential rains and devastating floods.

In the first branch of its track it crossed Navassa Island on October 21 and approached the coast of Cuba near Santiago early on the 22nd. Torrential rains occurred over extreme southwestern Haiti where the loss of life was placed at two thousand. In Jamaica property damage was put at $2,000,000. A schooner and its entire crew was lost off Port Antonio. There was considerable damage at Santiago.

Leaving Cuba with somewhat diminished force it crossed the Caribbean again with increasing force and struck Honduras near Cape Gracias on the 25th. Much damage to property and banana plantations occurred in Honduras. About one hundred fifty lives were lost there.

The track of the next storm was even more erratic than its predecessor. It was called the "Yankee storm" in Miami because it came from the north much later in the season than usual. It was seemingly of extratropical origin, since it appeared as a weak disturbance east of Bermuda early on October 30. It progressed west-by-north, passed close to but north of Bermuda, increased in intensity and threatened the Carolina coasts on the morning of November 1. During the night of November 1, however, it shifted its course to the southwest and then on the 2nd toward the south to the northern Bahamas from where it moved directly across Miami and into the eastern Gulf, where it finally dissipated.

The lowest pressure recorded was 28.46 inches on the S.S. *Queen of Bermuda* at 10 a.m. of November 3 at about 28°N., 76½°W.

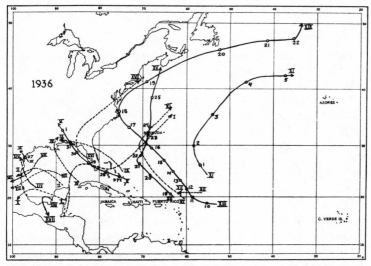

FIGURE 113.    Tracks of tropical storms of 1936. I. June 11 to 17; II. June 19 to 21; III. June 26, 27; IV. July 26 to 28; V. July 27 to August 1; VI. August 4 to 9; VII. August 8 to 12; VIII. August 15 to 19; IX. August 20 to 22; X. August 28 to 30; XI. August 28 to September 5; XII. September 7, 8; XVIII. September 8 to 26; XIV. September 11 to 13; XV. September 19 to 24; XVI. September 25 to October 1; XVII. October 9, 10.

At Miami, directly in the path of the hurricane, the lowest pressure was 28.73 inches, highest wind 75 miles an hour. The lull at the center lasted slightly more than an hour. In Florida and the Bahamas loss of life was placed at nineteen. Property loss in Miami and vicinity was estimated at $5,500,000. H. R. Byers, who investigated the unusual movement of this hurricane, found a strong north to south drift of the upper air which apparently accounts for the hurricane's unusual movement to lower latitudes beginning on November 1.

### 1936

Tropical disturbances were very frequent during the 1936 storm season but in average intensity these disturbances as a group were below normal. (Fig. 113.) The outstanding features were, first, the hurricane of great diameter about the middle of September and, second, the large expanse of the Caribbean Sea that was not visited, so far as reports disclose, by any tropical disturbance worthy of note;

the paths of the seventeen disturbances of the season lay almost entirely in the Gulf and Atlantic.

On the night of June 26-27, a hurricane of very small diameter but considerable force developed in the extreme western Gulf and moved inland over Port Aransas shortly before noon of the 27th. Wind was estimated at 80 miles an hour. There was no loss of life; property damage was placed at $550,000 mostly to oil refining property.

There were two tropical disturbances in July. The first moved from extreme western Cuba to southern Louisiana from the 25th to 27th. No loss of life and no important storm damage occurred in Louisiana. The second storm appeared north of Turks Island on the 26th, crossed Florida about 30 miles south of Miami at 8 p.m. of the 28th and on the 31st passed over Choctawhatchee Bay, about forty-five miles east of Pensacola. At the Miami airport the wind blew 49 miles an hour with gusts at 65. The calm center was over Fort Walton and Valparaiso about one hour and twenty minutes, lowest barometer 28.73 and wind estimated at 90 to 100. Damage in Florida was about $150,000. The fishing boat *Ketchum* was lost in the Gulf with four persons aboard.

On September 8 another disturbance was developing in the vicinity of 13°N., 50°W. It moved slowly northwestward, gaining in intensity. By the morning of the 15th this hurricane was of wide extent and marked intensity. On the 16th the area of winds of force 6 and higher (Beaufort scale) was about one thousand miles in diameter. By that criterion it was one of the largest tropical cyclones of record.

The storm center recurved near Hatteras early on the 18th and skirted the North Atlantic coast on the 19th and 20th. A considerable number of ships were heavily involved in or very near the hurricane center.

In the vicinity of Hatteras the hurricane was one of the most severe of record. The maximum wind was 80 miles, northwest (corrected). At Cape Henry the anemometer failed, hence the highest wind was not recorded. At Norfolk it was considered the worst storm that had ever visited that section. Extensive preparations had been made on Weather Bureau warnings and property loss was much reduced and loss of human life avoided. The total damage in the Norfolk area and the coastal area of North Carolina was about $1,600,000. Two deaths were indirectly attributed to the hurricane.

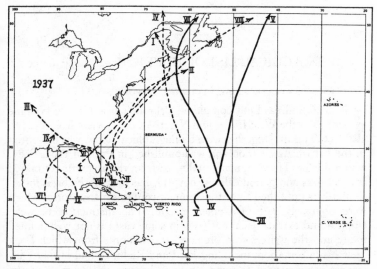

FIGURE 114. Tracks of tropical storms of 1937. I. July 29 to August 2; II. August 2 to 8; III. August 28 to September 2; IV. September 9 to 14; V. September 14 to 20; VI. September 16 to 21; VII. September 20 to 26; VIII. September 26 to 30; IX. September 30 to October 2.

## 1937

Tropical disturbances of 1937 were similar to those of 1936 in two particulars—a large proportion of them were not of hurricane force and practically all of the Caribbean Sea was unaffected. Only two of the ten disturbances of 1937 were known to be of full hurricane intensity (Nos. V and VII in Figure 114).

The storm which was in progress from the 9th to the 14th of September (No. IV) caused the British racing yacht *Endeavor I* to break loose from its tow when 200 miles east of Nantucket Lightship on the 13th; the yacht was lost until the 22nd when it was sighted 260 miles east of Fastnet Rock.

Four disturbances crossed the coast of the United States in low latitudes. Some damage to highways, bridges and electric wires resulted but none of them was of marked violence.

A moderate disturbance in the Gulf of Mexico from November 24 to 26 dissipated before reaching land. There is some doubt that it was of tropical origin, hence its track is not shown.

# CHAPTER XV

# CHRONOLOGICAL LIST OF HURRICANES, 1494 to 1900

## EXTRATROPICAL CYCLONES IN POËY'S LISTS

IN 1856 Andreas Poëy completed a chronological table of cyclonic storms of the West Indies and North Atlantic Ocean from 1493 to 1855. This list, together with bibliographical notes, was presented to the British Association and was published in Paris in 1862. Poëy, who resided at Havana, made up his list from the accounts contained in 450 books and periodicals. Although it has formed the basis for all similar lists published since that time, it contains many storms which were obviously not of tropical origin. The distinction between tropical and extratropical cyclones in some cases is not well defined today and the writers who prepared the accounts from which Poëy drew his information, including Reid and Redfield, had in many instances insufficient data upon which to base a conclusion as to the locality in which the cyclone originated. Many cyclones which are generated in temperate latitudes move to the subtropics, especially in winter, and on turning again to higher latitudes become storms of great energy. Many of these were included in Poëy's list. His first "hurricane," February 12, 1493, as has been previously stated, was one of this class.

Other lists have since been prepared by Blodgett, Finley, Alexander, Garriott, Fassig, and a number of others. Some have attempted to eliminate the extratropical cyclones from Poëy's table.

Without any exact information as to the point of origin of the doubtful storms, the time of year in which the storm occurred is used as a criterion for accepting or rejecting the record. This is only partially satisfactory because cyclones of undoubted tropical origin occur, though infrequently, in May and December. To a less degree the occurrences in June and November are doubtful.

There is another source of questionable data in Poëy's list. A hurricane may appear in one locality and at some later time in its path may show up in another region. Unless we have exact information as to the path of the storm after its first appearance, we may incorrectly conclude that the second appearance is that of a separate and distinct storm. No doubt there are errors of this kind in Poëy's list and in some of the accounts collected since that date.

### VALUE OF THE EARLY CHRONOLOGY

A chronological table is valuable, however, because it is reasonable to assume that all of the really great hurricanes which have been destructive to life and property on the islands of the West Indies and on the southern coasts of the United States have entered into the historical records of those regions. The dates are undoubtedly dependable. From these lists we can safely draw conclusions as to the frequency, the time of year, and the destructive character, of tropical storms which have visited sections inhabited since the early years of the record.

When such conclusions are drawn, they are found to be, in the main, in agreement with findings from the more exact records of recent years.

In the following table, the writer has used Poëy's list for the months from June to November, inclusive, and has eliminated all which occurred in other months. Where there is unquestioned evidence that the same storm has been listed twice, only one entry has been made in the table. The list has been extended to and including 1900, from every available source, but chiefly, for the period from 1871 to 1900, from the records of the U.S. Weather Bureau. In the years prior to 1856, there were some tropical storms not contained in Poëy's list and a number of additions have been made from various sources.

Dates are given in the table when known; in the later records, the dates include the entire period during which the storm was of sufficient importance to justify mention. In some of the earlier cases only one date is known; it usually applies to the first place named, e.g. if the entry is "1813, July 26, Bahamas, Bermuda" it does not mean that the storm was centered near both of those places during the course of one day. The date indicates the time the storm was near the first place named, though there is not much assurance in this respect in the earlier records.

Roman numerals refer to the number of the chapter in which a more extended account of the storm appears. All tropical storms worthy of note are discussed in Chapter XIV for the period 1901 to 1937, inclusive.

LIST OF TROPICAL STORMS OF THE NORTH ATLANTIC,
INCLUDING THE GULF OF MEXICO AND CARIB-
BEAN SEA, FROM 1494 TO 1900.

| Date of Storm | Principal Places Affected, and Remarks |
|---|---|
| 1494, June 16 | Santo Domingo. XII. |
| 1494, July 16 | Cape Santa Cruz. XII. Possibly same as preceding. |
| 1494, August | Santo Domingo. XII. |
| 1495, October | Santo Domingo. XII. |
| 1498, ——— | Cuba. Damaged fleet of Admiral Colon, en route Cuba to Spain. |
| 1500, August | West Indies. |
| 1502, July 1, 2 | Santo Domingo. XII. |
| 1504, October 19 | Atlantic. |
| 1508, August 3 | Santo Domingo. XII. |
| 1509, July 29 | Santo Domingo. XII. |
| 1510, July | Santo Domingo. |
| 1515, July | Puerto Rico. Caused the death of many Indians. |
| 1526, October 4, 5 | Puerto Rico and Santo Domingo. Great damage on both islands. |
| 1527, October 4 | Trinidad, Puerto Rico, Cuba. Destroyed naval fleet of Admiral Narvaez. |
| 1530, July 26 | Puerto Rico. |
| 1530, August 23 | Puerto Rico. |
| 1530, August 31 | Puerto Rico. This and the two preceding storms within six weeks blew down half the houses in San Juan; the remainder were unroofed. Great damage on the island; many cattle drowned. |
| 1537, July and August | Puerto Rico. Three hurricanes within two months; exact dates not known. Many slaves and cattle drowned. Great distress among the people. |
| 1548, ——— | Santo Domingo. |
| 1557, ——— | Cuba. Furious hurricane over the whole island. |
| 1565, ——— | West Indies. |
| 1568, August 24 | Puerto Rico. |
| 1575, September 21 | Puerto Rico. Known as "San Mateo." |
| 1583, September 9 | Atlantic. |

| Date of Storm | Principal Places Affected, and Remarks |
|---|---|
| 1588, ———— | Cuba. A furious hurricane at Havana. More destructive than that of 1557. |
| 1591, August 10 | Atlantic. Fleet en route from Havana to Spain. Commander and 500 men perished. |
| 1591, August 14 | Atlantic. Five or six ships lost. |
| 1591, August (end of month) | Atlantic. Twenty-two ships sunk. |
| 1591, September 6 | Atlantic. |
| 1609, July 25 | Atlantic. |
| 1615, September 12 | Puerto Rico. Severest hurricane in 40 years. |
| 1623, September 19 | Windward Islands. |
| 1635, August | Windward Islands. Violent gale between St. Kitts and Martinique. |
| 1642, ———— | Martinique. |
| 1642, ———— | St. Kitts, Martinique, Guadeloupe. Second hurricane of the year. Twenty-three vessels wrecked at St. Kitts. XII. |
| 1642, ———— | West Indies. |
| 1650, ———— | St. Kitts. |
| 1651, ———— | Martinique. |
| 1652, ———— | Martinique, Guadeloupe, St. Kitts. |
| 1653, July 13 | St. Vincent. |
| 1653, October 1 | St. Vincent. |
| 1656, ———— | Guadeloupe. XII. |
| 1656, ———— | Antilles. Possibly same as preceding. |
| 1657, ———— | Guadeloupe. |
| 1658, ———— | Antilles. |
| 1660, ———— | Antilles. |
| 1664, October 22, 23 | Guadeloupe, Antigua. XII. |
| 1665, August | Leeward Islands. |
| 1665, October | West Indies. |
| 1666, August 4, 5 | Guadeloupe, Martinique, St. Kitts. XII. |
| 1666, September 1 | Leeward Islands. |
| 1667, August 19 | Barbados, Nevis. |
| 1667, September 1 | St. Kitts. XII. |
| 1670, August 18 | Near Barbados. |
| 1670, October 7 | Jamaica. English fleet driven ashore. |
| 1674, June | Bay of Campeche. |
| 1674, August 10 | Barbados. XII. |
| 1675, August 31 | Barbados. Island devastated again. Crops destroyed. |
| 1680, August 14 | Santo Domingo. |

| *Date of Storm* | *Principal Places Affected, and Remarks* |
|---|---|
| 1681, August 27 | Antigua, St. Kitts. XII. |
| 1681, October 4 | St. Kitts. XII. |
| 1683, August 26-31 | Atlantic. Encountered by Dampier. |
| 1689, ———— | Jamaica. Not very severe. |
| 1691, ———— | Antilles. |
| 1692, June | Jamaica. |
| 1692, October 24 | Cuba. Storm of "San Rafael" in Havana. |
| 1694, August 13 | Barbados. |
| 1694, October 17 | Barbados. |
| 1695, October 2 | Martinique. |
| 1700, ———— | Barbados. |
| 1700, September 16 | Charleston. Inundation; many lives lost. |
| 1702, ———— | Barbados. |
| 1707, ———— | Nevis, Antigua. |
| 1711, September 11-13 | New Orleans. Destroyed St. Louis Cathedral. |
| 1712, August 28 | Jamaica. First great hurricane experienced by the English at Jamaica. |
| 1712, October | Havana. |
| 1713, ———— | Guadeloupe, St. Thomas. |
| 1713, September 16, 17 | Charleston. A great hurricane, attended by an immense inundation from the sea. Many vessels driven ashore. Possibly same as preceding. |
| 1714, August 13, 14 | Guadeloupe. |
| 1714, August 29 | Jamaica. Men-of-war driven ashore. |
| 1714, ———— | Cuba. Possibly same storm as preceding. |
| 1718, September | Nevis. |
| 1720, ———— | Barbados. |
| 1722, August 28 | Jamaica. XII. |
| 1722, August 31 | Antilles. |
| 1723, ———— | New Orleans. "A remarkable hurricane nearly destroyed all buildings." |
| 1725, ———— | Martinique. |
| 1726, October 22 | Jamaica. Blew down many houses; sank or wrecked many vessels. |
| 1728, August 19 | Antigua. |
| 1728, August | Charleston. |
| 1728, September 14 | Charleston. Town inundated. Twenty-three ships driven ashore. |
| 1730, ———— | Cuba. Destroyed the Paula Hospital in Havana. |
| 1731, ———— | Barbados. |

| *Date of Storm* | *Principal Places Affected, and Remarks* |
|---|---|
| 1732, ———— | Mobile. A destructive storm. |
| 1733, June | St. Kitts. |
| 1733, July 16 | Cuba. Strong storm throughout the island. |
| 1734, September 1 | Jamaica. |
| 1736, ———— | Pensacola. Village swept away. |
| 1737, September 9 | Santo Domingo, St. Kitts. |
| 1738, September 12 | Guadeloupe, St. Thomas, Puerto Rico. |
| 1739, September 9 | Antilles. |
| 1740, August | Antigua, Martinique, Dominica. |
| 1740, ———— | Puerto Rico. Probably same as preceding. |
| 1740, September 12 | Mouth of Mississippi, Pensacola. |
| 1742, ———— | St. Thomas. |
| 1743, September | West Indies. |
| 1744, October 20 | Jamaica. |
| 1744, November | Cuba. Hurricane followed by a plague of worms. |
| 1745, ———— | West Indies. |
| 1747, September 21 | Leeward Islands. Violent. |
| 1747, October 24 | Leeward Islands. This hurricane and the preceding one did great damage in the islands. Fifty ships lost. |
| 1751, July 6 | Haiti. |
| 1751, August 10 | Jamaica. |
| 1751, August 18 | Puerto Rico. |
| 1751, September 2 | Jamaica. |
| 1751, September 15 | Santo Domingo. |
| 1751, September 21-22 | Santo Domingo. |
| 1751, October | Jamaica, Santo Domingo. |
| 1752, September 15 | Charleston. All wooden houses above one story in height were either beaten down or shattered. |
| 1752, September | Charleston. Two hurricanes at Charleston in one month. Neither was felt 100 miles in the interior. |
| 1753, September 15 | Charleston. |
| 1754, September (13-15?) | Leeward Islands. Santo Domingo. Great damage to sugar and indigo plantations. Twelve ships driven ashore. |
| 1755, November 1 | Cuba. Gulf waters inundated Havana. |
| 1756, August 23 | Barbados. |
| 1756, September 12 | Martinique. |
| 1756, October 2, 3 | Cuba. |

| *Date of Storm* | *Principal Places Affected, and Remarks* |
|---|---|
| 1756, ——— | Coast of Georgia. Possibly one of the three preceding storms. |
| 1757, ——— | Atlantic coast, Florida to Boston. |
| 1757, August 29 | Barbados. |
| 1758, August 23 | Coast of South Carolina. |
| 1759, September | Gulf of Mexico, Florida. XII. |
| 1761, June 1 | Charleston. |
| 1765, July 31 | Martinique, Guadeloupe. |
| 1765, September | Martinique, St. Kitts, Guadeloupe. |
| 1765, November 13, 14 | Santo Domingo. |
| 1766, August 13 | Martinique. Town of St. Pierre ravaged. Ninety lives lost. Thirty-five ships wrecked. |
| 1766, August 16 | Jamaica. Probably same storm as preceding. |
| 1766, September 4 | Galveston. |
| 1766, September 11 | Virginia. |
| 1766, September 13, 14, 15 | St. Kitts and Montserrat. |
| 1766, September 21 | St. Eustatius and Tortugas. |
| 1766, October 6, 7 | Dominica, Guadeloupe, St. Kitts. Fifty-five ships driven ashore. |
| 1766, October 22 | Pensacola. Spanish fleet en route from Vera Cruz to Havana wrecked. |
| 1767, August 7 | Puerto Rico. Plantations destroyed and live stock drowned. |
| 1768, August 12 | Grenada. |
| 1768, ——— | Antigua. XII. |
| 1768, October 15 | Cuba. |
| 1768, October 25 | Cuba. Brief but violent in Havana. Over 4,000 houses destroyed, including 93 public buildings. One thousand lives lost. XII. |
| 1769, August 30 | Florida. |
| 1769, October 29 | Florida. |
| 1770, June 6 | Charleston. |
| 1771, August | St. Eustatius. |
| 1772, August 4 | Dominica. |
| 1772, August 16 | Cuba. |
| 1772, August 17 | Antigua. |
| 1772, August 28 | Puerto Rico, Jamaica. |
| 1772, August 31– September 4 | Leeward Islands, Antigua, Virgin Islands, Puerto Rico, Jamaica. XII. Louisiana. |
| 1772, October 18 | Leeward Islands. |

| *Date of Storm* | *Principal Places Affected, and Remarks* |
|---|---|
| 1772, November 22 | St. Kitts, St. Eustatius. |
| 1773, July | St. Thomas, Cuba. |
| 1773, August | Boston. |
| 1774, September 6 | Guadeloupe. |
| 1774, October 2 | Jamaica. |
| 1775, July 30-August 1 | St. Croix, Martinique, Puerto Rico. A furious hurricane. |
| 1775, August 25 | Martinique. |
| 1775, August 27 | Santo Domingo. Probably same storm as preceding. |
| 1775, September 14 | Cuba, Santo Domingo. |
| 1775, October 16 | St. Kitts. |
| 1776, ——— | New Orleans. |
| 1776, September 4, 5, 6, 7 | Martinique, Guadeloupe, St. Kitts, Puerto Rico, Antigua. Severe at Puerto Rico. |
| 1778, October 28 | Cuba. |
| 1779, October 7-10 | New Orleans. |
| 1780, June 13 | Puerto Rico, St. Lucia. Great destruction of property, especially crops. |
| 1780, August 24 | New Orleans. Swept over the province of Louisiana, destroying crops, tearing down buildings and sinking every vessel and boat afloat on the Mississippi River. |
| 1780, August 25 | St. Kitts. |
| 1780, October 3 | Jamaica, Cuba. The Savanna-la-Mar storm. XII. |
| 1780, October 10-18 | Barbados, Antigua, Dominica, Tobago, Grenada, St. Vincent, Santo Domingo, etc. "The Great Hurricane." X, XII. |
| 1780, October 16, 17 | Cuba. Solano's Storm. XII. |
| 1780, October 31 | Barbados. |
| 1781, August 1 | Jamaica. Passed near Kingston. Ninety vessels went ashore, 30 wrecked at Port Royal. |
| 1781, August 10 | North Carolina. |
| 1781, August 23 | New Orleans. |
| 1781, September 5 | Santo Domingo. |
| 1782, July 25 | Atlantic. |
| 1782, July 31, August 1 | Kingston, Jamaica. |
| 1782, September 16 | Atlantic. |
| 1783, ——— | Charleston. |

| *Date of Storm* | *Principal Places Affected, and Remarks* |
|---|---|
| 1784, July 30 | Jamaica, Santo Domingo. In Jamaica, buildings were destroyed, many lives lost and all vessels damaged or wrecked. |
| 1785, July 6 | West Indies. |
| 1785, July 25 | St. Croix. |
| 1785, August 25 | Guadeloupe, St. Kitts. Great damage to shipping. |
| 1785, August 27 | Jamaica. Possibly same as preceding. |
| 1785, August 31 | Guadeloupe, Barbados, Santo Domingo. |
| 1785, September 22-24 | Carolinas and Virginia. |
| 1785, September 25 | Puerto Rico. "A furious hurricane passed over the island." |
| 1785, September 27 | Santo Domingo. Probably same as preceding. |
| 1786, August 11 | Barbados, St. Eustatius, Santo Domingo. |
| 1786, August 29 | United States. |
| 1786, September 2 | Barbados. Many persons killed in ruins of their own houses. |
| 1786, September 10 | Guadeloupe. |
| 1786, October 5 | Barbados, Grenada. |
| 1786, October 20 | Jamaica. Shores were covered with aquatic birds killed by dashing against the mangroves. Storm followed by a great scarcity of food. |
| 1787, July | Guadeloupe, French Islands. |
| 1787, July 30 | United States. Possibly same as preceding. |
| 1787, August 3 | Dominica. |
| 1787, August 15 | Florida. |
| 1787, August 23 | Dominica. |
| 1787, August 29 | Dominica. Three gales in Dominica in one month. |
| 1787, September 2 | Honduras. |
| 1787, September 19 | Atlantic coast. |
| 1787, September 23 | Belize. A severe hurricane attended by heavy rains. Sea rose and great damage was caused by the overflow. Many lives lost. |
| 1788, July 22 | Atlantic coast. |
| 1788, August 14 | Martinique. |
| 1788, August 16 | Puerto Rico, Santo Domingo. Probably same as preceding. |
| 1788, August 19 | United States. This and two preceding storms possibly all the same one. |
| 1788, August 29 | Dominica. |

| *Date of Storm* | *Principal Places Affected, and Remarks* |
|---|---|
| 1788, September 19-20 | United States. |
| 1790, July 31 | Jamaica. |
| 1790, August | Nevis, Tobago. XII. |
| 1791, June 21 | Cuba. Greatest flood ever remembered in the country about Havana. Three thousand persons and 11,700 head of cattle perished. |
| 1791, September 27 | Cuba. |
| 1791, October 20 | Jamaica. |
| 1792, July 14 | St. Kitts. |
| 1792, August 1, 2 | Antigua, St. Kitts and (August 6th) Bermuda. A terrific flood at St. Kitts which caused loss of many lives and destruction of much property; made havoc with shipping. |
| 1792, September 10 | Antigua. |
| 1792, October 29 | Cuba. |
| 1793, August 12 | St. Kitts, St. Eustatius, St. Thomas. |
| 1794, August 27, 28 | Cuba. |
| 1794, October 27, 28 | Cuba. |
| 1795, August 10 | Jamaica. |
| 1795, August 18 | Antigua. |
| 1796, October 3 | Cuba, Bahamas. |
| 1796, October 24 | Cuba. |
| 1796, November 2 | Cuba. |
| 1797, September | Charleston. Wharves overflowed. |
| 1799, ———— | Cuba. On southern coast of island. |
| 1800, August | New Orleans. |
| 1800, October 14, 15 | Cuba. |
| 1800, November 2 | Santiago de Cuba. |
| 1801, July 22 | Nassau. |
| 1802, September 16 | Venezuela. |
| 1803, July 10 | Bahamas. |
| 1803, September 3 | West Indies. |
| 1804, August 29 | Jamaica. |
| 1804, September 3-9 | Antigua (3rd), Nassau (6th), Charleston (7th), Norfolk (8th), Boston (9th). Center kept near the coast and was very severe. Immense damage on the coasts of South Carolina and Georgia. XIII. |
| 1804, September 21 | Puerto Rico. A great hurricane known as "San Mateo," which long remained in the memory of the people. |
| 1804, September 22 | Jamaica. |

| *Date of Storm* | *Principal Places Affected, and Remarks* |
|---|---|
| 1804, October 4 | Savannah. |
| 1804, October 9 | United States. |
| 1805, July 27 | Jamaica. |
| 1805, July 29, 30 | Barbados. |
| 1806, August 30 | Bahamas. |
| 1806, September 9-11 | Dominica, Puerto Rico. XIII. |
| 1806, September 24 | Dominica. |
| 1806, September 27 | West Indies. Possibly same as preceding. |
| 1806, October 5 | Bahamas. |
| 1806, October 27 | Bahamas. |
| 1806, October 28 | Leeward Islands. |
| 1807, July 25 to 28 | St. Kitts, Montserrat. |
| 1807, August 17, 18, 19 | Puerto Rico. Severe hurricane from the east lasted 50 hours. |
| 1807, September 5 | Cuba, Bahamas. XIII. |
| 1809, July 27 | Dominica, Guadeloupe. |
| 1809, August 1-3 | Dominica, Guadeloupe. |
| 1809, September 2 | Guadeloupe, Puerto Rico. Probably same storm as the preceding one. |
| 1809, October 15 | Martinique. |
| 1809, October 18 | Trinidad. |
| 1810, June | Cuba. |
| 1810, August 12 | Trinidad, Barbados. |
| 1810, August 28 | Barbados. |
| 1810, September 28 | Cuba. |
| 1810, October 24, 25 | Cuba. Lowest barometer 29.35 inches at Havana. Called the "Salty Storm." |
| 1811, ———— | New Orleans. |
| 1811, September 7, 8 | Leeward Islands. |
| 1811, September 10 | Charleston. During the hurricane after the wind shifted from northeast to southeast, a tornado crossed the city, causing great destruction over a path 100 yards wide. Many lives lost. |
| 1812, July 23 | Puerto Rico. |
| 1812, August 14 | Jamaica. |
| 1812, August 19 | New Orleans. Possibly same as preceding. |
| 1812, August 21 | Puerto Rico. |
| 1812, October 12-14 | Jamaica, Cuba. Big storm at Trinidad, Cuba. At Jamaica there was great damage to houses, wharves and shipping. |
| 1813, July 20 | Bermuda. |

| *Date of Storm* | *Principal Places Affected, and Remarks* |
|---|---|
| 1813, July 22, 23 | Dominica, Martinique, Puerto Rico. |
| 1813, ——— | Dominica. The island suffered from two hurricanes which succeeded each other in a short time. XIII. |
| 1813, July 26 | Bahamas, Bermuda. |
| 1813, July 31, August 1 | Jamaica. Center passed over Kingston. |
| 1813, August 5-9 | Atlantic. May be same as preceding. |
| 1813, August 19 | Gulf coast. |
| 1813, August 25 | Dominica. Possibly the same as that at Jamaica on August 28. |
| 1813, August 27 | Charleston. Many persons drowned and vessels lost. Coast inundated. |
| 1813, August 28 | Jamaica. Storm at Savanna-la-Mar. |
| 1813, September 7, 8 | Leeward Islands. |
| 1813, November 19 | Nova Scotia. Storm may not have been of tropical origin. |
| 1813, ——— | Belize. |
| 1814, July 1 | Charleston. A tornado was reported within the hurricane area as was recorded in the case of the storm of 1811. |
| 1814, July 22, 23 | Puerto Rico. |
| 1815, July 25 | St. Kitts. |
| 1815, August 9 | Atlantic. |
| 1815, August 31 or September 1 | Leeward Islands. |
| 1815, September 18-24 | St. Bartholomews (18th), New York (22nd), coast of Rhode Island morning of 23rd. Very destructive. |
| 1815, September 20 | Turks Island. Doubtless same as preceding. |
| 1815, September 28 | South Carolina coast. |
| 1815, September 29 | Barbados. |
| 1815, October 18, 19 | Jamaica. Eastern half of island. Great damage by wind, flooding of rivers, and many lives were lost. |
| 1816, ——— | Puerto Rico. A hurricane of extraordinary violence. Great destruction of property. |
| 1816, September 15 | Barbados, Martinique, Dominica, St. Kitts. |
| 1816, October 16, 17 | Dominica, Bahamas. |
| 1817, September 8 | St. Kitts. |
| 1817, September 15 | Dominica. |
| 1817, October 21 | St. Vincent. |
| 1817, October 23 | Barbados, St. Lucia, Martinique. |

| Date of Storm | Principal Places Affected, and Remarks |
|---|---|
| 1818, August 28 | Bermuda. |
| 1818, September 10-12 | Cayman Islands, Bay of Campeche. |
| 1818, ———— | Galveston. Four of Lafitte's vessels sunk or driven ashore. |
| 1818, September 19 | Santo Domingo. |
| 1818, September 21, 22 | Barbados, Dominica, Puerto Rico. |
| 1818, September 27 | Barbados. |
| 1818, October 7 | Port Royal. |
| 1818, October 21 | St. Lucia. |
| 1818, November 18, 19, 20 | Jamaica. A hurricane swept over the west end of the island. Great damage. |
| 1819, August 25 | Dominica. |
| 1819, August 25 to 28 | Louisiana and Alabama. |
| 1819, September 21, 22 | St. Lucia, Barbados, Virgin Islands, Puerto Rico. Most destructive in the Virgin Islands but severe in Puerto Rico. |
| 1819, October 13, 15 | Barbados, St. Lucia. |
| 1819, October 28 | Cuba. |
| 1820, August 28 | St. Kitts. |
| 1821, September 1 | Guadeloupe. |
| 1821, September 1-4 | Turks Island, Long Island (U.S.). At New York there was great damage; the tide rose 13 feet in one hour. XIII. |
| 1821, September 9 | Antigua, St. Bartholomews, St. Kitts. |
| 1821, September 25 | New Haven, Conn. |
| 1821, ———— | Cuba. |
| 1821, ———— | New Orleans. |
| 1822, July 11 | Mobile. |
| 1822, August | Carolina coast. |
| 1822, September 27 | Carolinas. |
| 1824, ———— | Coast of Georgia. |
| 1824, July 26 | West Indies. |
| 1824, September 7, 8 | Guadeloupe. |
| 1825, July 25, 26, 27 | Dominica, Martinique, Guadeloupe, Puerto Rico. XIII. |
| 1825, October 1 | Cuba. Cienfuegos almost completely destroyed. |
| 1826, August 18 | Antilles. |
| 1826, November 6-9 | Atlantic. |
| 1826, ———— | Cuba. |
| 1827, July 30 | North Carolina coast. |

| *Date of Storm* | *Principal Places Affected, and Remarks* |
|---|---|
| 1827, August 17-28 | Windward Islands, near Hatteras. Very destructive in West Indies. XIII. |
| 1827, August 28 | St. Thomas, Virgin Islands. Not the same storm as preceding one. |
| 1827, September 7 | North Atlantic. |
| 1827, October 11 | Bahamas. |
| 1827, ——— | Belize. |
| 1828, September 18, 19 | Atlantic, northwest of Bermuda. |
| 1829, July 24 | Boston. |
| 1829, September 10 (?) | Mouth of Rio Grande. Coast inundated. |
| 1829, October 30 | St. Kitts. |
| 1830, August 7 | Jamaica. |
| 1830, August 11-18 | Dominica, St. Thomas, Atlantic coast. Off Boston on the 18th. XII. |
| 1830, August 19-24 | Martinique, United States. |
| 1830, September 29-October 2 | West Indies to Grand Banks. |
| 1831, ——— | Belize. |
| 1831, June 10 | Florida. |
| 1831, June 23 | Gulf of Mexico. |
| 1831, June 23-27 | Tobago, Grenada, Yucatan. XIV. |
| 1831, August 18 | Gulf coast, near mouth of Rio Grande. |
| 1831, August 10-18 | Barbados, Cuba, Louisiana. Terrible storm at Barbados. X, XIII. Severe in Cuba. Very destructive at mouth of Mississippi. |
| 1831, October 11 | Leeward Islands. |
| 1832, June 3-6 | Cuba, Bahamas, Bermuda. |
| 1832, August 7 | Jamaica. Violent storm. Lasted only 3 hours. |
| 1832, August 21 | Atlantic. |
| 1832, August 24 | Leeward Islands. |
| 1833, August 14 | Guadeloupe, Antigua, Bermuda. |
| 1833, September 20 | Dominica. |
| 1833, October 16-19 | Cuba, Gulf of Mexico. |
| 1834, September | South Texas. |
| 1834, September 20-23 | Dominica. XIII. Santo Domingo. |
| 1834, October 20, 21 | Martinique. |
| 1835, July 26 | Barbados. |
| 1835, August 12-18 | Antigua, Cuba, Galveston. At Antigua the barometer fell an inch in 1 hour and 27 minutes. |
| 1835, September 3 | Barbados. |
| 1835, September 18 | Matamoras. |

| *Date of Storm* | *Principal Places Affected, and Remarks* |
| --- | --- |
| 1835, November 10 | Nova Scotia. Possibly not of tropical origin. |
| 1837, July 9 | Barbados, St. Lucia. |
| 1837, July 26 | Barbados. Later approached Florida. |
| 1837, July 31 | Antigua, St. Thomas. |
| 1837, August 2-4 | Antigua, St. Thomas, Barbados, Puerto Rico. XIII. |
| 1837, August 12-21 | Turks Island. |
| 1837, August 24, 25 | Atlantic, east of Bermuda. |
| 1837, August 31 | Western Florida. |
| 1837, September 27-October 10 | Gulf of Mexico, "Racer's Storm," X, XIII. |
| 1837, October 1-3 | Bermuda. |
| 1837, October 25, 26 | Havana. Lowest barometer 28.06 inches. |
| 1838, ——— | Lower Texas coast. |
| 1838, September 2-4 | Atlantic. |
| 1838, September 7-10 | Bahamas. |
| 1838, September 28 | Atlantic. |
| 1838, November 1 | Vera Cruz. |
| 1838, November 13 (or 15) | St. Kitts. |
| 1838, November 26-28 | Atlantic coast. |
| 1838, November 26 | Vera Cruz. |
| 1839, June 9 | Antigua. |
| 1839, September 11-14 | Bermuda. X. |
| 1839, November 5 | Galveston. |
| 1840, ——— | Lower Texas. Villages destroyed at mouth of Rio Grande. |
| 1840, September 16 | Puerto Rico. |
| 1841, September 16 | South Carolina. |
| 1841, October 3-6 | United States. Nantucket. |
| 1841, October 6 | Barbados, St. Lucia. |
| 1841, October 21-28 | Bermuda. |
| 1841, November 28 | Cuba. |
| 1842, July 12 | Atlantic coast. |
| 1842, August 30 to September 9 | From Atlantic moved due west across Florida to Tampico. September 4 at Havana, barometer 28.93 inches. XIII. |
| 1842, September 18-22 | Gulf of Mexico. |
| 1842, October 5 | Galveston. |
| 1842, October 2-10 | Gulf of Mexico, Bermuda. Not same as preceding storm. |
| 1842, October 24-29 | Windward Islands. |
| 1842, November 3 | Atlantic. |

| Date of Storm | Principal Places Affected, and Remarks |
|---|---|
| 1843, August 17-19 | Bermuda. |
| 1843, October 13 | Florida. |
| 1844, August 4-6 | Mouth of Rio Grande. Not a vestige of a single house left at Brazos Santiago or at mouth of river. About 70 lives lost. |
| 1844, September 14 | Charleston. |
| 1844, October 4-7 | Cuba, Key West. Very destructive in Cuba on 5th. One hundred fifty-eight vessels wrecked. Over 2500 houses destroyed. XIII. |
| 1844, September 1 | East Gulf. |
| 1844, October 12 | Florida Straits |
| 1845, October 22 | Bermuda. |
| 1845, October 27 | Bermuda. |
| 1845, November 9 | Bermuda. |
| 1846, ——— | New Orleans. |
| 1846, August 16 | South Carolina coast. |
| 1846, September 11-21 | Barbados, Antigua, Guadeloupe. |
| 1846, September | Tampa. |
| 1846, October 6-18 | Cuba, United States. XIII. |
| 1847, October 10 | Tobago, Trinidad. |
| 1848, July 10 | Windward Islands. |
| 1848, August 22-<br>September 5 | Antigua, Turks Island, Nassau, off Florida. |
| 1848, September 19 | Barbados, St. Kitts. |
| 1848, September 25 | Tampa. Severe; lowest barometer reading, 28.18. |
| 1848, October 12 | Jacksonville. |
| 1848, October 16 | Tampa. |
| 1850, July 20 | Leeward Islands. Probably same as next. |
| 1850, July 14-16 | West Indies. |
| 1850, August 21-23 | Cuba, Apalachicola. |
| 1850, September 2-4 | Cape Verdes. |
| 1850, October 14 | Atlantic. |
| 1850, October 18 | Atlantic. |
| 1851, July 10 | Barbados, St. Kitts, Santo Domingo. |
| 1851, August 16-28 | Antigua, Puerto Rico, Havana, Florida. |
| 1851, September 18 | Gulf of Mexico. |
| 1852, August 23-27 | Cuba, Mobile. |
| 1852, September 22-26 | St. Kitts, St. Eustatius, Puerto Rico. |
| 1852, October 9 | Florida. |
| 1853, August 10 | Barbados. |

| *Date of Storm* | *Principal Places Affected, and Remarks* |
|---|---|
| 1853, August 30 to September 11 | Cape Verdes to Hatteras. XIII. |
| 1853, September 27 | Atlantic. |
| 1853, September 28 | Atlantic. Not same as preceding. |
| 1854, September 6-14 | Atlantic coast, Florida to New England. XIII. |
| 1854, September 16-19 | Matagorda, Tex. |
| 1854, September | Galveston. Probably same as preceding. |
| 1854, October 21 | Bermuda. |
| 1855, August 25, 26 | Martinique, Santo Domingo. |
| 1855, September 1, 2 | Atlantic, 50° N., 40° W. |
| 1856, August 9-12 | Louisiana coast. XIII. |
| 1856, August 21-22 | Cuba. |
| 1856, August 27- September 2 | Cuba to Mobile. Havana barometer 28.62. |
| 1857, September 12 | Atlantic, off Hatteras. |
| 1859, September 2 | St. Kitts. |
| 1859, October 2 | Cuba. |
| 1860, August 11 | Mobile. |
| 1860, September 15 | Mobile. |
| 1861, July 6-7 | Guadeloupe, St. Kitts. |
| 1864, August 31 | Belize. Calm center over town. Sea rose 5 feet, inundating town. |
| 1865, August 22-23 | Cuba. |
| 1865, September 6 | Leeward Islands. Serious damage at Guadeloupe and Dominica. Buildings carried away and vessels sunk. |
| 1865, September | Western Louisiana. |
| 1865, October 22, 23 | Cuba to Louisiana coast. |
| 1866, October 1 | Bahamas. XIII. |
| 1866, ——— | Galveston. |
| 1866, October 29, 30 | Leeward Islands. Unusually severe hurricane. |
| 1867, October 1-3 | Galveston. |
| 1867, October 29 | Puerto Rico. XIII. |
| 1869, September 8 | Atlantic, New England coast. |
| 1870, July 3 | Mobile. |
| 1870, September 10 | Near Bermuda. |
| 1870, October 7-8 | Cuba. |
| 1870, October 19, 20 | Cuba. |
| 1871, June 1-4 | Texas coast. Barometer at Galveston 29.51. |
| 1871, June 9 | East Texas coast. |
| 1871, August 16-18 | Florida, Georgia, South Carolina. |

| *Date of Storm* | *Principal Places Affected, and Remarks* |
|---|---|
| 1871, August 21-25 | St. Kitts, Jacksonville. |
| 1871, October 2-3 | Galveston. |
| 1872, September 13 | Leeward Islands, Atlantic. |
| 1873, June 2 | Jacksonville. |
| 1873, August 14-27 | West of Bermuda, Nova Scotia. XIII. |
| 1873, September 18-20 | Gulf and Southeastern States. Very severe along the coast. |
| 1873, September 22-24 | Gulf, Florida and South Atlantic coast. |
| 1873, October 3-8 | Western Cuba, Florida. Severe cyclone and many disasters at sea. Village of Punta Rassa, Fla., entirely destroyed. Wind velocity at Punta Rassa 90 miles an hour. |
| 1874, July 2-4 | Gulf, Indianola, Tex. |
| 1874, September 3-6 | Gulf coast of Mexico. Moved north-north-westward into Texas. |
| 1874, September 5-7 | Bermuda, Cape Breton Island. |
| 1874, September 9 | Atlantic between Bermuda and Hatteras. |
| 1874, September 25-30 | Gulf, Florida, Atlantic coast. Developed great force on Carolina coast. |
| 1874, November 1, 2 | Jamaica. |
| 1875, September 14-19 | Cuba, Gulf, Indianola, Tex. II, XIII. |
| 1875, October 13-15 | Atlantic Ocean, Halifax. |
| 1876, September 12 | Leeward Islands. |
| 1876, September 15-17 | Wilmington. Center passed over Washington, D.C., on 17th. Cape Lookout wind SW. 73. |
| 1876, October 7-10 | Gulf, Florida. |
| 1876, October 12-21 | St. Thomas, Puerto Rico, Cuba, southern Florida. Calm center passed over Havana, barometer 28.7 inches. Unusually severe in southern Florida, wind at Key West 88 miles. |
| 1876, November 18 | Leeward Islands. |
| 1877, August 2-4 | Florida, Nova Scotia. |
| 1877, September 15-21 | West Gulf, Louisiana, Georgia. |
| 1877, September 21 to October 5 | Barbados, Curaçao, St. Marks, Fla. Large loss of life at Curaçao; property damage $2,000,000. Most of the solid buildings at Curaçao swept down by waves. Tide 12 feet above mean at St. Marks. |
| 1877, October 13 | Cienfuegos. |
| 1877, October 27-29 | In Atlantic off the coast. |
| 1877, November 28-29 | Atlantic. |

| Date of Storm | Principal Places Affected, and Remarks |
|---|---|
| 1878, July 1-3 | Florida. |
| 1878, July 11, 12 | Jacksonville. |
| 1878, August 13-17 | Caribbean Sea and Gulf of Mexico. |
| 1878, August 24 | Atlantic. |
| 1878, September 1-14 | Trinidad, Santo Domingo, Cuba, Florida, Georgia. At Trinidad it was the most severe storm in 40 years. It was destructive at Santo Domingo. |
| 1878, September 13-18 | Atlantic. |
| 1878, September 26- October 6 | Santo Domingo, Atlantic. |
| 1878, October 9-13 | Gulf, North Florida. |
| 1878, October 18-24 | Cuba, Wilmington. Wind at Cape Lookout 100 miles. Portsmouth, N.C., 82 SE. Vortex passed over Washington, D.C. Barometer at Annapolis, 28.82. At Mt. Washington on 23rd, wind was 120 miles SE. A very destructive storm along coast. |
| 1878, October | Mid-Atlantic. |
| 1878, October | Northeast of Windward Islands. |
| 1878, November 25-28 | East of Puerto Rico. |
| 1879, August 16-20 | Atlantic coast. Very severe. I, XIII. |
| 1879, August 20-23 | Yucatan, Texas coast. |
| 1879, September 12-22 | Caribbean Sea, Florida. |
| 1879, October 4-5 | Cuba. |
| 1879, October 11-15 | Caribbean Sea, western Florida. |
| 1880, August 7-13 | Yucatan, Matamoras. |
| 1880, August 15-20 | Windward Islands, Cuba, Bahamas. |
| 1880, August 26-30 | Southern Florida, Alabama. |
| 1880, August 28-31 | Atlantic, near Bermuda. |
| 1880, October 3-9 | Cuba. |
| 1881, August 21-26 | Leeward Islands, Georgia and South Carolina. Much destruction and many lives lost. 335 dead in Savannah. |
| 1881, September 7-9 | Off Atlantic coast. |
| 1881, October 6 | Jacksonville. |
| 1881, October 27 | Manzanillo, Mexico. Every building in the city, without exception, completely destroyed. Lowest barometer 28.00 inches. |
| 1882, September 2-15 | Turks Island, Cuba, Gulf coast. Wind reached 92 miles NE. at Port Eads, La. |

| *Date of Storm* | *Principal Places Affected, and Remarks* |
|---|---|
| 1882, October 8-12 | Grand Cayman Island, Cuba. Florida. Town of Pinar del Rio practically all destroyed. |
| 1883, August 19-25 | Atlantic. |
| 1883, August 28-31 | Atlantic. |
| 1883, August 28-29 | Atlantic. Course somewhat west of Bermuda. |
| 1883, September 4-11 | Eastern Caribbean, Haiti, Nassau, North Carolina. Over 100 vessels wrecked in Bahamas and 50 lives lost. |
| 1883, October 22-23 | Bahamas, Atlantic. |
| 1884, September 3-11 | Atlantic. |
| 1884, October 7 | Jamaica, East Cuba. |
| 1884, October 11-17 | Eastern Cuba, Bahamas. |
| 1885, August 8 | Bermuda. |
| 1885, August 24-25 | Georgia and Carolinas. Greatest destruction occurred at Charleston; damage $1,690,-000; 21 lives lost. Wind at Smithville, N.C., 98 miles, estimated 125 after anemometer cups blew away. |
| 1885, September 17-21 | Brownsville, southern Louisiana, Georgia. |
| 1885, September 18-21 | Atlantic. |
| 1885, September 24-30 | Gulf, Louisiana. |
| 1885, September 27-28 | Atlantic, east of Bermuda. |
| 1885, October 10-11 | Florida. |
| 1886, June 13-14 | Sabine, Tex. Inundation. XIII. |
| 1886, June 15-20 | Yucatan Channel, Florida. Much damage at Cedar Keys. Wind 68 miles east. |
| 1886, June 27-31 | Yucatan, Florida. Great destruction in the Apalachicola-Tallahassee section. |
| 1886, July 14-19 | Yucatan Channel, Florida. |
| 1886, July 30 | East Gulf. |
| 1886, August 16-28 | Grenada, Cuba. |
| 1886, August 13-20 | East Caribbean, Cuba, Indianola, Tex. Very severe in Cuba; destroyed Indianola. II, XIII. |
| 1886, August 12-18 | Eastern Caribbean, Cuba, Gulf. |
| 1886, September 7 | Pinar del Rio. |
| 1886, September 15-25 | Martinique, Jamaica, Brownsville, Tex. XIII. |
| 1886, September 26-30 | Atlantic. |

| *Date of Storm* | *Principal Places Affected, and Remarks* |
|---|---|
| 1886, October 8-13 | Western Cuba, extreme East Texas. Center passed near Sabine Pass, Tex. Johnson's Bayou and Sabine Pass inundated; overflow extending 20 miles inland. Nearly every house moved from its foundation. One hundred fifty lives lost. Second overflow at this point in 1886; first occurred in June. XIII. |
| 1886, October 22-23 | Santo Domingo. |
| 1887, July 20-28 | Martinique, Yucatan, Apalachicola. |
| 1887, July 30 to August 7 | Windward Islands, Caribbean Sea. |
| 1887, August 16-20 | Atlantic east of Florida. Hurricane winds of exceptional violence along the coast. |
| 1887, August 19-30 | Recurved east of Florida. |
| 1887, September 1-7 | Far out in Atlantic. |
| 1887, September 11-21 | Dominica, Yucatan, Brownsville. Moved very slowly on passing inland at Brownsville on 21st and 22nd. Barometer 28.93; was below 29 inches several hours. Wind 78 miles N. |
| 1887, September 15-18 | Far out in Atlantic. |
| 1887, October 6-8 | Yucatan. |
| 1887, October 9-11 | Western Cuba. |
| 1887, October 9-24 | Recurved in Gulf. |
| 1887, October 11 | Far out in Atlantic. |
| 1887, October 16-29 | Far out in Atlantic. |
| 1887, October 29-November 8 | Gulf, over Florida to Atlantic. |
| 1887, November 27-December 6 | Described loop in Bahamas and turned northeastward into Atlantic. |
| 1888, June 17 | North Texas coast. |
| 1888, July 5 | Galveston. |
| 1888, August 14-24 | Florida, middle Gulf coast. Wind estimated at 90 miles at New Orleans. |
| 1888, August 31-September 8 | Turks Island, Great Inagua, Cuba, Mexico. Great damage; loss of life at Turks Island, Great Inagua, and in Cuba more than 1000. Whole towns along coast of Cuba swept out of existence by gigantic waves. XIII. |
| 1888, September 7-17 | Bahamas, off Atlantic coast. Gales on coast. |
| 1888, September 23-27 | Florida Straits, Atlantic. |

*Date of Storm*          *Principal Places Affected, and Remarks*

| | |
|---|---|
| 1888, October 8-12 | Bay of Campeche, Atlantic. |
| 1888, November 1-8 | St. Vincent, Antigua, Atlantic. |
| 1888, November 17- December 2 | Atlantic, recurved near North Carolina coast. Hurricane winds at sea. |
| 1888, November 21-23 | South of Bermuda, Atlantic. Slight force. |
| 1889, June 15-25 | Extreme western Cuba, Florida. |
| 1889, September 1-13 | St. Kitts, St. Thomas, Hatteras. Severe in West Indies and considerable damage along Atlantic coast. |
| 1889, September 2-11 | Far out in Atlantic. |
| 1889, September 12-19 | Far out in Atlantic. |
| 1889, September 12-26 | Guadeloupe, west Gulf. |
| 1889, September 29- October 6 | East of Tobago, recurved near Bermuda. |
| 1889, October 5-11 | Isle of Pines, northeastward to Atlantic. |
| 1890, August 26- September 4 | Leeward Islands, Atlantic. |
| 1891, July 3-13 | Bay of Campeche, Texas-Louisiana coasts. |
| 1891, August 17-29 | Martinique, Bahamas, Florida. At Martinique it was one of the most disastrous of West Indian hurricanes; damage $10,-000,000, 700 lives lost. Severe in Bahamas. Lost force before reaching Florida; dissipated. XIII. |
| 1891, September 2-11 | Atlantic. |
| 1891, September 16- October 3 | Atlantic. |
| 1891, September 29- October 10 | Atlantic; recurved between Hatteras and Bermuda. |
| 1891, October 1-9 | Puerto Rico, Haiti, Cuba, Florida. |
| 1891, October 6-11 | Western Caribbean, Florida, Atlantic coast. |
| 1891, October 8-24 | Atlantic, between Bermuda and Hatteras. |
| 1891, October 12-22 | Tobago, Puerto Rico, Bermuda. |
| 1891, November 3-9 | Atlantic. |
| 1891, November 5-15 | Western Caribbean, Atlantic. |
| 1892, June 10-16 | Southern Florida. |
| 1892, August 16-26 | Atlantic. |
| 1892, September 4-17 | Atlantic. |
| 1892, September 9-17 | Middle Gulf coast. |
| 1892, September 12-23 | Atlantic. |
| 1892, September 25-27 | Bay of Campeche, Mexico. |
| 1892, October 6-15 | Windward Islands, Bermuda. |

| *Date of Storm* | *Principal Places Affected, and Remarks* |
|---|---|
| 1892, October 13-30 | Atlantic. |
| 1892, October 21-31 | Gulf, Florida. |
| 1893, June 12-30 | Bay of Campeche, Atlantic coast. |
| 1893, July 4-6 | Western Caribbean Sea. |
| 1893, August 13-26 | Windward Islands, Puerto Rico, Atlantic. |
| 1893, August 15–September 1 | Middle Atlantic coast. |
| 1893, August 22-30 | Carolina coast. XIII. Disastrous on coast of Georgia and South Carolina. Reached Charleston and Savannah on 27th. "Accompanied by a tremendous wave which submerged islands." Property damage $10,000,000; 1,000 lives lost. Ravage at Charleston was said to be terrific. |
| 1893, August 20-29 | Atlantic. |
| 1893, September 6-10 | Gulf of Mexico. |
| 1893, September 25–October 15 | Cape Verdes, Atlantic coast. |
| 1893, September 27–October 6 | Louisiana. Reached Gulf coast on October 1 and 2. Wind estimated at 100 miles an hour. Loss of life placed at 2,000. XIII. |
| 1893, October 6 | Leeward Islands. |
| 1893, October 20-23 | Southern Florida, Middle Atlantic coast. |
| 1894, August 6-8 | Middle Gulf coast; of small force. |
| 1894, August 30–September 11 | Atlantic. |
| 1894, September 18-30 | Haiti, Cuba, Florida. Considerable damage from wind in Cuba and rivers overflowed. |
| 1894, October 1-13 | Western Caribbean Sea, Gulf and Atlantic coast States. Moved northeastward inside coast line. Winds exceeded 80 miles an hour at some places. |
| 1894, October 11-19 | Windward Islands, Bermuda. |
| 1894, October 21–November 7 | Atlantic. Described loop southwest of Bermuda and moved northeastward near Bermuda. |
| 1895, August 16 | Middle Gulf coast. Of slight force. |
| 1895, August 22-29 | Caribbean, Gulf, near mouth of Rio Grande. |
| 1895, September 28–October 15 | Yucatan, Florida Straits, Atlantic. Of slight intensity. |
| 1895, October 2-7 | Gulf, southern Florida, Bermuda. |

| *Date of Storm* | *Principal Places Affected, and Remarks* |
|---|---|
| 1895, October 5-26 | Cape Verdes, Caribbean, western Cuba, southern Florida, Atlantic. Wind was 80 miles an hour at Havana. Very high tides on South Atlantic coast. |
| 1895, October 13-16 | Bay of Campeche, southern Florida, Atlantic. |
| 1896, July 4-6 | Western Caribbean. |
| 1896, September 3-11 | Cuba, Bahamas. |
| 1896, September 19-29 | Atlantic. |
| 1896, September 22-October 1 | Windward Islands, extreme western Cuba, Florida. Increased in intensity as it reached Florida and moved through Atlantic States, inside coast line. Center passed over District of Columbia. Principal damage in Florida. Total $7,000,000; 114 lives lost. XIII. |
| 1896, November 27-29 | Leeward Islands. |
| 1897, August 31-September 10 | Cape Verdes, eastern Atlantic. |
| 1897, September 11-13 | Gulf, Louisiana. |
| 1897, September 20-25 | Near Atlantic coast; slight force. |
| 1897, October 10-26 | Caribbean Sea, western Cuba, southern Florida, Atlantic. |
| 1897, October 23-November 7 | Atlantic. Described loop near Hatteras. Was not of much force. |
| 1898, September 5-20 | Windward Islands, Atlantic. |
| 1898, September 12-25 | Yucatan, Louisiana. |
| 1898, September 20-28 | Puerto Rico, Bahamas. |
| 1898, September 21-28 | Western Caribbean, Yucatan, east Texas coast. Not of much force. |
| 1898, September 25-October 7 | Atlantic, Carolina coast. |
| 1898, October 10-26 | Caribbean Sea, western Cuba, Florida. |
| 1898, October 26-November 9 | Caribbean Sea, Yucatan. |
| 1899, August 3-September 8 | Cape Verdes, Puerto Rico, recurved off Atlantic coast. Disastrous at Puerto Rico. V, XIII. Skirted South Atlantic coast; at Hatteras was most violent storm in the memory of oldest inhabitants. |
| 1899, August 29-September 10 | Puerto Rico, Bahamas. |

| *Date of Storm* | *Principal Places Affected, and Remarks* |
|---|---|
| 1899, September 3-21 | Atlantic. |
| 1899, October 2-9 | Gulf, Florida, Atlantic. Of small force. |
| 1899, October 26–<br>November 5 | Western Caribbean, Cuba, inland over North Carolina. |
| 1900, August 27–<br>September 22 | Atlantic, Haiti, Cuba, Galveston. Disaster at Galveston, Sept. 8. II, XIII. |
| 1900, September 9-25 | Atlantic. VIII. |
| 1900, September 13-20 | Atlantic. |
| 1900, October 4-14 | Atlantic. |
| 1900, October 9-15 | Western Caribbean, Yucatan, Gulf, Atlantic coast. Not of much intensity. |
| 1900, October 23–<br>November 2 | Windward Islands, Puerto Rico, Bahamas, Bermuda. |
| 1901-1937 | Tropical storms from 1901 to 1937, inclusive, are described chronologically in Chapter XIV. |

# BIBLIOGRAPHY

ABBE, CLEVELAND. "Winds and Waves," *Monthly Weather Review,* 33: 261-262, 1905.

ALEXANDER, W. H. *Hurricanes: Especially Those of Puerto Rico and St. Kitts,* Washington, 1902.

ALGUÉ, JOSÉ. *Cyclones of the Far East.* Manila, 1904.

AMERICAN NATIONAL RED CROSS. *Report of Relief Activities.* Washington, 1928.

AMERICAN SOCIETY OF CIVIL ENGINEERS. "Final Report of the Committee of the Structural Division," *Transactions,* 1931.

BALLOU, S. M. "The Eye of the Storm," *American Meteorological Journal,* 1902.

BIGELOW, FRANK H. *Storms, Storm Tracks and Weather Forecasting.* Washington, 1897.

BLANFORD, H. F. *Indian Meteorologist's Vade-Mecum.* Calcutta, 1876.

BLODGETT, LORIN. *Climatology of the United States.* Philadelphia, 1857.

BOWIE, E. H. "Formation and Movement of West Indian Hurricanes." *Monthly Weather Review,* 50:173-179, 1922.

————. "Hurricane of October 25, 1921, at Tampa, Fla." *Monthly Weather Review,* 49:567-570, 1921.

————. and WEIGHTMAN, R. H. *Types of Storms of the United States and Their Average Movements.* Washington, 1914.

BOYER, H. B. *Atmospheric Circulation in Tropical Cyclones as Shown by Movements of Clouds.* Washington, 1896.

————. "Destructive Gust at Jupiter, Fla., following the Miami Hurricane," *Monthly Weather Review,* 54:416, 1926.

BRENNAN, J. F. *A Report on the Hurricane of Western Jamaica, October 29, 1933.* Kingston, 1934.

————. "Relation of May-July Weather Conditions in Jamaica to the Caribbean Tropical Disturbances of the Following Season," *Monthly Weather Review,* 63-13, 1935.

BROOKS, C. F. "Some Excessive Rainfalls," *Monthly Weather Review,* 47:302, 1919.

————. *Why the Weather?* New York, 1924.

BUCHAN, A. *Handy Book of Meteorology.* Edinburgh and London, 1868.

BYERS, H. R. "On the Meteorological History of the Hurricane of November 1935," *Monthly Weather Review,* 63: 318-322, 1935.

CALVERT, E. B. "History of Radio in Relation to the Work of the Weather Bureau," *Monthly Weather Review,* 51: 1-9, 1923.

CALVERT, E. B. "The Hurricane Warning Service and Its Reorganization," *Monthly Weather Review*, 63: 85-88, 1935.

CHAPEL, L. T. "Winds and Storms on the Isthmus of Panama," *Monthly Weather Review*, 55: 519-530, 1927.

————. "The Significance of Air Movements Across the Equator in Relation to the Development and Early Movement of Tropical Cyclones," *Monthly Weather Review*, 62: 433-438, 1934.

CHU, CO-CHING. "Some New Facts about the Centers of Typhoons," *Monthly Weather Review*, 46: 417-419, 1918.

CLAYTON, H. H. *World Weather*. New York, 1923.

CLAXTON, T. F. "The Climate of the Pamplemousses in the Island of Mauritius," *Report of the 8th International Geographical Congress*. Washington, 1904.

CLINE, I. M. *Tropical Cyclones*. New York, 1926.

————. "Tides and Coastal Currents Developed by Tropical Cyclones," *Monthly Weather Review*, 61: 36-38, 1933.

COLLINS, A. E. "Chronological Data of Hurricanes Recorded as Having Caused Damage in the Leeward Islands Colony," *Leeward Islands Gazette*, pp. 175, 176, June 20, 1935.

CORNISH, VAUGHN. *Waves of the Sea and Other Water Waves*. Chicago, 1910.

CORONAS, J. *The Climate and Weather of the Philippines*. Manila, 1920.


DALLAS, W. L. *Cyclone Memoirs*. Calcutta, 1891.

DAMPIER, Wm. *Dampier's Voyages*. Edited by John Masefield. New York, 1906.

DARWIN, G. H. *The Tides*. Cambridge, 1898.

DAVIS, W. M. *Elementary Meteorology*. Boston, 1894.

————. *Whirlwinds, Cyclones and Tornadoes*. Boston, New York, 1884.

DEL MONTE, ENRIQUE. *La Tormento Tropical y la Armonia entre Dos Centros Tempestuosos*. Havana, 1905.

DEPPERMANN, C. E. *Outlines of Philippine Frontology*. Manila, 1936.

DOBERCK, W. *The Law of Storms in the Eastern Seas*. Hongkong, 1904.

DOVE, HEINRICH WILHELM. *The Law of Storms*. London, 1862.

DRUM, W. M. "The Pioneer Forecasters of Hurricanes," *The Messenger*, June 1905.

DRYDEN, H. L. and HILL, G. C. "Wind Pressure on a Model of the Empire State Building," Research paper 545, *Bureau of Standards Journal of Research*. Washington, April 1933.

DYKE, R. A. "Excessive Rainfall of July 22-25, in Louisiana and Extreme Eastern Texas," *Monthly Weather Review*, 61: 202-203, 1933.


EASTMAN, J. R. *Discussion of the West India Cyclone of October 29 and 30, 1867*. Washington, 1868.

ELIOT, J. *Cyclones of the Bay of Bengal.* Calcutta, 1900.
ESPY, J. *The Philosophy of Storms.* Boston, 1841.

FASSIG, O. L. "Discussion of Tropical Cyclones," *Monthly Weather Review*, 57: 331, 1929.
————. *Hurricanes of the West Indies.* Washington, 1913.
FERRELL, W. *A Popular Treatise of the Winds.* New York, 1889.
FINLEY, J. P. *The Sailors Handbook of Storm Tracks, Fog and Ice Charts of the North Atlantic Ocean and Hurricanes of the Gulf of Mexico.* Boston, 1889.
FLEMING, J. A. *Waves and Ripples.* London, 1912.
FLEMING, ROBINS. *Wind Stresses in Buildings.* London, 1930.
FORTIER, EDOUARD. *Un Cyclone dans les Antilles, l'Ouragan de 1891 à la Martinique.* Paris, 1892.
FRANKLIN, BENJAMIN. *The Ingenious Dr. Franklin.* Edited by Nathan G. Goodman. London, 1931.
FRAZIER, R. D. "Early Records of Tropical Hurricanes on the Texas Coast in the vicinity of Galveston," *Monthly Weather Review*, 49: 454-457, 1921.
FROC, L. *Typhoon Highways in the Far East.* Zikawei, 1896.
————. *Atlas of the Tracks of 620 Typhoons, 1893-1918.* Shanghai, 1920.

GARRIOT, E. B. *West Indian Hurricanes.* Washington, 1900.
GRAY, R. W. "Tornado within a Hurricane Area, Goulds, Fla.," *Monthly Weather Review*, 47: 639-641, 1919.
————. "Florida Hurricanes," *Monthly Weather Review*, 61: 11-13, 1933.
GREGG, W. R., TANNEHILL, I. R., and others. "Testimony regarding the Hurricane of September 2, 1935," *Hearings before the Committee on World War Veterans' Legislation*, H.R. 9486. Washington, 1936.

HALL, MAXWELL. *Notes of Hurricanes, Earthquakes.* Kingston, 1916.
————. "West Indian Hurricanes as Observed at Jamaica," *Monthly Weather Review*, 45: 578, 1917.
HALLENBECK, CLEVE. "A Hurricane at Trinidad, 1527." *Bulletin of American Meteorological Society*, 17: 263.
HAURWITZ, B. "The Height of Tropical Cyclones and the 'Eye' of the Storm," *Monthly Weather Review*, 63: 45-49, 1935.
HECK, N. H. *Earthquakes.* Princeton, 1936.
HENRY, A. J. "The Frequency of Tropical Cyclones That Closely Approach or Enter Continental United States," *Monthly Weather Review*, 57: 328-331, 1929.
HORIGUTI, Y. "The Typhoon of the Far East," *Memoirs of the Imperial Marine Observatory*, Kobe, Japan, 1926.

HUMPHREYS, W. J. *Physics of the Air*. Philadelphia, 1929.

HURD, W. E. "The North Atlantic Hurricane of October 13-29, 1926," *Pilot Chart of the North Atlantic Ocean*, October 1926.

————. "Tropical Storms of the Eastern North Pacific," *Pilot Chart of North Pacific Ocean*, May 1923.

IRVING, WASHINGTON. *The Life and Voyages of Christopher Columbus*. New York, 1893.

JARBOE, J. H. "The San Antonio Flood of September 10, 1921," *Monthly Weather Review*, 49: 494-496, 1921.

KIMBALL, H. H. "What Is a Storm Wave?" *Monthly Weather Review*, 29: 461-463, 1901.

KREBS, WILHELM. "The Lowest Barometric Minima at Sea Level," *Monthly Weather Review*, 39: 471, 1911.

LEHMANN-NITSCHE, R. *Das Sternbild des Orkans, Forschungen und Fortschritte*. 1931.

LOOMIS, ELIAS. *A Treatise on Meteorology*. New York, 1868.

McAULIFFE, J. P. "Excessive Rainfall and Flood at Taylor, Texas," *Monthly Weather Review*, 49: 496-497, 1921.

McDONALD, W. F. "Low Barometer Readings in West Indian Disturbances of 1932 and 1933," *Monthly Weather Review*, 61: 273, 274, 1933.

————. "Lowest Barometer Reading in the Florida Keys Storm of September 2, 1935," *Monthly Weather Review*, 63: 295, 1935.

MARVIN, C. F. "The Law of the Geoidal Slope and Fallacies in Dynamic Meteorology," *Monthly Weather Review*, 48: 565-582, 1920.

————. "A Rational Theory of the Cup Anemometer," *Monthly Weather Review*, 60: 43-56, 1932.

MAURY, M. F. *Physical Geography of the Sea and Its Meteorology*. London, 1855.

MELDRUM, C. *On the Rotation of Wind between Oppositely Directed Currents of Air in the Southern Indian Ocean*. London, 1869.

————. *Notes on the Forms of Cyclones in the Southern Indian Ocean, and on Some of the Rules Given for Avoiding Their Centres*. London, 1873.

MILHAM, W. I. *Meteorology*. New York, 1920.

MILLÁS, JOSÉ. *Memoria del Huracan de Camaguey de 1932*, Havana, 1933.

————. *Un Esayo sobre los Huracanes de los Antillas*. Havana, 1928.

MILLER, ERIC. "American Pioneers in Meteorology," *Monthly Weather Review*, 61: 189-193, 1933.

MITCHELL, C. L. *West Indian Hurricanes and Other Tropical Cyclones of the North Atlantic Ocean.* Washington, 1924.

————. *Hurricanes of the South Atlantic and Gulf States, 1879-1928.* Washington, 1928.

*Monthly Weather Review.* Accounts of individual storms, usually in the issue of the month in which the storm occurred, 1873 to 1934.

MOORE, W. L. *Descriptive Meteorology.* New York, 1910.

————. "I am Thinking of Hurricanes," *American Mercury,* September 1927.

NEWNHAM, E. V. *Hurricanes and Tropical Revolving Storms.* London, 1922.

NORMAND, C. W. B. *Storm Tracks in the Bay of Bengal.* Calcutta, 1925.

NORTON, GRADY. *Florida Hurricanes.* Washington, 1936.

OKADA, T. "On the Eye of the Storm," *Memoirs of the Imperial Marine Observatory,* Kobe, Japan, 1922.

ORTIZ, O. R. *Breve Estudio del Huracan del 1ro al 11 de Noviembre de 1932.* Havana, 1933.

PAGLIUCA, SALVATORE. "Measurement of Winds of Super-Hurricane Force on Mt. Washington, N.H. The Low-Pressure Disturbance of April 11-12, 1934, on Mt. Washington, N.H." Papers presented to American Meteorological Society, 1934.

PIDDINGTON, HENRY. *The Sailors Hornbook for the Law of Storms.* London, 1876.

————. *Conversations about Hurricanes: for the Use of Plain Sailors.* London, 1855.

POËY, ANDREAS. *Table Chronologique des Quatre Cents Cyclones.* Paris, 1862.

RAY, C. L. "Relation of Tropical Cyclone Frequency to Summer Pressures and Ocean Surface-Water Temperatures." *Monthly Weather Review,* 63: 10-12, 1935.

RECLUS, ELISE. *The Ocean, Atmosphere and Life.* New York, 1874.

REDFIELD, W. C. *On Three Several Hurricanes of the Atlantic and Their Relations to the Northers of Mexico and Central America.* New Haven, 1846.

REID, W. *The Law of Storms.* London, 1850.

RODEWALD, M. "Die Entstehungsbedingungen der tropischen Orkane," *Meteorologischen Zeitschrift,* Heft 6. Berlin, 1936.

SARASOLA, S. *Los Huracanes de las Antillas.* Bogotá, 1925.

SCHUBART, L. *Praktische Orkankunde mit Anweisungen zum Manouvrieren in Sturmen.* Berlin, 1934.

SHAW, NAPIER. "The Birth and Death of Cyclones," *Geophysical Memoirs no. 19*. Meteorological Office, London, 1922.
————. *Manual of Meteorology*. Cambridge, 1926.
STEARNS, W. D. "Storms of the Gulf of Mexico and Their Prediction," *American Meteorological Journal*, 1894.

TANNEHILL, I. R. "Some Inundations Attending Tropical Cyclones," *Monthly Weather Review*, 55: 453-456, 1927.
————. "The Hurricane," *U.S. Department of Agriculture Misc. Publication no. 197*. Washington, 1934.
————. "Preparation and Use of Weather Maps at Sea," Chapter VII, "Tropical Storms," *U.S. Weather Bureau Circular R*. Washington, 1935.
————. "A Relation between Temperature and Cyclone-Frequency in the Tropics," *Transactions of the American Geophysical Union*, Part I. Washington, 1935.
————. "Sea Swells in Relation to Movement and Intensity of Tropical Storms," *Monthly Weather Review*, 64: 231-238, 1936.
TAYLOR, GRIFFITH. *Australian Meteorology*. Oxford, 1920.
THOM, A. *An Enquiry into the Nature and Course of Storms in the Indian Ocean South of the Equator*. London, 1845.
TINGLEY, F. G. "The Genesis of a Tropical Cyclone," *Monthly Weather Review*, 59: 340-347, 1931.
TOYNBEE, H. "On the Great Hurricanes, the Tracks of American Storms and the Ordinary Winds of the North Atlantic Ocean in August 1873," *Nautical Magazine*. London, December 1877.
TRUE, A. E. "The Structure of Tropical Cyclones," *Proceedings of the U.S. Naval Institute*. Annapolis, March 1937.

UNION GÉODÉSIQUE ET GÉOPHYSIQUE INTERNATIONALE. *Annales de la Commission pour l'Étude des Raz de Marée*. No. 3. Paris, 1933.
U. S. NAVY DEPARTMENT. "Disaster at Apia, Samoa," *Annual Report of the Secretary of the Navy, 1889*.
U.S. WEATHER BUREAU. *The Hurricane Warning Service*. Washington, 1933.

VIÑES, B. *Cyclonic Circulation and Translatory Movement of West Indian Hurricanes*. Washington, 1898.
VISHER, S. S. "Notes on Typhoons with Charts of Normal and Aberrant Tracks," *Monthly Weather Review*, 50: 583-589, 1922.
————. *Tropical Cyclones of the Pacific*. Honolulu, 1925.
————. "Tropical Cyclones in the Eastern North Pacific between Hawaii and Mexico," *Monthly Weather Review*, 50: 295-297, 1922.

WALDO, FRANK. *Modern Meteorology*. New York, 1893.

WALTER, A. *The Sugar Industry of Mauritius*. London, 1910.

WEIGHTMAN, R. H. See BOWIE, E. H.

WEIGHTMAN, R. H. "The West Indian Hurricane of September, 1919, in the Light of Sounding Observations," *Monthly Weather Review*, 47: 717-720, 1919.

WHEELER, W. H. "Effect of a Gale upon the Tides," *Nautical Magazine*, 1895.

————. *A Practical Manual of Tides and Waves*. London, 1906.

WILLETT, H. C. "Dynamic Meteorology," *Physics of the Earth*, III. Washington, 1931.

# INDEX

*(Names in italics are ships involved in hurricanes. For dates of hurricanes and places affected see chronological list in Chapter XV.)*

Abbe, Cleveland, 8, 49

Adjuntas, P. R., rainfall at, 70

*Adler*, wreck of, 132

advisory warnings, 139, 140

air currents, and hurricane movements, 99-109, 217

*Albert Watts*, 212

Alexander, W. H., 141-6, 220

Algué, the Rev. José, clouds, 88; height of cyclones, 59; precursory signs, 88; temperatures in central calm, 22

Altapass, N.C., rainfall at, 72

anemometer, cup, 12-15; invention of, 12; pressure tube, 12

aneroid barometer, *see* barometer

*Angelina*, 214

anticyclone, 1, 3; affecting hurricane movements, 61, 100-9, 171

*Antje's* hurricane, 155

Apia, Samoa, hurricane of 1889, 131-3

*Aquitania*, in high hurricane seas, 190

*Arethusa*, low barometer reading on, 85

Arias, Clemente, 30

Backergunge, India, cyclone and storm wave, 38, 39

Baguio, P.I., heavy rainfall at, 72

balloon soundings, 9, 106, 108

Ballot, Buys, 82

bar, of the hurricane, 96

Barbados, 1831 hurricane, 127, 128, 152, 153

barograph, *see* barometer

barometer and the weather, 4, 78; and forecasting, 79; aneroid, 78-80; discovery of, 4, 78; low readings of, in cyclone centers, 82-7; "pumping" of, 87; rate of fall of, 80, 81, 211; reduction to sea-level, 78, 84; *see also* pressure

barometric gradient, 80, 81

Beaufort scale, 11, 44, 45

Beaufort, Francis, 44

Bermuda, 1839 storm, 130, 154

*Berwyn*, 187

Bigelow, Frank, 49

birds, in storm center, 20

birth of hurricanes, 44-54

Black River, Jamaica, hurricane at, 18

Blanford, H. F., 40

Blodgett, L., 148, 220

Bobadillo, fleet of, 142

bore, tidal, 38

Bowie, E. H., 58, 62, 108

Brandes, H., 5

broadcasts, by radio, 135, 139, 140

Brooks, C. F., 129

buoys, moved by cyclone currents, 54

Byers, H. R., 217

Cabre, Antonio, 112

Calcutta, India, 38, 41

*Calliope*, in hurricane at Samoa, 132

calm center of hurricane, 17-24; diameter of, 17; in relation to storm wave, 41; pressure in, 87

calms, belt of, *see* doldrums

Cape Lookout, N.C., hurricane at, 15

Cape Verde-Hatteras hurricane, 156

*Cartago*, 52, first hurricane report by radio from, 8, 174

charts, weather, synoptic, 5, 8, 50, 79, 135

Cherrapunji, India, rainfall at, 72

Chief Signal Officer, 7

Chittagong, India, cyclone at, 38

Chu, Co-ching, 22

cirro-stratus clouds, 96

cirrus clouds, 95-7

Cline, I. M., rainfall in tropical cyclones, 74-6; storm tides, 36

clouds, as precursory signs, 88, 95

Columbus, Christopher, 44, 110, 141, 142

*Commack*, 198

condensation, 75

convection, 48

Coringa, storm wave, 31

corrections, for barometers, 78; for wind velocities, 12

countercurrent theory, 48, 49